PRELIMINARY CHECKLIST OF THE NAVAL RECORDS COLLECTION OF THE OFFICE OF NAVAL RECORDS AND LIBRARY 1775-1910

Record Group 45

THE NATIONAL ARCHIVES

LITTERA SCRIPTA MANET

1934

OF THE UNITED STATES

Compiled by
James R. Masterson
Records Control Unit

HERITAGE BOOKS
2011

HERITAGE BOOKS

AN IMPRINT OF HERITAGE BOOKS, INC.

Books, CDs, and more—Worldwide

For our listing of thousands of titles see our website
at
www.HeritageBooks.com

A Facsimile Reprint
Published 2011 by
HERITAGE BOOKS, INC.
Publishing Division
100 Railroad Ave. #104
Westminster, Maryland 21157

Originally published
National Archives Library
1946

Reprinted 1994
Scott Genealogical
Lovettsville, Virginia

International Standard Book Numbers
Paperbound: 978-0-7884-3404-4
Clothbound: 978-0-7884-8672-2

CONTENTS

INTRODUCTION

The subject of this checklist is a body of records comprising all records in Record Group 45, Naval Records Collection of the Office of Naval Records and Library, that are in the custody of the Archivist of the United States. They consist of 6,726 bound volumes and binders, 1,188 boxes of loose papers in folders and envelopes, and other loose papers in 196 wrappers, with a total linear measurement of 1,890 feet and a total bulk of 1,767 cubic feet. The earliest record dates from 1648 and the latest from 1913, but very few are previous to 1775 or subsequent to 1910.

Legal custody of these records was transferred to the Archivist on November 19, 1942, as Accession 1212 of the National Archives. This accession included most of the records assembled by the Office of Naval Records and Library that originated before January 1911 with the exception of records filed by the Office in its correspondence and of photographs and other pictorial records collected by the Graphic Branch (formerly the Pictorial Branch) of the Office. At the time of the accession the whole of the Naval Records Collection, including records of date as recent as 1942, was removed to the National Archives Building and was accompanied by members of the staff of the Office of Naval Records and Library. The staff has arranged and shelved the whole of the Collection and has performed reference services in connection with all the records, including those in the custody of the Archivist.

The records that constitute Record Group 45 cannot be properly understood apart from the history of the office that collected them. This office was originally a library; later it undertook the publication of manuscript naval records; and ultimately, though retaining its earlier functions, it developed into an archival agency, authorized to acquire records from all units of the Navy and the Navy Department and also from sources outside the Department.

The history of the agency now known as the Office of Naval Records and Library began with General Order 292, issued by the Secretary of the Navy on March 23, 1882, establishing the Office of Naval Intelligence in the Bureau of Navigation and placing the Library of the Navy Department within this office. The Library contained some 7,000 printed volumes, chiefly relics of ships' libraries. James Russell Soley, Professor of Mathematics, USN, was attached to the Library as officer in charge on June 15, 1882. He not only improved and expanded the Library but began to collect and prepare for publication the manuscript naval records relating to the American Civil War. An act of Congress of July 7, 1884, appropriated $2,640 for the salaries of one clerk and two copyists to collect, compile, and arrange the naval records of the "War of the Rebellion," in addition to $1,800 for the salaries of one clerk and one messenger for duty in the Library. The staff compiling war records constituted the Naval War Record Office, which in the naval appropriation acts from July 11, 1890, to July 16, 1914, was designated as "Office of Naval Records of the Rebellion." In a circular to chiefs of bureaus, October 31, 1889, the Secretary of the Navy directed that "The officer in charge of the Naval War Record Office will hereafter be designated Superintendent of Naval War Records."

Though this Office and the Library received separate appropriations, they functioned from the beginning under one head and as a single organization, usually referred to as the Office of Library and Naval War Records. It was transferred from the Office of Naval Intelligence to the Office of the Secretary of the Navy by an order of October 19, 1889. Professor Soley's successors as Superintendent, previous to World War I, were Lieutenant Commander Frederick May Wise (attached October 30, 1889), Lieutenant Commander Richard Rush (attached May 8, 1893), Edward K. Rawson, Professor of Mathematics (attached March 31, 1897), and Charles W. Stewart, formerly Chief Clerk of the Office (appointed September 20, 1902). An act of March 4, 1915, consolidated the two appropriations formerly made for the Library and the Naval War Record Office into a single sum for the "Office of Naval Records and Library." Since 1915 this title has remained unchanged.

A transformation in the Office had its origin when Admiral William S. Sims, Force Commander, United States Naval Forces Operating in European Waters, conceived an admiration for the practices of the Historical Section of the British War Cabinet, directed by Sir Julian Corbett. Admiral Sims recommended the formation of such a unit in the Navy Department; and in a despatch dated June 22, 1918, he was informed by the Chief of Naval Operations that his recommendation had been approved. In a circular of July 19, 1918, the Secretary of the Navy announced that a "History Section" had been established under the Chief of Naval Operations, with Rear Admiral William W. Kimball in charge.

By an order of July 1, 1919, the Secretary restored the Office of Naval Records and Library to the Office of Naval Intelligence (which in May 1915 had become part of the newly established Office of the Chief of Naval Operations), and attached Captain Charles C. Marsh (who had relieved Admiral Kimball in the Historical Section on May 31, 1919) to the Office of Naval Records and Library as officer in charge of both the Office and the Historical Section. An incidental effect of the order was to terminate the seventeen-year service of Charles W. Stewart as Superintendent, though he remained as librarian till June 1920. Captain Marsh was succeeded as officer in charge by Captain William D. McDougall (attached May 18, 1920) and Captain (now Commodore) Dudley W. Knox (attached August 1, 1921), the present incumbent. The work of the two units was merged from the beginning of this reorganization. All official distinction between them virtually disappeared when the appropriations for the Historical Section and the Office of Naval Records and Library were combined into a single appropriation, which became available on July 1, 1927, of $40,000 for the twenty-five employees of the Office of Naval Records and Library.

The naval appropriation act authorizing the first appropriation for printing the naval records of the Civil War ($15,000) took effect on

July 1, 1894. In the same year was published the first volume of <u>Official Records of the Union and Confederate Navies in the War of the Rebellion</u>. The thirtieth and last volume was issued in 1922, and a general index to the series in 1927. These volumes included documents from the files of the Navy Department and also correspondence, journals, and other materials borrowed or acquired as gifts by the Office from naval officers or their heirs. The publication was followed by <u>Naval Documents Related to the Quasi-War Between the United States and France</u> (Washington, 7 vols., 1935-38) and <u>Naval Documents Related to the United States Wars With the Barbary Powers</u> (Washington, 6 vols. to date, 1939-).

The Naval Records Collection consisted originally of manuscript records covering the period of the Civil War, acquired by the Naval War Record Office to be abstracted or printed in <u>Official Records of the Union and Confederate Navies in the War of the Rebellion</u>. The gathering of such records was begun by Professor Soley in 1882. At a later date, probably in or shortly after 1889, the main body of the bound records of the Office of the Secretary of the Navy (comprising most records of the Office previous to 1886) was transferred to the Library, which thus became in a sense the archival unit of the Secretary's Office. An act of April 27, 1904, directed that "all naval records, such as muster and pay rolls, orders, and reports relating to the personnel and operations of the Navy of the United States" from the beginning of the Navy Department to the Civil War in any of the executive departments should be delivered to the Secretary's Office. Only scattered volumes were received from the bureaus, offices, and shore establishments of the Navy Department, which retained most of their early records.

An act of June 29, 1906, provided that all records "relating to the personnel and operations of public and private armed vessels of the North American colonies" in the Revolution in any of the executive departments should be transferred to the Secretary of the Navy to be preserved, indexed, and prepared for publication. It was soon learned, however, that few of the naval records before 1789 were in the custody of the Federal Government. Most papers of this sort were found to be widely dispersed, in both public and private possession. An act of March 2, 1913, authorized the collection of military and naval records of the Revolution with a view to their publication. The funds appropriated to the Navy Department were spent in photostating documents in Massachusetts, Virginia, and North Carolina, but were exhausted long before work in these States was completed. No further appropriation for this purpose has been made. The naval photostats have been added to the Naval Records Collection (chiefly in its Area File). Since 1923 the Office of Naval Records and Library has obtained originals or copies of many other public and private papers of the period of the Revolution and subsequent periods.

Before 1918 the Naval Records Collection consisted chiefly of old records. Upon the establishment of the Historical Section, which was designed as an agency to compile the naval history of the World War, the collection of contemporary records was undertaken on a large scale. Within twelve months after July 1918 the Secretary of the Navy, in various circular letters, had directed all ships and stations to forward materials of historical value to the Historical Section, had established a Pictorial Branch of the Section to collect and file naval photographs of the World War, and had required that as each war-time unit of the Navy was abolished its records should be transmitted to the Historical Section. On July 1, 1919, the first appropriation became available for "the collection or copying and classification, with a view to publication, of the naval records of the War with the Central Powers of Europe."

During the first three years after its establishment, the Historical Section received records at such a rate that most of them remained unexamined and inaccessible. When not engaged in answering inquiries from the records, the staff of the Historical Section was occupied chiefly in the compilation of monographs concerning the World War. When appropriations for printing were discontinued in June 1922, seven monographs had been published and about fifteen, which remain in manuscript, were in course of preparation. The policy of the Historical Section had been to write history from the records rather than to collect, copy, and classify the records with a view to their publication.

Captain Knox introduced systematic methods of examining and arranging records. These methods had been developed in England, where, on December 12, 1918, Admiral Sims had been directed by the Chief of Naval Operations to designate officers to gather records illustrating the character of the naval service in the World War. For this purpose a unit in charge of Captain Knox, assisted by other active and Reserve officers, had been established in the London Headquarters of the Force Commander, United States Naval Forces Operating in European Waters.

The procedure evolved by this unit was later described by Captain Knox in an undated memorandum, written probably in 1922:

> Since demobilization was impending, and was expected to include the headquarters in London, the work of the Historical Section abroad was limited necessarily to the selection, copying, arrangement, indexing, and filing, of appropriate documents from the voluminous and varied headquarters files. After preliminary study of French and British systems, it was decided to follow the latter closely. Selections were limited to papers relating to the operations of naval forces. All papers were arranged by geographical areas, and placed in chronological order within each area. Subdivision by subjects was avoided when possible; since the British were most emphatic in stating that any attempt to collect and permanently bind records by subjects was a mistake and would handicap historical writing greatly. Necessarily some documents, such as reports covering a long period of time, statistical data, etc., had to be filed by subjects; but even then the geographical-chronological system was followed as closely as practicable. This work occupied a large clerical force for about six months, after which the historical collection was transferred to Washington.

This procedure was later applied to the records that had accumulated in the Historical Section in Washington. As Captain Knox wrote in a communication to the Director of Naval Intelligence, May 6, 1929:

> In 1921, after considerable study, an archive system was adopted, patterned on the arrangement of the large collection received from the London Headquarters, which had examined into and followed the general principles of the British archive system for naval historical documents. The major part of the office force was then put to work archiving the heterogeneous collections on hand, and those being constantly received, into a uniform system. This was indispensable not only to be able to answer inquiries with sufficient accuracy and completeness, some of them involving claims for large sums of money, but also as a preliminary to the publication of the records themselves, to which end the money for the office force was being annually appropriated.

In a memorandum of June 16, 1928, to the Director of Naval Intelligence, Captain Knox had explained that his object was to devise

> an appropriate scheme of archives into which all of the heterogeneous matter could be permanently incorporated systematically. This was obviously necessary to avoid tremendous future losses of time in accomplishing the immediate task which Congress had set as well as in all future research work. The most eminent archivists in the city were consulted and a comprehensive plan adopted which was appropriate for the old records as well as the new. The office personnel was then reorganized to handle archiving in a systematic way (which had not previously been undertaken seriously) so that there would be a steady and orderly flow of documents from the selection desks, through the classifiers, into the archive files.

The method adopted, he continued, "has involved the examination of papers of great bulk, the selection out of those suitable for preservation, and the systematic arrangement of them in permanent archives. Rejections have been boxed and stored." Of the "rejections" 42,080 pounds were sold as waste paper in April 1931 for $42.08; and 24 boxes, weighing from 150 to 350 pounds each, were accessioned on March 25, 1937, by the National Archives.

The methods and doctrines illustrated by the passages cited above have guided and still guide the Office of Naval Records and Library in the selection and organization of contemporary records. Until 1941 the Office was largely occupied with records of World War I, and since that date it has received official records relating to World War II, which are in process of selection and consolidation. Naval records that originated between the two wars have been only partly organized; but the Office plans to integrate all the records that it has retained into a single system, composed of a single Area File and a single Subject File. No project for publishing the records has been undertaken.

Until 1923 no effort had been made to apply these methods to records of date earlier than World War I, including those that comprise Record Group 45. They consisted of boxes and parcels of loose papers and series of bound volumes, approximately as described by Claude H. Van Tyne and Waldo G. Leland in their Guide to the Archives of the Government of the United States in Washington (Washington, 1904). In 1923 the Library and its holdings, both printed and manuscript, were moved from the State, War, and Navy Building to the quarters of the Historical Section in the New Navy Building, and, as Captain Knox wrote in his memorandum of June 16, 1928, "the archiving of this material" was begun under his immediate supervision.

By an order of January 10, 1924, he established in the Historical Section of the Office of Naval Records and Library of the Office of Naval Intelligence of the Office of the Chief of Naval Operations a Division of Records to "have cognizance over all material from the beginning of American Naval History to the beginning of the World War Period." The Division (as well as the Section to which it belonged) soon lost its separate identity; but with slight changes the procedures prescribed in the order have governed the selection and arrangement of these records ever since. Two classes of procedures were necessary: one for loose papers and one for bound volumes.

The loose papers were "archived" by the methods already established in organizing the papers of the London Headquarters and of World War I in general. In applying these methods the Office of Naval Records and Library has regarded series as accumulations to be disintegrated into their ultimate elements. These elements are individual papers. Each element is scrutinized. The rejected elements may substantially retain their original order or may survive as masses of amorphous matter. The elements in which historical value is deemed to inhere are combined in new arrangements determined by the form in which subjects define themselves in the archivist's mind. This process of disintegration, selection, and recombination is designated by the Office as "archiving," and a series that has been subjected to the process is described as having been "archived." Series are conceived as temporary arrangements made by file clerks for convenience in performing their assigned duties. The papers that compose the series are considered as the raw materials from which a permanent product is digested by archivists.

For the loose papers in Record Group 45 the application of these methods resulted in an Area File and a Subject File (described in Entries 463 and 464 of this checklist). The papers are filed in labeled folders and labeled envelopes, which occupy 1,185 cardboard file boxes, each labeled with some designation of its contents. The novelty of these files in the history of record-keeping in the Navy Department does not lie in the belief that there should be a uniform system to which all filing must conform. Such systems had been incompletely applied in most of the bureaus and offices of the Department long before 1924; and during the years from 1923 to 1926 they culminated throughout the Department in the mandatory subject-numeric system prescribed by the Navy Filing Manual. The difference between the system embodied in the Manual and that embodied in the Area and Subject Files is that the former is designed only as a guide to the current filing of records when they are produced, while the latter is designed to be applied retroactively to old records, already filed according to other systems.

The papers in the Area and Subject Files, forming about a fifth of the bulk of Record Group 45, have undergone every part of the process of "archiving." It cannot be applied, however, to bound records without dismantling them. A few volumes and binders have been taken to pieces and "archived," but most are intact. These were arranged in 1924 according to the following scheme:

                    Class 1
                        Logs and journals
                        Watch, station, and quarter bills

                    Class 2
                        Indexes and keys
                        Matériel
                        Miscellaneous
                        Personnel
                            Acceptances
                            Appointments, orders, etc.
                            Courts and investigations
                            General
                            Muster and pay rolls
                            Officers of ships and stations
                            Prisoners
                            Resignations
                    Signals
                    Uniforms

                    Class 3
                    Operations

The volumes of Class 3, relating to naval operations, form about four fifths of the total number of volumes. All volumes of this class are arranged on the shelves as a single chronological sequence from 1691 to 1910. All series of more than one volume are thus distributed among similarly separated volumes of other series. A volume of "Captains' Letters" may be followed by one volume each of "Commanders' Letters," "Miscellaneous Letters," "General Letter Book," the Navy Commissioners' Journal, the private letter book of an officer, letters received by the Navy Commissioners from the commandant of the New York Navy Yard, and letters received by the commandant of the New York Navy Yard from officers. All volumes that begin in 1845 follow the volumes that begin in 1844 and precede those that begin in 1846. All volumes beginning in 1845 and extending beyond the end of that year are shelved after those that are confined to 1845. A volume labeled as beginning April 15, 1845, is shelved to the right of a volume labeled as beginning April 14, 1845. A volume labeled simply "1845" is shelved at the beginning of the volumes for 1845.

The original plan for the volumes in Classes 1 and 2 was that the subclasses in each should be arranged alphabetically by title of subclass, and the volumes of each subclass (or, for "personnel," each division of a subclass) should be arranged chronologically. When the volumes were removed to the National Archives, the alphabetical arrangement was partly abandoned, though most of the subclasses themselves remain distinct. The logs and journals are still a single group, so completely chronological that the first volume of a journal is separated from the second by alien volumes of intermediate dates. A similar arrangement has been preserved for the few volumes of watch, station, and quarter bills, of signals, of uniforms, and of prisoners. On the other hand, the muster rolls and pay rolls, the records of proceedings of general courts martial and courts of inquiry, the indexes and "keys," and some smaller groups are arranged by series, all the volumes of a series being shelved together, not intermingled with volumes of any other series.

One large group of records, nominally part of the Subject File, is physically separate. The group consists of loose muster rolls and pay rolls of ships and shore establishments of the United States and Confederate States Navies, filed in heavy paper sheets folded once to form covers 18 x 24 inches. The covers and their contents are arranged by names of ships and shore establishments in two alphabets, for naval personnel (NA) and civil personnel (PA).

The scheme of the Area File and the subject designations of the Subject File are set forth in an unpublished manual of the Office of Naval Records and Library and are copied in this checklist under Entry 463 and in Appendix F. A more complete guide to the Subject File, listing the designation on each envelope, would be useful. Thorough control over the Area File and the Subject File could be established only by the preparation of a calendar, with an entry for each document. The only lists of the loose muster rolls and pay rolls are contained in this checklist. A card catalogue (Entry 465) consists of two typed cards (ribbon copy and carbon copy) for nearly every manuscript or photostated volume in the Naval Records Collection previous to 1911. The ribbon copies are in chronological order; the carbon copies are arranged according to the classes and subclasses of the scheme and thereunder, to some extent, by series. Thus the 845 cards for the volumes of "Officers' Letters" are filed together in this part of the catalogue, though the volumes themselves are scattered among thousands of volumes of other series.

This checklist is designed as a classified and annotated list of all the series that make up Record Group 45. These are distinguished as they are presumed to have been distinguished by the offices, bureaus, boards, shore establishments, and private persons that created the records. It is obvious, for instance, that the 811 volumes of "Miscellaneous Letters" (Entry 21) were regarded as a series; the volumes are nearly uniform in contents, organization, and format, and they bear identical backstrip labels. Some series, however, are artificial in that their original organization is unknown and their present organization has been imposed either physically, by the Office of Naval Records and Library (as in the Area and Subject Files), or metaphysically, for the purposes of this checklist (as in the listing of muster rolls and pay rolls).

Indeed, nearly all the series except one-volume series are metaphysical or ideal in that the volumes composing series of bound records are not in juxtaposition on the shelves; but the entries for such series are presumed to correspond to a juxtaposition that existed formerly and that, if reconstituted, would conform to the general pattern by which the arrangement of bound records in all units of the naval establishment except the Office of Naval Records and Library has always been governed. If series entries for bound volumes and binders conformed to the system of arrangement adopted by the Office of Naval Records and Library, this checklist would contain more than 6,000 series entries. On the other hand, if the Office had found it feasible to apply the process of "archiving" to all the records in the collection, the 474 series listed would have been consolidated and diminished to two—an Area File and a Subject File.

Each entry describes a record or body of records conceived as forming a series, designated by a serial number at the end of the first paragraph of the entry. Subseries are designated by numerals in parentheses. When the backstrip title of a bound series is not identical or nearly identical with the title assigned to the series in this checklist, the backstrip title is cited within quotation marks if it appears useful as a brief designation or as a means of physically identifying volumes. The word "indexed," when entered in the first paragraph, indicates that the volume or volumes forming the series contain an index in each volume. The quantity of each series is expressed by its linear measurement, regarded as the height of the pile that would be formed if the records constituting the series were laid one upon another.

The general system of arrangement of entries in this checklist, as exhibited in the table of contents, is determined by the known or presumed origin of the records, classified as records (1) created by the Office of the Secretary of the Navy, (2) created by the Board of Navy Commissioners, (3) created by bureaus of the Navy Department, (4) created by naval shore establishments, (5) created by boards and commissions, (6) created outside the Navy Department, by the Federal Government, other governments, or private citizens, (7) assembled from both official and private sources and combined by the Office of Naval Records and Library to form new series, and (8) prepared by that Office as indexes and registers for records in the Naval Records Collection. Series begun by one office and continued by another are treated as records of the successor office. The Collection proper consists of records brought together by the Office from sources outside itself, but the records in Section (8) are attached to the Collection and have no relevance apart from it. Administrative records of the Office of Naval Records and Library that are in the custody of the Archivist of the United States are allocated to Record Group 38, Records of the Office of the Chief of Naval Operations.

All records described in Sections (I)-(V) and some of those in Sections (VI) and (VII) would have been parts of record groups other than Record Group 45 if they had not been separated by the Office of Naval Records and Library from other records of the units that created or inherited them. Many of the papers in the Area File and the Subject File have been derived from series of loose papers of which the rejected remnants are in other record groups, but the original identities and affinities of many papers in these two files are virtually irrecoverable. The records of unknown origin in these files, and the records known to have been created by foreign governments and by private citizens, are presumed to have had no connection with any unit of the Navy Department other than the Office of Naval Records and Library.

The greater part of the Collection consists of records that originated in the Office of the Secretary of the Navy, including nearly all its bound records of dates previous to 1886. Nearly all the records of the Board of Navy Commissioners are in the Collection. Records created by other units of the Navy Department form only a small part of the Collection; and some units, such as the Bureau of Medicine and Surgery and the Bureau of Supplies and Accounts, are not represented among the volumes or binders. The builders of the Collection have been convinced that logistical records have little historical value and that such value is most fully present in records relating to naval operations.

Many of the records in the Collection have been printed in the publications of the Navy Department described above, in the annual reports of the Secretary of the Navy and other volumes of the Congressional Series, and elsewhere. About 1,600 volumes of the Collection have been reproduced on microfilm, the file negatives of which are in the custody of the Archivist of the United States. From these file negatives positive microcopies can be printed at cost for individuals or institutions desiring them.

PRELIMINARY CHECKLIST

I. OFFICE OF THE SECRETARY OF THE NAVY, 1776-1913

The Navy Department was established by an act of Congress of April 30, 1798. The act provided

> That there shall be an executive department under the de-
> nomination of the Department of the Navy, the chief officer
> of which shall be called the Secretary of the Navy, whose
> duty it shall be to execute such orders as he shall receive
> from the President of the United States, relative to the
> procurement of naval stores and materials and the construc-
> tion, armament, equipment and employment of vessels of war,
> as well as all other matters connected with the naval
> establishment of the United States.

The act repealed such parts of the act of August 7, 1789, establishing the War Department, as vested control over naval matters in the Secretary of War; and it empowered the Secretary of the Navy "to take possession of all the records, books and documents and all other matters and things appertaining to this department, which are now deposited in the office of the Secretary at War."

Before 1815 the records of the Office of the Secretary of the Navy included all the central records of the Navy Department except those of the Marine Corps (established in 1798). Since 1815 various functions of the Secretary's Office have been transferred to other units of the Navy Department. Separate bodies of records relating exclusively to these functions have been transferred with the functions, while pertinent records retained by the Secretary's Office were retained in that Office.

Functions relative to naval procurement, construction, and equipment were transferred in 1815 to the Board of Navy Commissioners, from which they were inherited by several of the bureaus established in 1842 and 1862. Functions relative to courts martial and courts of inquiry, to boards for the promotion and retirement of officers, and to prisoners of war, prize vessels and cargoes, contracts, claims, and legal matters in general were transferred to the Office of the Judge Advocate General, established in 1880. Functions relative to officer personnel were transferred in 1889 to the Bureau of Navigation (now the Bureau of Naval Personnel), established in 1862, and in large part had been in charge of the Chief of that Bureau, though not under the cognizance of the Bureau itself, since 1865. Functions relative to enlisted personnel had been transferred to the Bureau of Equipment and Recruiting in 1862, from which in 1889 they were transferred to the Bureau of Navigation. Functions relative to the planning and coordination of naval operations were transferred to the Office of the Chief of Naval Operations, established in 1915. The Secretary's Office has retained not only the general direction and administration of the Navy but also various functions relative to finance and civil personnel. The records concerning these subjects in the Naval Records Collection are scattered and fragmentary, consisting largely of one-volume series that cannot be described in general terms.

The general system of record-keeping before 1885 was to bind letters received and to enter handwritten copies of letters sent in letter books, both in series determined by classes of correspondents and arranged within each series by date, with separate indexes or registers in most volumes and also with consolidated indexes or registers for letters received and letters sent. New series were detached from old series when it became convenient to file certain classes of correspondence separately, and other new series were begun when new classes of correspondents appeared. In 1832 and 1833 a number of press-copy books were prepared, containing copies of letters sent that were also copied in handwritten letter books. It is not known whether press copies were prepared in the Secretary's Office before 1832 or during the period from 1834 to 1858. In and after the latter year several series of press copies were begun, few of which are part of the Collection. In addition to correspondence and the accompanying indexes and registers, there were daybooks, ledgers, lists, and various other types of records.

This general system of record-keeping prevailed not only in the Secretary's Office but in the other offices and the bureaus of the Navy Department until 1885. A different system was established for the Department by a regulation issued by the Secretary of the Navy on January 14 of that year. Letters received and press copies or carbon copies of related letters sent were folded, stamped, and briefed as serially numbered units, usually $3\frac{1}{2}$ inches wide and 8 inches long, which were filed in numerical order in narrow wooden boxes. Bound series of letters sent and of letters received, classified and labeled according to classes of correspondents, were thus succeeded, with some exceptions, by a single general file in each office.

In the Secretary's Office most of the exceptions were discontinued by a special order of October 30, 1886, directing that on and after November 15 "the following record books will be dispensed with, viz:—General Letter, Officers, Commandants of Yards and Superintendent of Naval Academy, Squadrons, Bureaus, Marine Corps, Executive and Congress." After this date only occasional small series of letters received relating to special subjects or forming bulky enclosures were bound separately; and handwritten copies of letters sent were replaced by series of press-copy books, containing duplicates of press copies that were inserted in the general file.

Bound indexes were continued in the Secretary's Office till June 1897, after which date they were replaced by card indexes. Chronological registers ("briefing records"), the preparation of which had been required by the regulation of January 14, 1885, were also continued till June 1897, after which date they were replaced by card registers ("history cards"). The preparation of press-copy books was discontinued in December 1911 and that of history cards in August 1926; after 1915 all correspondence was filed flat in stapled and labeled folders; and in August 1926 the system of filing correspondence by serial numbers was succeeded by the subject-numeric system prescribed by the Navy Filing Manual, which still prevails. A similar sequence of changes occurred at various dates in the other offices and the bureaus of the Navy Department.

The Naval Records Collection contains nearly all the bound records that originated in the Office of the Secretary of the Navy before 1886. Only a few bound volumes of later date are included. Quantities of individual papers, however, have been removed from the general files by the Office of Naval Records and Library and have been incorporated into its Area and Subject Files (Entries 463 and 464). These files also contain loose papers from the Secretary's Office of dates previous to 1885. All papers in the Area File and the Subject File are arranged by subject only, without regard to the series of which they were formerly part or to the offices and bureaus in which they originated. Such papers, therefore, can no longer be distinguished as records of offices and bureaus.

Records created by the Office of the Secretary of the Navy that are in the National Archives and are not included in the Naval Records Collection are allocated to Record Group 80, General Records of the Department of the Navy, with the exception of certain records that are in Record Group 24, Records of the Bureau of Naval Personnel, and in Record Group 125, Records of the Office of the Judge Advocate General (Navy).

A. General Records, 1798-1910

The records described below are general in that they relate to most or all functions of the Office of the Secretary of the Navy, and are not confined to particular subjects. They consist chiefly of correspondence, bound in separate series of letters sent and letters received, with accompanying indexes.

1. Copies of Letters Sent, 1798-1910

LETTERS TO OFFICERS. Mar. 1798 - Sept. 1886. 93 vols. 23 ft. Handwritten copies. Arranged chronologically. Indexed.
Vols. 1-84 (Mar. 1798 - Sept. 1868) are entitled "Letters to Officers, Ships of War"; vols. 85-87 (Sept. 1868 - Sept. 1871), "Letters to Port Admirals, Command'ts of Yards, &c., Naval Academy, Commanding & Other Officers"; and vols. 88-93 (Sept. 1871 - Sept. 1886), "Letters to Commandants of Navy Yards & Stations." In the earlier volumes the instructions, appointments, permissions, and other communications issued by the Secretary of the Navy are addressed to officers of all ranks from flag officer to boatswain. Later volumes are progressively less inclusive as a result of the establishment of new series consisting of classes of materials no longer bound in this primary series. Such series comprise letters to officers of the Marine Corps, 1804-86 (formerly part of the Naval Records Collection but now in Record Group 80, General Records of the Department of the Navy); letters to commandants and naval agents, 1808-65 (Entry 6); letters to flag officers, 1861-86 (Entry 16); and letters to Naval Academy, commanding, and other

(handwritten margin notes: 1; Vols. 1-84 (1798-1868); M149)

3

officers, 1869-84 (Entry 17). The series described in Entry 6, consisting originally of letters to commandants, changed gradually till the series contained only letters to navy agents; and in proportion as the change occurred, letters to commandants reappeared in the present series. The series consisted almost exclusively of such letters after 1869, when most letters to officers who were neither flag officers nor commandants began to be bound in the series described in Entry 17.

REGISTER OF LETTERS TO PORT ADMIRALS AND COMMANDANTS. Nov. 1869 –
    Jan. 1877. 1 vol. 3/4 in. Arranged by ports, thereunder
    chronologically.   **2**

MISCELLANEOUS LETTERS SENT ("General Letter Book"). June 1798 –
    Nov. 1886. 107 vols. 25 ft. Handwritten copies. Arranged
    chronologically. Indexed.   **3**
    Originally this series consisted of copies of letters to all classes of correspondents except executive agents (Entry 4) and officers of the Navy and Marine Corps (Entry 1). The later letters are addressed to applicants for appointment, claimants, inventors, inquirers, and others. Many of the letters would seem appropriate for inclusion in other series.

LETTERS TO FEDERAL EXECUTIVE AGENTS. June 1798 – June 1824. 5 vols.
    10 in. Handwritten copies. Arranged by classes of correspondents,
    thereunder chronologically. Indexed.   **4**
    To the President ("Nominations for Appointment of Officers" and other subjects, July 1798 – June 1824, 2 vols.), the Secretary of State (July 1798 – June 1824), the Secretary of War (June 1798 – June 1824), and the Secretary of the Treasury ("Requisitions upon U. S. Treasury" and other subjects, June 1798 – Aug. 1803). For later letters to executive agents, see Entry 10.

LETTERS TO CONGRESS ("Congress"). Dec. 1798 – July 1886. 18 vols.
    3 ft. 7 in. Handwritten copies. Arranged chronologically.
    Indexed.   **5**
    Chiefly to presiding officers and to chairmen of committees. From 1820 to 1831, letters to individual members of Congress were bound separately (Entry 9). Letters in reply to Congressmen who recommended candidates, urged mitigation of court-martial sentences, or otherwise corresponded with the Secretary of the Navy in favor of individuals were usually entered in the "General Letter Book" (Entry 3).

LETTERS TO COMMANDANTS AND NAVY AGENTS. Jan. 1808 – Dec. 1865.
M441   10 vols. 2 ft. 3 in. Handwritten copies. Arranged chronologi-
    cally. Indexed.   **6**
    Vols. 1-5 are entitled "Navy Yards"; vols. 6-10, "Navy Agents." The earlier volumes consist chiefly of letters to commandants; the middle volumes of letters to both commandants and navy agents; and the later volumes of letters to navy agents. The numbering, binding, and dates of the volumes permit no doubt that they were maintained as a single series. Before 1808, letters to navy agents had been entered in the

"General Letter Book" (Entry 3) and those to commandants in "Officers, Ships of War" (Entry 1). As letters to commandants became infrequent in this series, they reappeared in "Officers, Ships of War." The office of navy agent was abolished by an act of April 17, 1866. For letters from the Board of Navy Commissioners to commandants and navy agents, see Entries 216 and 215.

CONFIDENTIAL LETTERS SENT ("Private Letters"). Feb. 1813 - Mar. 1822, Jan. 1840. 1 vol. 3 in. Handwritten copies. Arranged chronologically. Typed index.   7
    No other series of confidential letters sent is known to have been maintained before that described in Entry 14.

LETTERS TO THE BOARD OF NAVY COMMISSIONERS. Apr. 1815 - Aug. 1829, Jan. 1836 - Apr. 1842. 2 vols. 4¼ in. Handwritten copies. Arranged chronologically. Indexed.   8
    First volume entitled "Naval Board"; second, "Letters to Navy Commrs." As the second volume is numbered "3," it is clear that a middle volume existed. The original letters received by the Navy Commissioners from the Secretary form the series described in Entry 222, which seems complete. The letters relate chiefly to the manufacture and repair of vessels and parts of vessels and the procurement and disbursement of supplies.

LETTERS TO MEMBERS OF CONGRESS. Nov. 1820 - Dec. 1851. 3 vols. 6 in. Handwritten copies. Indexed.   9
    Chiefly in reply to Congressmen who recommended candidates, urged mitigation of court-martial sentences, or otherwise addressed the Secretary of the Navy in favor of individuals. See Entry 5 for other letters to Congress.

LETTERS TO FEDERAL EXECUTIVE AGENTS ("Executive Letter Book").   M472
    July 1821 - Nov. 1886. 41 vols. 10 ft. Handwritten copies. Arranged chronologically. Indexed by titles of correspondents.   10
    Includes letters to the President, the heads of departments, and other executive agents outside the Navy Department. See Entry 4 for earlier letters to executive agents.

INDEX TO LETTERS SENT. Dec. 1823 - Dec. 1861. 69 vols. 10 ft. 3 in. Arranged chronologically by volumes, thereunder by first letter of correspondents' names or titles, thereunder chronologically.   11
    "Key to Office Letters," vols. 1-42, ending July 1843; and "Key to Letters," vols. 1-16, 18-28, beginning Aug. 1843 (vol. 17 lacking). No difference between the two is perceptible except in dimensions of volumes. Both give date of letter sent, name and address of correspondent, and abstract. The index does not indicate the series of bound volumes in which the letters are copied. Successor volumes are in the National Archives in Record Group 80, General Records of the Department of the Navy.

LETTERS SENT. Jan. 1832 - Dec. 1833. 7 vols. 1 ft. 5 in. Press
    copies. Arranged by classes of correspondents, thereunder
    chronologically. Indexed.   12
    To commanders (Feb. 1832 - Nov. 1833, 1 vol.), other officers
(Jan. 1832 - Nov. 1833, 4 vols.), applicants for office (Jan.-Dec.
1833, 1 vol.), and other correspondents (July-Dec. 1832, 1 vol.).
Duplicated in series of handwritten copies. These volumes may be
remnants of an extensive series.

LETTERS TO BUREAUS OF THE NAVY DEPARTMENT ("Letters to Heads of
M480   Bureaus"). Sept. 1842 - Nov. 1886. 7 vols. 1 ft. 6 in.
    Handwritten copies. Arranged chronologically. Indexed.   13
    In effect a continuation of the series described in Entry 8, the
bureaus having succeeded to the functions of the Board of Navy
Commissioners.

CONFIDENTIAL LETTERS SENT ("Record of Confidential Letters").
    Sept. 1843 - Dec. 1879. 5 vols. 1 ft. Handwritten copies.
    Arranged chronologically. Indexed.   14
    See Entry 7 for earlier confidential letters.

CONFIDENTIAL LETTERS TO THE SECRETARY OF WAR AND TO OFFICERS OF THE
    ARMY, THE NAVY, AND THE MARINE CORPS. Nov. 1861 - Sept. 1875.
    1 vol. 3 in. Press copies. Arranged chronologically. Indexed. 15

LETTERS TO OFFICERS COMMANDING SQUADRONS OR VESSELS ("Letters to Flag
    Officers"). Sept. 1861 - May 1886. 8 vols. 2 ft. Hand-
    written copies. Arranged chronologically. Indexed.   16
    Chiefly to commanders, captains, commodores, and rear admirals in
command of either squadrons or single vessels. For similar letters
of earlier date see Entry 1.

LETTERS TO NAVAL ACADEMY, COMMANDING, AND OTHER OFFICERS. Nov. 1869 -
    Aug. 1884. 15 vols. 3 ft. 2 in. Handwritten copies.
    Arranged chronologically. Indexed.   17
    Chiefly to officers not addressed in the series described in
Entries 1 and 16—that is, to officers not in command of shore establishments, vessels, or squadrons. Each of the three series contains
occasional letters appropriate for inclusion in one of the other two.
The title, from the backstrips of the volumes, is not closely related
to their contents; but precise designation seems impossible.

LETTERS TO OFFICERS GENERALLY. Oct. 1884 - Nov. 1886. 3 vols. 7 in.
    Handwritten copies. Arranged chronologically. Indexed.   18
    To officers of all ranks from rear admiral to boatswain. Apparently
a continuation of the preceding series (Entry 17). Title from backstrips of the volumes.

TRANSLATIONS OF MESSAGES SENT IN CIPHER. Oct. 1888 - Jan. 1910.
    1 vol. and 3 adhesive binders. 8 in. Arranged chronologically.   19
    Press copies (Oct. 1888 - Jan. 1910, 3 binders, indexed) and typed
copies (Oct. 1888 - July 1895), probably prepared by the Office of
Naval Intelligence.

CONFIDENTIAL LETTERS SENT. Sept. 1893 - Oct. 1908. 4 vols. 8 in.
Press copies. Arranged chronologically. Indexed.   20
Dated Sept. 1893 - Jan. 1897, July 1894 - Mar. 1900, Sept. 1899 -
June 1904 (labeled "No. 3"), and June 1904 - Oct. 1908. Many letters
in the last 2 vols. bear numbers preceded by "G. B." (General Board);
and some of these, though signed by the Secretary of the Navy, were
typed on stationery with the letterhead of the Board. The volumes may
be fragments of three series.

2. Letters Received, 1801-1910

MISCELLANEOUS LETTERS RECEIVED ("Miscellaneous Letters"). Jan. 1801 -
Dec. 1884. 811 vols. 217 ft. Arranged chronologically.
Indexed.   21
The first volume of this series contains letters from all classes
of correspondents. The series became increasingly limited as more
specialized series were separated from it. These include letters from M124
Congress, 1825-61 (Entry 27); from the Navy Commissioners, 1827-42
(Entry 28), and from their successors, the chiefs of bureaus, 1842-85
(Entry 32); from Federal executive agents, 1837-86 (Entry 29); from
navy agents and naval storekeepers, 1843-65 (Entry 33); and from the
Fourth Auditor and the Second Comptroller of the Treasury, 1847-84
(Entry 57). By 1884 the letters were chiefly from applicants for employment, inventors, senders of bills, persons requesting copies of
publications, and other correspondents whose letters were not appropriate for inclusion in other series. According to a card catalogue
prepared by the Office of Naval Records and Library (Entry 465), a volume entitled "Miscellaneous Letters, 1794-1800" was "broken up and
archived" in Apr. 1931, and "Miscellaneous Letters (& Captains' Letters),
1798-1826" received similar treatment in Feb. 1930. The papers formerly
in these two volumes are now distributed through the "Area File" and the
"Subject File" (Entries 463 and 464). The earliest volume of "Miscellaneous Letters" on the shelf is "Vol. 2"; in the catalogue volume 1 is
marked as missing.

LETTERS FROM OFFICERS OF RANK BELOW THAT OF COMMANDER ("Officers'
Letters"). Apr. 1802 - Dec. 1884 (volume for Nov. 1884 lacking).
845 vols. 231 ft. Arranged chronologically. Most vols. indexed. 22
From lieutenants, ensigns, midshipmen, and staff and noncommissioned officers. For the period of the Civil War the series includes M148
letters from both regular and volunteer officers. Most of the letters
concern only their writers, who request orders, detachment, transfer,
leave of absence, or extension of leave, or acknowledge appointment or
orders, report obedience to orders, announce change of address or state
of health, transmit copies of requested papers, or tender resignation.
Some of the letters recommend candidates for appointment or promotion;
and some, particularly from lieutenants, are reports of naval actions.
Originally the series contained letters from all classes of officers,
but more specialized series were separated from it, including letters
from commanders, 1804-86 (Entry 23); from captains, 1805-61, 1866-85
(Entry 24); and from officers of the Marine Corps, 1828-86 (formerly
part of the Naval Records Collection).

LETTERS FROM COMMANDERS. Apr. 1804 - Dec. 1886 (volume for 1823
    lacking). 217 vols. 52 ft. Arranged chronologically. Indexed. 23
    Entitled "Masters Commandant" through Dec. 1837, thereafter "Com-
manders' Letters." The rank of master commandant, abolished by an act
of Mar. 3, 1837, was intermediate between those of lieutenant and
captain, and was replaced by that of commander. In this series, as
in the preceding one, many letters concern only the writers; but a
higher proportion are reports of naval actions.

LETTERS FROM CAPTAINS ("Captains' Letters"). Jan. 1805 - Dec. 1861,
    Jan. 1866 - Dec. 1885, with the volume for Aug. 1843 lacking.
    413 vols. 96 ft. Arranged chronologically. Indexed.   24
    For letters from captains, 1862-65, see Entry 57; from captains
commanding squadrons, 1841-86, Entry 30; from captains commanding
shore establishments, 1848-86, Entry 34. This series consists largely
of reports of activities at sea.

LETTERS FROM OFFICERS COMMANDING EXPEDITIONS. Jan. 1818 - Dec. 1885,
    with gaps. 23 vols. 4 ft. 8 in. Arranged in 14 subseries
    (listed in Appendix A), thereunder chronologically. Some
    volumes indexed.   25
    Scattered volumes or groups of volumes of letters relating to the
Pacific Exploring Expedition of 1838-42, the North Pacific Exploring
Expedition of 1852-56, and other expeditions. Usually designated as
"Exploring Expedition Letters," though not all the expeditions were
concerned with exploration. Most of the letters are from lieutenants
and commanders.

INDEX TO LETTERS RECEIVED ("Key to Letters Received"). Dec. 1823 -
    Dec. 1866. 81 vols. 13 ft. 4 in. Arranged chronologically by
    volumes, thereunder by first letter of correspondents' names or
    titles, thereunder chronologically.   26
    Gives date when each letter was received; date of writing; name and
rank of writer; his ship, station, or residence; clerk with whom letter
was deposited; and abstract. Does not indicate the series of volumes in
which the letters were bound. Successor volumes are in the National
Archives in Record Group 80, General Records of the Department of the
Navy.

LETTERS FROM CONGRESS. Dec. 1825 - Dec. 1861. 6 vols. 1 ft. 1 in.
    Arranged chronologically in overlapping volumes. Indexed.   27
    Chiefly resolutions, with covering letters, and also requests for
information, with some letters from chiefs of bureaus providing information thus requested. Similar letters of earlier and later date are
in "Miscellaneous Letters" (Entry 21), which also contains most letters
from individual Congressmen as distinguished from committees or the
Senate and the House in general. The first and the last volume are
entitled "Resolutions"; the others, "Congress." All the volumes, however, consist chiefly of resolutions and obviously form one series.

LETTERS FROM THE BOARD OF NAVY COMMISSIONERS ("Navy Commissioners'
    Letters"). Jan. 1827 - Aug. 1842. 27 vols. 6 ft. 3 in.
    Arranged chronologically. Indexed.   28
    Previous letters from the Navy Commissioners are in "Miscellaneous
Letters" (Entry 21); copies retained by the Board, 1815-42, are
described in Entry 213. The letters relate chiefly to estimates of
funds, accounts and contracts, stores and supplies, civil personnel
in navy yards, and the building and repairing of ships and parts of
ships.

LETTERS FROM FEDERAL EXECUTIVE AGENTS ("Executive Letters"). May 1837 -
    Dec. 1886. 131 vols. 35 ft. Arranged chronologically.   M517
    Indexed in fronts of volumes by agencies, beginning with the
    Executive Mansion and proceeding to departments in order of
    their founding.   29
    Similar letters of earlier date are in "Miscellaneous Letters"
(Entry 21).

LETTERS FROM OFFICERS COMMANDING SQUADRONS (orally designated as
    "Squadron Letters"). Feb. 1841 - Nov. 1886. 309 vols. 77 ft.
    Arranged by squadrons in 24 subseries (listed in Appendix B),
    thereunder chronologically. Indexed.   30
    Reports usually numbered separately by each commanding officer
during his period of command, with enclosed letters from subordinate   M89
officers, officers of foreign navies, ministers and consuls of the
United States and sometimes of foreign states, American citizens in
distress, and other persons. Some of the letters from subordinate
officers were delivered directly to the Secretary of the Navy without
passing through the hands of a commanding officer, and therefore were
not enclosures. Many letters from subordinate officers that might
have been included in this series as enclosures were bound instead in
"Commanders' Letters" and "Officers' Letters" (Entries 23 and 22).
Before 1841 most letters from commanding officers of squadrons were
bound in "Captains' Letters" (Entry 24). Before 1857 the officer commanding a squadron was regularly a captain, the highest rank in the
United States Navy, but was addressed by the honorary title of commodore.
An act of Jan. 16, 1857, provided that captains in command of squadrons
should be denominated flag officers. By an act of July 16, 1862, the
rank of rear admiral was created and that of commodore was established
as a regular rather than an honorary rank; thereafter the commanding
officer of a squadron was regularly a rear admiral or a commodore.
Before the Civil War the United States Fleet was distributed in six
squadrons: the Home Squadron, the Mediterranean Squadron, the African
Squadron, the Brazil Squadron, the Pacific Squadron, and the East India
Squadron. All but the Pacific Squadron were disbanded or virtually disbanded during the Civil War. The squadrons of the Civil War were the
Atlantic Blockading Squadron (divided in 1861 into the North Atlantic
Blockading Squadron and the South Atlantic Blockading Squadron, the
former centering its activities off the coasts of Virginia and North
Carolina and the latter off South Carolina), the Gulf Blockading Squad-
ron (divided in 1862 into the East Gulf Blockading Squadron and the West
Gulf Blockading Squadron, recombined in 1865 to form the Gulf Squadron,

disbanded in 1867), the West India Squadron, the Mississippi Squadron, and the Pacific Squadron, in addition to the Potomac Flotilla. The squadrons established after the Civil War were the North Atlantic Squadron, the South Atlantic Squadron, the European Squadron, the Asiatic Squadron, and the Training Squadron, besides the surviving Pacific Squadron. Others, maintained for short periods of time, were the Eastern Squadron (1853), the James River Flotilla and the Mortar Flotilla (1862), the Atlantic Squadron (1865-66), and the Special Squadron (1865).

INDEX TO LETTERS RECEIVED RELATING TO SQUADRONS ("Key to Letters Received"). Jan 1848 - July 1858. 8 vols. 1 ft. Arranged chronologically by volumes, thereunder by first letter in alphabets for squadrons and for correspondents outside squadrons, thereunder chronologically.   31

Volumes numbered from A through H, probably to prevent confusion with those described in Entry 26. The register gives number of letter received, dates of writing and receipt, writer's name, his ship, station, or residence, and abstract of letter.

LETTERS FROM BUREAUS OF THE NAVY DEPARTMENT ("Letters from Bureaux," later "Bureau Letters"). Sept. 1842 - Dec. 1885. 86 vols. 23 ft. Arranged chronologically. Most volumes indexed.   32

1518

Letters from all bureaus form a single sequence, but the indexes in the fronts of the volumes are arranged according to bureaus. In effect this series is a continuation of that described in Entry 28, the bureaus having succeeded to the functions of the Board of Navy Commissioners.

LETTERS FROM NAVY AGENTS AND NAVAL STOREKEEPERS. Jan. 1843 - Nov. 1865. 28 vols. 5 ft. 10 in. Arranged chronologically. Indexed.   33

528   Chiefly concerning supplies and accounts. Similar letters of earlier date are in "Miscellaneous Letters" (Entry 21). Most letters from navy agents between 1815 and 1842 were addressed to the Navy Commissioners (Entry 223).

LETTERS FROM COMMANDANTS OF NAVY YARDS AND SHORE STATIONS ("Commandants' Letters"). Jan. 1848 - Dec. 1886, with 1885 lacking. 332 vols. 82 ft. Arranged in groups of volumes by shore establishments, with 42 vols. containing letters from 2 or more shore establishments; thereunder chronologically. Most volumes indexed.   34

Chiefly concerning movements and repairs of ships; appointment, detachment, and leave of naval and Marine Crops personnel; and employment of laborers. Many letters acknowledge orders, request information or orders, or forward enclosures. The prevailing practice was to bind the letters from each yard or station for each calendar year as one or more volumes, but letters from two or more yards or stations might be bound together if the bulk of letters was small. The letters are distributed as follows (number of volumes being indicated only for volumes that are confined to one shore establishment): Norfolk (39 vols.),

Pensacola (24 vols.), Portsmouth (24 vols.), and Washington (36 vols.),
1848-84, 1886; Boston (35 vols.) and New York (61 vols.), 1848-84;
Memphis, 1848-50, 1853-55; Philadelphia (35 vols.), 1848-75; Sackett's
Harbor, 1850, 1853-59; Mare Island (19 vols.), 1854-58, 1860-63,
1866-84; Baltimore (4 vols.), 1862-65; Mound City (2 vols.), 1864-73;
League Island (10 vols.), 1868-73, 1876-84; New London, 1872-73,
1882-84, 1886; Beaufort, 1882; and Key West and Newport, 1882-84,
1886. Similar letters of earlier date are in "Captains' Letters"
(Entry 24), most of the commandants being captains. Most letters
from commandants between 1815 and 1842 were addressed to the Navy Commissioners (Entry 220).

REGISTER OF LETTERS FROM COMMANDANTS. Jan. 1877 - Oct. 1881. 1 vol.
    1 in. Arranged by yards and stations, thereunder chronologi-
    cally.   35
    Gives serial number of letter, date, and abstract.

SUPPLEMENTAL LETTERS RECEIVED ("Supplemental Letters From All
    Sources"). June 1860 - Dec. 1861, Mar. 1862 - Dec. 1863,
    Jan. 1871 - Dec. 1879. 14 vols. 3 ft. 5 in. Arranged
    chronologically. Indexed.   36
    Materials apparently overlooked or missing at whatever time the
main series of letters received were bound. Some former volumes of
this series have been dismantled by the Office of Naval Records and
Library, and their contents have been distributed among the papers in
the Area File and the Subject File (Entries 463 and 464).

LETTERS FROM REAR ADMIRALS, COMMODORES, AND CAPTAINS ("Admirals',
    Commodores', and Captains' Letters"). Jan. 1862 - Dec. 1865.
    26 vols. 6 ft. 10 in. Arranged chronologically. Indexed.   37
    Letters from officers serving in squadrons or commanding shore
establishments are usually to be found not in this series but in
those described in Entries 30 and 34. Before and after the period
of this series, letters from captains form a series apart (Entry 24).

LETTERS FROM REAR ADMIRALS AND COMMODORES ("Admirals' and Commodores'
    Letters"). Jan. 1866 - Dec. 1884. 30 vols. 6 ft. 3 in.
    Arranged chronologically. Indexed.   38
    Continuation of the preceding series except that letters from
captains were not included.

REGISTER OF LETTERS RECEIVED AND REFERRED TO BUREAUS. May 1874 -
    Nov. 1884. 3 vols. 4 in. Arranged chronologically.   39
    The first volume ("Index to Letters Referred") gives name of writer
of letter, abstract, to whom referred, and date of referral. The
other volumes ("Key to Letters Received and Referred to Bureaus") give
also the rank and residence or station of the writer, the date of the
letter, and the date of its return to the Secretary of the Navy.

TRANSLATIONS OF MESSAGES RECEIVED IN CIPHER. Nov. 1888 - Aug. 1910.
    5 adhesive binders. 10 in. Arranged chronologically. Indexed. 40

B. Directives, 1776–1913

The records described below consist of orders, circulars, instructions, and regulations issued by the Secretary of the Navy to several or all units of the Navy and the Navy Department.

DIRECTIVES ("Orders, Circulars, Instructions, Regulations"). Apr. 1776 –
    Dec. 1863. 1 vol. 1 in. Arranged chronologically.   <u>41</u>
    Printed copies and a few handwritten copies, in addition to samples of blank forms. Before 1812 the only papers in the volume are printed instructions from Congress to commanders of privateer vessels, Apr. 3, 1776, and instructions from the President concerning prize goods, July 10 and Dec. 29, 1798. Few of the directives are of date previous to 1835.

DIRECTIVES ("Circulars and General Orders"). May 1798 – July 1895.
    4 vols. 1 ft. 2 in. Arranged chronologically.   <u>42</u>
    Chiefly handwritten copies, with some carbon copies and printed copies. Many directives are omitted; perhaps the intention was to include only the more important. The printed copies in the preceding and the following series are of course to be preferred to handwritten copies. For circulars issued by the Board of Navy Commissioners, see Entry 212.

DIRECTIVES ("General Orders, John Cassin"). Jan. 1863 – Feb. 1870.
    1 adhesive binder. 2 in. Printed copies. Arranged chronologically. Indexed.   <u>43</u>
    Uniform circulars, general orders 1–150, unnumbered regulations, and unnumbered circulars. John Cassin was appointed as a clerk in the Office of the Secretary of the Navy in Feb. 1873. Presumably the binder was compiled after that date. It serves (and may have been designed) as a continuation of the series described in Entry 41.

REGISTER OF DIRECTIVES ("Numerical Index to General Orders, Circulars, &c."). Jan. 1863 – Oct. 1913. 1 vol. 3/4 in.   <u>44</u>
    The date of beginning of this register is the date on which was begun the issuance of numbered directives. The register gives numbers, dates, and subjects (but not abstracts) of the following:

See M984

General orders, 1–552 (Jan. 10, 1863 – June 28, 1900), 1–80 (June 30, 1900 – Dec. 1, 1908), 1–228 (Jan. 1909 – Oct. 19, 1913)
Circulars, unnumbered (June 10, 1863 – Jan. 4, 1907)
Special circulars, unnumbered (Nov. 7, 1891 – Feb. 1, 1900)
Orders and special circulars, unnumbered (Apr. 17, 1865 – Feb. 16, 1891)
Special orders, 1–98 (Apr. 15, 1891 – Apr. 10, 1900), 1–80 (July 3, 1900 – July 3, 1905), 1–105 (Aug. 10, 1905 – Dec. 30, 1908), 1–118 (Jan. 11, 1909 – Dec. 1, 1911)
Navy regulation circulars, unnumbered (Jan. 30, 1866 – Dec. 9, 1870), [-]–19 (Dec. 1, 1871 – Oct. 17, 1876), 1–123 (Mar. 15, 1877 – Feb. 13, 1893), 1–19 (Mar. 13, 1893 – Nov. 27, 1895), 1–17 (Feb. 25, 1897 – Sept. 2, 1899), unnumbered (June 30, 1900 – Dec. 27, 1911)

Changes in uniform regulations, 1-9 (Feb: 7, 1906 - Oct. 19, 1911)
Bureau of Navigation orders, 1-20 (Oct. 1, 1889 - Jan. 1, 1892)
Bureau of Navigation information circulars, 1-17 (Feb. 15, 1890 -
    July 26, 1892)
Departmental orders, 1-61 (Dec. 16, 1893 - Mar. 27, 1908)

DIRECTIVES ("G. O. Letters"). Aug. 1890 - Oct. 1896. 1 vol. ("No. 3").
    2 in. Press copies. Arranged chronologically. Table of
    contents.   45
    Vols. 1 and 2 have not been found. These copies were prepared from
typed copies, perhaps from those that were sent to the printer. Successor volumes are in the National Archives in Record Group 80, General
Records of the Office of the Secretary of the Navy.

C. Fiscal Records, 1794-1893

    The records described below concern the receipt and disbursement of·
funds by the Office of the Secretary of the Navy. The records are fragmentary, and some can be identified only in part. A few records of similar character are among the records of the Office of the Secretary in
Record Group 80, General Records of the Secretary of the Navy; but these,
too, are scanty and fragmentary, suggesting that many of the fiscal records that must have been maintained by the Office of the Secretary have
not survived. Some records may have been transferred to the General Accounting Office.

INVENTORY OF STORES IN NAVY YARDS ("Naval Ledger, U. S. Navy Yards").
    Dec. 1794 - Mar. 1800. 1 vol. 1½ in. Arranged by yards
    (Baltimore, Boston, New York, Philadelphia, Portsmouth, N. H.,
    and Portsmouth, Va.).   46
    Probably compiled in Philadelphia before the Government removed to
Washington, and probably begun by the War Department before the Navy
Department was established in 1798.

LETTERS SENT BY THE ACCOUNTANT OF THE NAVY. Sept. 1798 - May 1800.
    1 vol. 2 in. Handwritten copies. Arranged chronologically.
    Indexed.   47
    The Office of the Accountant of the Navy was established in the
Navy Department by an act of July 16, 1798. It was his duty to settle
"all accounts for monies advanced and stores issued or distributed by
or under the direction of the Secretary of the Navy," and to "report
from time to time, all such settlements . . . for the inspection and
revision of the accounting officers of the treasury." The office was
abolished by an act of Mar. 3, 1817. The letters in this volume are
addressed to the Comptroller of the Treasury and to naval agents,
pursers, private claimants, and others, notifying them that warrants
drawn in their favor have been issued or that their accounts are found
unsatisfactory.

RECEIPT BOOK OF THE ACCOUNTANT OF THE NAVY. July 1809 - Jan. 1820.
1 vol. 1¼ in. Arranged chronologically.   48
   Contains the original signatures of persons receiving payment.
The entries after Mar. 1817 were made in the Office of the Secretary
of the Navy.

LEDGER OF THE ACCOUNTANT OF THE NAVY. Jan. 1811 - Jan. 1813. 1 vol.
3/4 in. Arranged by objects of expenditure, thereunder chronologically. Table of contents.   49

REGISTER OF WARRANTS DRAWN BY THE SECRETARY OF THE NAVY UPON THE
SECRETARY OF THE TREASURY. Dec. 1811 - June 1820, July 1822 -
Sept. 1842. 19 vols. 2 ft. 7 in. Arranged by warrant number.   50
   Gives date of warrant, to whom issued, distribution of the moneys
involved under each object of appropriation, and total sum of warrant.
Apparently in three subseries: (1) volumes labeled "Warrant Book,"
beginning with vol. 10 but not consistently numbered thereafter, containing warrants 1675-6363 (Dec. 2, 1811 - Mar. 3, 1817), 1-2730
(Mar. 12, 1817 - June 30, 1820), 1-5308 (July 1, 1822 - Dec. 30, 1826),
and 1-7368 (Jan. 1, 1827 - Sept. 29, 1832); (2) vols. 18, 16, and 17
(in chronological order), the first labeled "Refunding," containing
warrants 1-628 (July 3, 1822 - Dec. 29, 1826) and 1-1560 (Jan. 1, 1827 -
Feb. 28, 1837); and (3) "Warrant Book No. 18," containing warrants
1561-2322 (Mar. 9, 1837 - Sept. 26, 1842). In dimensions and format
the three subseries have little resemblance, and the numbers affixed to
the volumes seem inexplicable. Possibly fragments of more than three
subseries are present. At least two numbering systems or series of
warrants existed concurrently between 1822 and 1832.

DAYBOOK OF THE TREASURER OF THE NAVY. May 1816 - Sept. 1817. 1 vol.
½ in. Arranged chronologically.   51

SUMMARY OF ACCOUNTS OF NAVY AGENTS AND PURSERS. Jan. 1824 - Jan. 1826.
1 vol. 1/3 in. Arranged chronologically. Table of contents.   52
   Chiefly in pencil.

EXHIBIT OF APPROPRIATIONS FOR THE NAVY AND MARINE CORPS AND THE EXPEN-
DITURE THEREOF. June 1828 - Nov. 1830. 1 vol. 3/4 in.
Arranged chronologically.   53

REGISTER OF BILLS OF EXCHANGE DRAWN UPON THE SECRETARY OF THE NAVY
("Bill Book, Navy Department"). Aug. 1830 - May 1865. 3 vols.
2½ in. Arranged chronologically.   54
   Gives date and place of drawing of bill, by whom drawn, in whose
favor, for what amount, from what appropriation, requisition number,
and to whom paid. The bills were drawn chiefly by ships and stations.

ACCOUNTS OF EXPENDITURES UNDER VARIOUS CONTRACTS ("Memoranda, Naval
Contracts"). Oct. 1838 - Aug. 1854. 1 vol. 1 in. Arranged
chronologically. Indexed.   55
   In the absence of other volumes, it seems impossible to determine
what distinguished the few contracts referred to from other contracts.

LEDGER OF CONTINGENT EXPENSES OF THE NAVY DEPARTMENT AND ITS BUREAUS.
    May 1845 - July 1851. 1 vol. ½ in. Arranged chronologically.   <u>56</u>

LETTERS FROM THE FOURTH AUDITOR AND THE SECOND COMPTROLLER OF THE
    TREASURY. Jan. 1847 - Dec. 1884. 59 vols. 12 ft. 8 in.
    Arranged chronologically. Indexed.   <u>57</u>
    Chiefly form letters notifying the Secretary of the Navy that
accounts submitted by him have been passed, transmitting papers relating to claims for travel expenses to be acted upon by him, requesting
copies of documents, acknowledging receipt of contracts, inquiring as
to rank or promotions of naval officers, or requesting or transmitting
other information. Before 1847 the letters from the Fourth Auditor
and the Second Comptroller were bound in "Miscellaneous Letters" (Entry
21). The offices of the Fourth Auditor and the Second Comptroller were
established in the Treasury Department by an act of Mar. 3, 1817. The
act provided that the Fourth Auditor should receive all accounts accru-
ing in or relative to the Navy Department, examine the accounts and
certify the balance, transmit the accounts (with their vouchers and
certificates) to the Second Comptroller for his decision, receive from
him and preserve the accounts that had been finally adjusted, record all
warrants drawn by the Secretary of the Navy, report to the Secretary of
the Navy when requested by him, and report annually to the Secretary of
the Treasury. It was the duty of the Second Comptroller to examine all
accounts settled by the Fourth Auditor, to certify the balance to the
Secretary of the Navy, to countersign all warrants lawfully drawn by the
Secretary of the Navy, to report to him the official forms to be used
for disbursing the public money and the manner and form of keeping accounts, and to supervise the preservation of the public accounts subject
to his revision. The Fourth Auditor was concerned only with accounts of
the Navy Department; the Second Comptroller handled also those of the War
Department.

LEDGER OF RECEIPTS AND DISBURSEMENTS OF FUNDS FROM WAR DUTIES LEVIED
    IN MEXICO ("Mexican War Duties Ledger"). May 1847 - Jan. 1849.
    1 vol. 2½ in. Arranged chronologically. Indexed.   <u>58</u>

MONTHLY SUMMARY STATEMENTS OF RECEIPTS AND EXPENDITURES SUBMITTED BY
    NAVY AGENTS, PURSERS, AND QUARTERMASTER'S DEPARTMENTS OF THE
    MARINE CORPS. Jan. 1849 - Jan. 1850. 2 vols. 2¼ in. Arranged
    by disbursing authority (agents in one vol., pursers and quarter-
    masters in the other), thereunder chronologically.   <u>59</u>

DAYBOOK OF CONTINGENT EXPENSES OF THE NAVY DEPARTMENT. Jan. 1849 -
    Dec. 1856. 1 vol. ½ in. Arranged chronologically.   <u>60</u>

INVENTORY OF PROPERTY IN SHORE ESTABLISHMENTS ("Inventory of Public
    Property"). 1878. 4 vols. 10 in. Arranged by shore establish-
    ments.   <u>61</u>
    Inventories, some on printed forms, submitted to the Secretary of
the Navy at his request, consisting of one volume for Boston and Mare

Island; one for Norfolk, Key West, and Pensacola; one for Portsmouth, New York, and League Island; and one for Washington, Newport, Naval Academy, Naval Asylum, New London, Marine Corps, and Miscellaneous.

WEEKLY STATEMENTS OF PURCHASES BY BUREAUS. Jan. 1883 - June 1890.
    7 vols. 1 ft. 3 in. Arranged chronologically by volumes,
    thereunder by bureaus, thereunder chronologically.   62
Transmitted by heads of bureaus to the Secretary of the Navy.

LETTERS FROM THE SECRETARY OF THE TREASURY CONCERNING CUSTOMS DUTIES
    ON NAVAL MATERIALS ("Treasury Department Letters"). Jan.-Nov.
    1884. 1 vol. 1½ in. Arranged chronologically. Indexed.   63
    Acknowledgment, on a printed form, of requests from the Secretary
of the Navy that specified articles be admitted at ports of entry free
of duties and charges for the use of the Navy.

INVENTORIES OF THE PERSONAL PROPERTY OF THE NAVY DEPARTMENT IN
    BUREAUS AND OFFICES AT WASHINGTON AND IN PAY OFFICES. Mar. 1885 -
    Mar. 1893. 2 vols. 3 in.   64
    The first volume covers March-June 1885; the second is a continua-
tion to December 1887, with one inventory of March 1893. "Personal
property" is apparently understood as movable public property exclu-
sive of charts, maps, books, stationery, models, and drawings.

D. Personnel Records, 1798-1890

The records described below concern the appointment, employment,
resignation, and retirement of naval, Marine Corps, and civil personnel,
the orders issued to officers, and the numbers and distribution of personnel. As explained in Section III-F, various functions relative to
naval (but not Marine Corps) officers were centered in an Office of
Detail within the Office of the Secretary of the Navy in or before 1861;
in 1865 the Office of Detail was placed under the Chief of the Bureau of
Navigation (without ceasing to be part of the Office of the Secretary);
and in 1889 most functions relative to naval officers were transferred
to the Bureau of Navigation. Most functions relative to enlisted men
of the Navy were transferred from the Office of the Secretary to the
Bureau of Equipment and Recruiting in 1862, and thence to the Bureau of
Navigation in 1889. Functions relative to civil personnel are retained
by the Office of the Secretary. Most of the records described below
would normally have been transferred to the Bureau of Navigation in 1889,
with the functions to which they relate; but apparently some of the records were transferred directly from the Office of the Secretary to the
Office of Naval Records and Library.

1. Correspondence, 1803-1890

LETTERS OF RESIGNATION FROM OFFICERS. Mar. 1803 - June 1877. 14 vols.
    4 ft. 8 in.   65
    (1) Alphabetical subseries, 1803-25 (1 vol.); (2) alphabetical
subseries, 1810-25 (2 vols.); and (3) "Resignations of Officers of the

U. S. Navy," 1812-77, arranged chronologically, indexed (11 vols.).
The papers in the three subseries appear to be identical in character.
Those in (3) were probably bound contemporaneously; the others were
probably assembled and bound at two later times, possibly because
they had been previously lost or overlooked. See Entries 76 and 85
for other letters of resignation.

LETTERS FROM OFFICERS ACKNOWLEDGING RECEIPT OF COMMISSIONS AND
    WARRANTS AND ENCLOSING OATHS OF ALLEGIANCE ("Acceptances").
    July 1804 - Oct. 1864. 50 vols. 11 ft. 6 in.   66
    (1) Alphabetical subseries, 1804-23 (3 vols.); (2) alphabetical
subseries, 1809-39 (4 vols.); and (3) chronological subseries, indexed, 1812-64. As in the preceding series, the papers in the three
subseries are apparently identical in character. See Entry 78 for
similar letters of volunteer officers.

LETTERS FROM OFFICERS ACCEPTING, DECLINING, AND RESIGNING APPOINT-
    MENTS AND STATING PLACES OF BIRTH AND RESIDENCE ("Acceptances,
    Resignations, Place of Birth"). Jan. 1804 - Dec. 1826. 1 vol.
    1½ in.   67
    Acceptances, Sept. 1805 - Apr. 1812, arranged chronologically;
resignations and declinations, Jan. 1804 - July 1820, arranged chronologically; letters relating to death and dismissal, Apr. and July 1804;
and letters indicating places of birth, appointment, and residence,
1826, arranged alphabetically. These papers were probably omitted by
oversight from other series of bound records.

LETTERS FROM MIDSHIPMEN ACCEPTING APPOINTMENT AND ENCLOSING OATHS OF
    ALLEGIANCE ("Officers, Acceptances of Appointments, Midshipmen").
    Jan. 1810 - Dec. 1814. 1 vol. 5 in. Arranged chronologically.
    Indexed.   68

STATEMENTS OF PLACE OF BIRTH FROM APPOINTEES. Aug.-Dec. 1816. 1 vol.
    1 in. Arranged chronologically.   69

LETTERS OF APPOINTMENT TO CIVIL APPOINTEES. Dec. 1825 - June 1829,
    Apr. 1841 - June 1855. 1 vol. 1¼ in. Handwritten copies.
    Arranged chronologically. Indexed.   70
    According to a note in the front of the volume, civil appointments
from 1829 to 1841 were entered in the "General Letter Book" (Entry 3).

STATEMENTS OF PLACE OF BIRTH AND RESIDENCE FROM APPOINTEES. Jan.-June
    1826. 2 vols. 8 in. Arranged alphabetically.   71
    Gives name of applicant and State or Territory in which born, from
which appointed, and of which a citizen. A printed form.

STATEMENTS OF SERVICE FROM OFFICERS ("Returns of Services of Officers").
    Aug. 1842 - Aug. 1843. 2 vols. 6 in. Arranged by officers'
    rank, thereunder by date of receipt of statements. Indexed.   72
    Two printed forms: "A. Statement of the Services of _____, U. S.
Navy, from the Time of His Entrance (or First Appointment) to the
31st December, 1841" and "B. Statement of the Departure and Arrival of
the Several U. S. Vessels of War, on Board of Which _____, of the

U. S. Navy, Has Served at Different Periods." These records refer
to naval services as early as 1798.

TABULAR SUMMARY OF OFFICERS' STATEMENTS OF SERVICE ("Services of
     Officers, 1798-1842"). Aug. 1842 - Aug. 1843. 1 vol. $2\frac{1}{4}$ in.
     Arranged by officers' rank. Indexed.   73
  Gives officer's name, dates of service in each station, dates of
holding of each rank, and number of days of sea service and of other
duty.

WARRANTS ISSUED TO NAVAL ENGINEERS ("Warrants, Naval Engineers").
     Oct. 1860 - June 1868. 2 vols. ("2" and "3"). 4 in. Handwritten
     copies on printed forms. Arranged chronologically. Indexed.   74

INDEX TO VOL. 2 OF WARRANTS ISSUED TO NAVAL ENGINEERS. Oct. 1860 -
     June 1864. 1 vol. $\frac{1}{2}$ in. Arranged by first letter of names,
     thereunder chronologically.   75

LETTERS FROM OFFICERS TENDERING THEIR RESIGNATIONS BUT DISMISSED
     INSTEAD. Nov. 1860 - Dec. 1861. 1 vol. and loose papers.
     4 in. Unarranged. Indexed.   76
  The volume is labeled "Resignations and Dismissals of Officers
from the U. S. Navy"; the loose papers are of the same character.
The resignations were submitted by officers unwilling to engage in
action against the Confederate States. The fact and date of each
dismissal are indicated in endorsements.

OATHS OF ALLEGIANCE FROM OFFICERS ("Oaths of Allegiance"). May 1861 -
     Dec. 1862. 2 vols. 5 in. 1 vol. arranged by first letter of
     names; 1 vol. unarranged. Indexed.   77

LETTERS FROM VOLUNTEER OFFICERS ACKNOWLEDGING RECEIPT OF COMMISSIONS
     AND WARRANTS AND ENCLOSING OATHS OF ALLEGIANCE ("Acceptances").
     May 1861 - July 1871. 38 vols. 10 ft. 5 in. Indexed.   78
  Received by the Secretary of the Navy. Arranged chronologically
in each subseries: (1) lieutenant commanders and lieutenants,
May 1861 - Feb. 1867 (1 vol.); (2) masters, May 1861 - Oct. 1867
(4 vols.); (3) ensigns, July 1862 - Aug. 1867 (8 vols.); (4) master's
mates, Sept. 1861 - May 1870 (7 vols.); (5) mates, Mar. 1865 -
Jan. 1871 (1 vol.); (6) chief engineers, Jan. 1862 - Jan. 1867 (1 vol);
(7) first ass't engineers, Jan. 1863 - Sept. 1866 (1 vol.); (8) second
ass't engineers, July 1862 - Feb. 1867 (3 vols.); (9) third ass't
engineers, Jan. 1862 - July 1867 (7 vols.); (10) ass't paymasters,
July 1861 - Aug. 1866 (2 vols.); (11) ass't surgeons, July 1862 -
July 1871 (2 vols.); and (12) admiral's secretaries, commodore's
clerks, captain's clerks, masters at arms, first-class pilots, gunners,
carpenters, and boatswains, 1862-65 (1 vol.).

LETTERS TRANSMITTING APPOINTMENTS AND ORDERS TO VOLUNTEER OFFICERS.
     May 1861 - June 1879. 10 vols. 2 ft. 3 in. Handwritten copies.
     Arranged chronologically. Indexed.   79
  Vols. 1-7 ("Acting Appointments"), May 1861 - June 1879, contain
copies of letters sent by the Secretary of the Navy. Vols. 8-10

("Orders, Volunteer Officers, General Service"), May 1865 - June 1879, contain copies of letters sent by the Chief of the Bureau of Navigation, who was ex officio head of the Office of Detail. In both format and contents the 10 volumes appear to form a single series.

CORRESPONDENCE AND DATA CONCERNING APPOINTMENTS OF VOLUNTEER OFFICERS ("Volunteer Service"). Aug. 1861 - Nov. 1867. 1 vol. 3 in. Arranged chronologically. Indexed. 80
  Applications, testimonials, copies of letters of appointment, original confirmations received from the Senate, and printed forms listing officers who joined the Navy.

ORDERS AND OTHER LETTERS TO ACTING MASTERS' MATES AND TO MATES. Jan. 1862 - Feb. 1890. 3 vols. 8 in. Handwritten copies. Arranged chronologically. Indexed. 81
  Issued by the Secretary of the Navy. The last communication to an acting master's mate is dated Mar. 11, 1865; the first to a mate, Mar. 13, 1865. By act of Congress of March 3, 1865, the title "acting master's mate" had been changed to "mate." See Entry 86 for letters and orders to mates from the Office of Detail.

ORDERS TO VOLUNTEER OFFICERS OF THE MISSISSIPPI SQUADRON ("Acting Appointments, Miss. Squadron"). Nov. 1862 - Jan. 1866. 2 vols. 4½ in. Handwritten copies. Arranged chronologically. Indexed. 82
  Issued by the Secretary of the Navy.

REGISTER OF CORRESPONDENCE. May-Oct. 1865. 2 vols. 1 in. Arranged chronologically. 83
  A rough preliminary register of letters, reports, and orders, apparently kept in the Office of Detail.

ORDERS TO VOLUNTEER OFFICERS OF THE MISSISSIPPI SQUADRON ("Orders to Volunteer Officers, Mississippi Squadron"). May-Nov. 1865. 1 vol. 3 in. Arranged chronologically. Indexed. 84
  Issued by the Office of Detail.

LETTERS OF RESIGNATION FROM VOLUNTEER OFFICERS. May 1865 - Nov. 1875. 2 vols. 6 in. Arranged chronologically. Indexed. 85
  Received by the Secretary of the Navy.

LETTERS AND ORDERS TO MATES ("Orders to Mates, General Service"). May 1865 - Aug. 1884. 1 vol. 3 in. Handwritten copies. Arranged chronologically. Indexed. 86
  Sent by the Office of Detail. At the end are two letters dated Jan. 23, 1896.

LETTERS FROM THE COMMISSIONER OF PENSIONS ("Letters from Commissioner of Pensions, Supplemental . . . Services of Officers, Volunteer and Regular"). Jan. 1870 - May 1872. 1 vol. 1¼ in. Arranged chronologically. Indexed. 87
  Requests, chiefly on printed forms, for addresses and service records. Received by the Bureau of Navigation and Office of Detail.

LETTERS OF APPLICATION FOR APPOINTMENT AS VOLUNTEER OFFICERS
("Applications for Appointment as Volunteer Officers").
Nov.-Dec. 1873. 1 vol. 2 in. Arranged chronologically.
Indexed.
Received by the Secretary of the Navy.

88

LETTERS TO THE COMMISSIONER OF PENSIONS. Dec. 1882 - Mar. 1890.
6 vols. 7½ in. Press copies. Arranged chronologically.
Indexed.
Five volumes, covering the whole period, consist of letters signed
by the Chief Clerk; one volume, May 1883 - Aug. 1885, consists of
letters sent by the Office of Detail, but seems indistinguishable
from the others in contents. The letters give either the name and
latest known address of a single officer or a list of the officers
attached to a given vessel at a given date, with rank and latest
known address.

89

2. Muster Rolls, Pay Rolls, and Rosters, 1798-1889

MUSTER ROLLS AND PAY ROLLS OF VESSELS. July 1798 - Dec. 1859, with
rolls as early as 1779 and as late as 1885. 138 vols., and
loose sheets and booklets in 111 labeled wrappers. 36 ft.
(1) Bound rolls, July 1798 - June 1847, 127 vols., arranged
alphabetically by ships' names (121 vols., with one or more volumes
to a ship) and unarranged (6 vols.); (2) bound rolls, June 1813 -
Dec. 1860, 11 vols. (with several ships to a volume), arranged by
first letter of ships' names; and (3) loose rolls, Mar. 1805 -
June 1885 (with 2 photostated rolls of 1779 and 1798-99), in 111
labeled wrappers, arranged alphabetically by ships' names. In general,
(1) includes nearly all vessels between 1798 and 1845; (2) extends
from 1846 through 1859, with a few rolls of earlier and later date;
and (3) is composed of rolls that were never bound, were bound or
merely sewed to form thin booklets, or were derived from the dismantling of large volumes that had become dilapidated. The materials in
the three subseries are identical in character, consisting of muster
rolls and pay rolls so much intermingled that they cannot conveniently
be listed separately. The muster rolls give the name of each officer
or enlisted man, his date of entry, whence he came, and his rate or
rank. The pay rolls give for an enlisted man his number on the ship's
books, his name, rate or rank, date of commencement of service or of
this settlement, term of service for which enlisted, amount of pay in
this settlement, and other details regarding pay, credit, allotments,
deductions, and refunds, with remarks. For an officer, only a part of
this information is applicable. For certain vessels of the Navy before
the Civil War no muster rolls or pay rolls are known to exist; for
many others only a few rolls survive. Commanding officers, in disobedi-
ence to rules and regulations of the Navy, often neglected to transmit
rolls to the Navy Department. A circular letter of Oct. 10, 1817,
called the attention of various commanding officers to the regulations
requiring each "to send every month, one Muster Book complete, to the
Navy Office, signed by himself and Purser," and asserted that these
regulations "have been too long neglected by many of the Officers, whose

90

duty it is to see them executed," and that the lack of rolls "has occasioned great delays and difficulties in settlements, as well as expense to Government and individuals." As late as 1865 Capt. Cicero Price was found guilty by a general court martial of failure to transmit muster and pay rolls to the Department, and the finding was published in a general order to be read aloud in all vessels of the Navy. A list of the vessels included in this series is furnished in Appendix C. Except for a few rolls in (3), the rolls of naval vessels subsequent to 1859 form a series of bound volumes in Record Group 24, Records of the Bureau of Naval Personnel.

ARREARAGE ABSTRACTS OF BALANCES DUE FOR PAY. May 1800 - June 1835.
    3 vols. 10 in. Indexed.   91
    Volumes labeled respectively "Roster of Vessels of U. S. Navy," "Roster of All Vessels of U. S. Navy," and "Roster of Vessels and Yards." Each volume, however, consists of forms headed "Arrearage Abstract of Balances Due to Individuals for Pay." The uniformity of handwriting and format in the lists for the various vessels indicates that the lists were compiled in Washington and are not original rolls received from the vessels. They include name of individual, rate or rank, dates of service, sum due, and place and date of payment.

MUSTER ROLLS AND PAY ROLLS OF SHORE ESTABLISHMENTS OF THE UNITED STATES
    NAVY. Aug. 1800 - Dec. 1842, with rolls as late as Dec. 1887.
    48 vols., and loose sheets and booklets in 17 labeled wrappers.
    14 ft. 4 in.   92
    (1) Bound rolls, 48 vols., Aug. 1800 - Dec. 1842, arranged more or less alphabetically by names of places, thereunder chronologically; and (2) loose rolls and booklets in 17 labeled wrappers, Apr. 1812 - Dec. 1887, arranged alphabetically by names of shore establishments, thereunder chronologically. (1), which includes all but 1 cubic foot of the rolls, consists of volumes labeled as follows: Baltimore, 1809-36, including Gunboats 136-144; Boston, 1812-26; Boston Navy Yard, 1824-25, 1830-38; Lake Champlain and Whitehall, 1813-14; Battle of Lake Champlain, September 11, 1814; Chesapeake Flotilla, including Asp, Scorpion, Shark, and Gunboat 137, 1807-14; Delaware Flotilla, 1812-14; Lake Erie, 1812-23; New London, Newport, and Savannah, 1804-06, 1814-15; New Orleans and the Viper, 1805-26; New York, 1800-33, including the receiving ship Hudson, 1833-39; New York Gunboat Flotilla, 1805-13; Newport, Norfolk, and New York, 1815-30; Norfolk, including Gunboats 4, 7, 10, 59, 60, 63, 66, and 67-69, 1807-38; Norfolk Navy Yard, 1815-42; Pensacola, 1826-37; Pensacola Navy Yard, 1829-31, 1834-40; Philadelphia, 1810-37; Philadelphia Navy Yard, 1825, 1828, 1830-40; Portland, 1809-13; Portsmouth, N. H., 1812-28; Portsmouth (N. H.) Navy Yard, 1830-39; St. Mary's and Gunboats, 1811-14; Washington, including Gunboats 2 and 137, 1806-28; and Wilmington, N. C., including Gunboats 7 and 166-168, 1809-14. (2) consists of one wrapper each for Baltimore Naval Station, 1818; Black Rock Naval Station on the Niagara River, 1812-13; Boston (Charlestown) Naval Station, 1833-38; Gosport Naval Station, 1815-31; Lake Erie Naval Station, 1815; Mare Island Navy Yard, 1865; Mound City Naval Station, 1864-70; Naval Academy, 1865; New Orleans Naval Station, 1815-24; New

York Naval Station, 1831-37; Philadelphia Naval Station, 1817-42; Portsmouth Navy Yard, 1818-65; Sackett's Harbor Navy Yard and Hospital, 1813-26; Savannah Naval Station, 1813; Washington Naval Station, 1812-62; West Indies Naval Station, 1823-24; and Whitehall Navy Yard, 1818-24. The rolls are similar in character to those described in Entry 90, and many are for receiving ships.

RETURNS OF BOYS ENTERED AS NAVAL APPRENTICES. July 1837 - Aug. 1842.
  2 vols. 3 in. Arranged by rendezvous, thereunder chronologi-
  cally.   93
    Printed form, prepared by recruiting officers in naval rendezvous
at Baltimore, Boston, New York, Norfolk, and Philadelphia, giving date
of entrance, name, rating, wages monthly, date of birth, and time of
expiration of service. An act of March 2, 1837, provided "that it
shall be lawful to enlist boys for the navy, with the consent of their
parents or guardians, not being under thirteen, nor over eighteen years
of age, to serve until they shall arrive at the age of twenty-one years."

CERTIFICATES OF ENLISTMENT OF SEAMEN AND LANDSMEN ON THE RECEIVING
  SHIP COLUMBUS, CHARLESTON NAVY YARD. July-Aug. 1839. 1 vol.
  3/4 in. Arranged in roughly alphabetical order.   94
    Printed forms signed by recruiting officer, commanding officer of
ship, purser, and enlisted man, and giving date of enlistment, rate,
advanced wages paid, amount of monthly pay, term of service, date of
expiration of leave of absence, date when received on board, date when
entered by purser on the ship's books, and receipt for advanced wages.

LISTS OF NAVAL, MARINE, AND CIVIL OFFICERS OF SHORE ESTABLISHMENTS OF
  THE UNITED STATES NAVY. Mar. 1855 - Dec. 1889, with some lists
  as early as 1845. 26 vols. 6 ft. 7 in.   95
    (1) Volumes arranged alphabetically by shore establishments,
Mar. 1855 - Jan. 1878 ("Lists of Officers of Navy Yards"), 10 vols.;
(2) 3 vols. containing various lists, 1855-74, 1865-72, and 1874-86; and (3)
13 vols. arranged chronologically by volumes, thereunder by shore establishments, thereunder chronologically, 1876, 1878, 1880-89. The
lists themselves are of uniform character in all the volumes, and consist chiefly of four printed forms: "Naval, Marine, and Civil Officers,
and Attachés" is divided into sections for Commandant's Office; Departments of Yards and Docks, Navigation, Ordnance, Construction and Repair,
Steam Engineering, Equipment and Recruiting, Provisions and Clothing and
Paymaster of Yard, and Medicine and Surgery; Receiving Ship; and Office
of the Purchasing and Disbursing Paymaster. This form gives only names
and ranks. "Monthly Return of Commissioned and Warrant Officers" gives
name, rank, and remarks. "Clerks and Writers" and "Master Workmen"
give name, rate, department, date of appointment, by what authority appointed, and pay. (1) consists of a volume each for Boston (1855-78),
League Island (1867-77), Mound City (1869-73), Mare Island (1865-77),
New York (1865-77), Pensacola (1863-77), Norfolk (1866-77), Philadelphia
(1861-75), Portsmouth (1861, 1866-77), and Washington (1863, 1865-77).
In (2) the earliest volume contains lists of officers at Baltimore (1855),
Bay Point, S. C. (1865-66), Beaufort, N. C. (1865), Jefferson Barracks
(1865-67), Mound City (1866-73), New London (1877), and Port Royal (1866)

and in the coast survey (1845, 1854, 1874); the second volume contains lists for League Island, Mount City, and New Orleans (December 1865 - December 1872); and the third contains various lists, too numerous to itemize (1874-86).

LISTS OF OFFICERS OF VESSELS OF THE UNITED STATES NAVY. Aug. 1861 - Dec. 1877. 34 vols. 5 ft. 3 in.   96
    Consists of a printed form in five sections: line officers, staff officers, marine officers, passengers, and changes since last report (names added to or removed from the ship's roll, with date of change and place whence or whither made). Bound as five subseries: (1) "List of Officers of Vessels," Aug. 1861 - July 1869, 25 vols., alphabetical by ships' names; (2) "Lists of Officers of Squadrons and Fleets," Nov. 1862 - Oct. 1872, 1 vol., alphabetical by ships' names, with list of ships in front; (3) "List of Officers of Vessels," July 1864 - June 1865, 3 vols., alphabetical by ships' names, with list of ships in front; (4) "List of Officers of Vessels," Jan. 1865 - Dec. 1877, 3 vols., alphabetical by ships' names, with list of ships in front; and (5) "List of Officers of Vessels, etc.," 1874-76, 2 vols., roughly chronological. In this series, as in those described in Entries 90, 92, and 95, the multiplicity and overlapping of subseries are probably due to premature binding rather than to deliberate classifications designed to distinguish rolls or other lists according to differences in their character or purpose.

3. Registers and Indexes of Applications and Appointments, 1814-1887

REGISTER OF MARINE CORPS AND CIVIL PERSONNEL ("Marine Corps and Civil Register"). 1814-52. 1 vol. 1 in. Arranged by title of office, thereunder chronologically. Indexed.   97
    Gives employee's name, date of appointment, and date of promotion or resignation. Arranged under the following heads: Marine Corps, Storekeepers, Pension Agents, Live Oak Agents, Commissioners, Constructors, Navy Agents, and Agents to Coast of Africa.

REGISTER OF APPLICATIONS FOR CIVIL APPOINTMENTS ("List of Applicants for Appointments, With Names of Those Recommending Them"). Feb. 1834 - Aug. 1842. 1 vol. 2 in. Arranged by serial numbers of applications, 534-2600. Indexed.   98
    Gives applicant's name, position applied for, place of residence or station, action taken on application, and name of person recommending applicant. A successor volume is in the National Archives in Record Group 80, General Records of the Department of the Navy.

REGISTER OF APPLICATIONS FOR APPOINTMENT AS SURGEON'S MATE AND ASSISTANT SURGEON. Oct. 1834 - Dec. 1875. 2 vols. 3½ in. Arranged by serial number of application, 505-3758. Indexed.   99
    First volume labeled "Surgeon's Mates"; second, "Assistant Surgeons." Gives application number, applicant's name, date of application, date of permit to take examination, and name of person recommending applicant.

REGISTER OF APPLICATIONS FOR APPOINTMENT AS PAY OFFICER. June 1837 -
    Nov. 1873. 3 vols. 7 in. Arranged by serial number of appli-
    cation, 488-4159. Indexed.   100
   First two volumes labeled "Pursers"; third, "Acting Assistant
Paymasters." The title of purser was changed to paymaster by an act
of June 22, 1860. Gives application number, applicant's name, date of
application, position applied for, action taken, and name of person
recommending applicant.

REGISTER OF APPLICATIONS FOR APPOINTMENT AS MIDSHIPMAN ("Midshipmen").
    Jan. 1840 - May 1852. 1 vol. 2 in. Arranged by State from
    which application was made, thereunder by Congressional district,
    thereunder by serial number of application.   101

REGISTER OF APPLICATIONS FOR APPOINTMENT AS MIDSHIPMAN ("Midshipmen").
    Jan. 1840 - Dec. 1857. 2 vols. 5 in. Arranged by serial number
    of application, 2960-5323 (to June 1847) and 1-2142 (beginning
    July 1847). Indexed.   102
   Gives application number, name of applicant, date of application,
State from which appointment is applied for, date of appointment (if
made), and name of person recommending applicant.

REGISTER OF APPLICANTS FOR OFFICE ("Applicants for Office"). Mar. 1849 -
    Jan. 1854. 2 vols. 4 in. Arranged in sections for single
    stations and yards, for timber agents, for miscellaneous appli-
    cations (alphabetical), and for "applicants for advertising."   103
Apparently working papers.

REGISTER OF APPLICATIONS FOR APPOINTMENT AS PAY OFFICER, CHAPLAIN, OR
    OFFICER IN THE MARINE CORPS ("Pursers, Chaplains, & Marine
    Corps, Applicants by States . . . from 1853"). 1853 et seqq.
    1 vol. 2 in. Arranged by States.   104
   Gives State, number, and name, without other information.

REGISTER OF APPLICATIONS FOR APPOINTMENT AS ENGINEER OFFICER ("Engi-
    neers"). Sept. 1853 - July 1862. 1 vol. $1\frac{1}{2}$ in. Arranged by
    serial number of application, 1-1099. Indexed.   105
   Gives application number, applicant's name, date of application,
position applied for, action taken, and nature or source of testimonials.

REGISTER OF APPLICATIONS FROM OFFICERS FOR REINSTATEMENT IN THE NAVY
    ("Reinstatements"). Sept. 1853 - May 1868. 1 vol. 1 in. Ar-
    ranged chronologically. Indexed.   106
   Gives officer's name, rank or rate, State from which appointed, and
writer of letter of application (whether the officer or another person).

REGISTER OF APPLICATIONS FOR APPOINTMENT AS VOLUNTEER OFFICER ("Appli-
    cations for Appointment as Volunteer Officers"). Jan. 1854 -
    Mar. 1871. 5 vols. 1 ft. Arranged numerically (vols. 1-4), and
    by first letter of applicant's name, thereunder numerically
    (vol. 5). Vols. 1-4 indexed.   107
   Gives serial number of application, applicant's name, rank applied
for, date of application, and State from which to be appointed. The

serial numbers begin with 1 and end with 10225.

REGISTER OF APPLICATIONS FOR APPOINTMENT AS MASTER'S MATE, ACTING
 MASTER, AND ACTING ENSIGN ("Applications, &c., Vol. 1st").
 June 1861 - Apr. 1865. 1 vol. 1½ in. Arranged by rank of
 officer, thereunder by date of application.   108
   Gives date of application, applicant's name and address, and
sometimes action taken on application, for master's mate (Aug. 1861 -
Apr. 1863), acting master (June 1861 - June 1862), and acting ensign
(July 1862 - Apr. 1865). At the front of the volume is a daily register of letters received, Apr. 19 - May 7, 1861. On the flyleaf is
written "Bureau of Orders & Detail" (apparently an early designation
for the Office of Detail).

INDEX TO EXAMINATION PERMITS OF APPLICANTS FOR APPOINTMENT AS VOLUNTEER
 OFFICERS ("Volunteer Officers' Permits"). Jan. 1863 - Apr. 1865.
 1 vol. 1½ in. Arranged by first letter of applicants' names,
 thereunder chronologically.   109
Permits to report to commandants of navy yards for examination.

REGISTER OF APPLICATIONS FOR CLERKSHIPS OF CLASS 1 ("Civil Service").
 May 1872 - May 1874. 1 vol. 2 in. Arranged by serial number of
 application, 1-66.   110
   Gives application number, applicant's name, residence, age, date of
application and of its receipt, abstract of replying notification, date
of reply, and remarks.

REGISTER OF APPLICATIONS FOR POSITIONS ("Applications for Positions").
 July 1872 - May 1875. 2 vols. 4 in. Arranged by first letter of
 applicants' names, thereunder chronologically.   111
   Gives date of receipt of application; applicant's name; ship, station,
or residence; date of application; clerk to whom referred; and abstract.

REGISTER OF APPLICATIONS FOR POSITIONS. Jan. 1885 - Mar. 1887. 1 vol.
 2 in. Arranged chronologically. Indexed.   112
   Gives date of receipt of application, applicant's name, date of
application, to what clerk referred, action taken, and abstract.

4. Registers and Indexes of Regular Officers, 1798-1874

REGISTER OF SEA DUTY OF OFFICERS. Mar. 1798 - Dec. 1823. 1 vol.
 1/3 in. Arranged by officers' rank, thereunder chronologically.   113
   Gives officer's name, date of entry into Navy, date of present commission, vessels on which officer has served, and dates of service on
each.

REGISTER OF APPORTIONMENT OF MIDSHIPMEN AMONG THE STATES ("Midshipmen").
 Mar. 1834 - Dec. 1847. 1 vol. 3/4 in. Arranged by States in
 order of admission to the Union, thereunder chronologically.   114
   Gives name of midshipman and whether he died, resigned, was expelled,
or was promoted.

REGISTER OF ENGINEER OFFICERS ("Register, Engineer Corps"). Oct. 1842 -
       May 1861. 1 vol. 2 in. Arranged by date of beginning of service.
       Indexed.   115
       Gives dates of service and of orders and amount of sea duty, shore
duty, and unemployment. The volume begins with the beginning of the
Engineer Corps, established by an act of Aug. 31, 1842. At the front are
handwritten copies of orders issued by the Chief of the Bureau of Construction, Equipment, and Repairs to engineer officers, Dec. 1850. At
the end are a classified list of engineers, giving present duty of each;
a list of the steamers in the United States Navy; and the names and
duties of the engineer officers on each. These lists are undated. Reference is made to a second volume of the register. The series described
in Entry 282, which begins with May 1861, is apparently not a continuation of this volume.

INDEX TO SERVICE RECORDS OF CAPTAIN'S CLERKS, PAYMASTER'S CLERKS, AND
       PAY STEWARDS. Apr. 1844 - Feb. 1871. 3 vols. 2 in. Arranged
       alphabetically. Indexed.   116
       Gives dates of service on each ship, and sometimes biographical
information. The smallest volume ("List of Paymasters and Captains
Clerks"), consisting of one alphabet, was apparently copied with many
additions into the other two volumes ("Captain's and Paymaster's Clerks"),
which form one alphabet and are in part in the same hand as the
smallest volume.

REGISTER OF APPOINTMENTS OF MIDSHIPMEN AND OF VACANCIES IN THE LIST OF
       MIDSHIPMEN ("Naval Academy, Midshipmen"). July 1850 - May 1853.
       1 vol. 2 in.   117
       A chronological list of vacancies, numbered serially 1-225, July
1850 - Apr. 1853, giving State for which vacancy exists, date of
occurrence of vacancy, name of midshipman whose removal from the list
of appointments created the vacancy, and serial number of vacancy; a
chronological list of appointments, numbered serially 1-173, Jan. 1851-
May 1853, giving State, date, name, serial number of appointment, date
on which to report, and by whom recommended; and list of appointments
arranged by States, giving name of each midshipman appointed, Congressional district, and sequel of appointment (promotion, resignation,
reinstatement, or dismissal).

REGISTER OF APPOINTMENTS MADE BY RECOMMENDATIONS OF MEMBERS OF
       CONGRESS. Ca. 1861 - ca. 1865. 1 vol. 1¼ in. Arranged by
       State, thereunder by name of Congressman, thereunder chronologi-
       cally. Indexed.   118
       The serial number of each appointment, but not its date, is given.
Names of some Congressmen are followed by blanks.

REGISTER OF OFFICERS AVAILABLE ("Officers Available"). May 1861 -
       May 1865. 2 vols. 4 in. Arranged by rank of officer.   119
       The first volume contains a list of officers, their stations, and
the locations and dates of sailing of vessels. The second volume
gives for each officer included in the volume his name, station, date
and place of birth, date of appointment, place of which a citizen,
date of original entry into the Navy, date of present commission, and
total amount of service in each type of duty. The second volume is
labeled on its flyleaf, in pencil, "Statement of Services of Officers,
U. S. Navy."

BIOGRAPHIES OF NAVAL OFFICERS. Ca. 1865. 3 vols. 8½ in. No arrangement apparent. Indexed.   120
     This compilation was probably begun in or soon after 1865 and was
probably left unfinished. A different officer's name is written (always
in the same hand) at the head of each page. Some names are followed by
fragmentary information concerning dates of appointment and concerning
services in the Navy during the War with Mexico and the Civil War. Other
names stand alone.

REGISTER OF APPOINTMENTS OF CADET MIDSHIPMEN ("Cadet Midshipmen").
     July 1866 - Oct. 1874. 1 vol. 2 in. No arrangement apparent.   121
     Probably bound working papers; partly in pencil. Among the subjects
included are distribution of cadet midshipmen by States and Congressional districts, names of persons nominating cadet midshipmen, lists
of midshipmen at the Naval Academy, dates of appointment, and file
numbers (apparently referring to numbers on service records).

5. Registers of Volunteer Officers, 1861-1879

REGISTER OF ACTING OFFICERS OF THE UNITED STATES NAVY. 1861-65. 1 vol.
     1 in. Arranged chronologically.   122
     Gives name of officer, by whom recommended, and station. The name of
Capt. Thornton A. Jenkins is on the title page. The register seems in-
complete.

REGISTER OF ACTING OFFICERS OF THE UNITED STATES AND CONFEDERATE STATES
     NAVIES ("Lists of Names, Acting Officers"). 1861-65. 1 vol.
     3/4 in. Arranged alphabetically.   123
     Gives date and nature of appointment, later occurrences (death,
resignation, and the like), and the number of the document containing
the information cited. The method of citation is too cryptical to per-
mit identification of the documents. Officers of the United States Navy
are entered in red; those of the Confederate States Navy, and other
officers, in black.

REGISTER OF VOLUNTEER OFFICERS ("Acting Volunteer Officers"). May 1861 -
     June 1866. 1 vol. 2 in. Arranged in order of descending rank
     (act'g volunteer lieutenants, act'g masters, act'g ensigns, act'g
     ass't surgeons, act'g ass't paymasters), thereunder by date of
     appointment.   124
     Gives date of appointment, details to which assigned, and dates of
service on each vessel to which assigned.

REGISTER OF VOLUNTEER OFFICERS. May 1861 - Oct. 1867. 2 vols. 5½ in.
     Arranged in order of descending rank (same ranks as in Entry 124,
     with the addition of act'g volunteer lieutenant commander), there-
     under chronologically by date of appointment.   125
     Gives date of appointment, State of birth, State from which appointed,
State of which a citizen, duty or station, and date and circumstances of
end of volunteer service.

REGISTER OF VOLUNTEER OFFICERS ("Voluntary Officers' Records").
May 1861 - Oct. 1879. 1 vol. 2 in. Arranged in order of
descending rank from volunteer lieutenant commanders to carpenters, thereunder by first letter of names, thereunder chronologically.   126
Gives date of original entry into service, date of present appointment, State of birth, State of which a citizen, duty or station, and
date and circumstances of end of volunteer service.

REGISTER OF VOLUNTEER OFFICERS ON LEAVE. July 1861 - May 1865. 1 vol.
2 in. Arranged by first letter of officers' names, thereunder
chronologically.   127
Gives rank of officer, name, date of original entry into the Navy,
date when leave expires, and address. The volume is labeled on its
front cover "Journal No. 6, Ringgold, U. S. N.," and was originally a
blank book prepared for but not used by the expedition to the North
Pacific under the command of Comdr. Cadwalader Ringgold.

REGISTER OF DISMISSALS OF VOLUNTEER OFFICERS WITH NAMES BEGINNING WITH
A OR B ("Register of Volunteer Officers, U. S. N., Dismissals").
Dec. 1861 - Nov. 1865. 1 vol. 2 in. Arranged by first letter of
officers' names, thereunder chronologically.   128
Gives name, rank, and date of dismissal. The volume is labeled on its
front cover as Journal 7 of the Ringgold Expedition (see Entry 127).

REGISTER OF HONORABLE DISCHARGES OF VOLUNTEER OFFICERS. May 1865 -
May 1866. 1 vol. 2 in. Arranged by rank of officer, thereunder
chronologically. Indexed.   129
Gives name, date of original entry into the Navy, rank, and date of
honorable discharge. The volume is labeled on its front cover as Journal
8 of the Ringgold Expedition (see Entry 127).

REGISTER OF HONORABLE DISCHARGES OF VOLUNTEER OFFICERS ("Honorably Discharged Officers"). July 1865 - Oct. 1870. 1 vol. 2½ in.
Arranged by rank of officers. Indexed.   130
Gives name of officer, address when discharged, date of original
entry into service, original rank, date of discharge, and remarks.

6. Registers and Indexes of Officers' Orders, 1823-1873

REGISTER OF APPLICATIONS OF OFFICERS FOR ORDERS. Apr. 1823 - Sept. 1825.
1 vol. ½ in. Arranged by rank of officers.   131

INDEX TO ORDERS ISSUED TO OFFICERS ("Key to Orders"). Jan. 1828 -
Apr. 1851. 9 vols. 8 in. Arranged chronologically by volumes,
thereunder by first letter of officers' names, thereunder
chronologically.   132
Includes very brief abstracts of the orders.

REGISTERS OF APPLICATIONS OF OFFICERS FOR ORDERS. Aug. 1850 - Apr. 1861.
2 vols. 1¼ in.   133
The first volume, Aug. 1850 - Mar. 1861, is arranged chronologically

to Oct. 1851 and thereafter alphabetically by first letter of officers'
names. The second volume, Jan. 1856 - Apr. 1861, is arranged by rank
of officers, thereunder chronologically. Each gives date of application, name and rank of officer, station, and what is applied for.

REGISTER OF ORDERS ISSUED TO ACTING VOLUNTEER OFFICERS ("Acting Volun-
     teer Officers"). May 1861 - July 1863. 1 vol. 2 in. Arranged
     chronologically.   134
  Information concerning orders, details of officers, discharges,
deaths, and miscellaneous matters. Probably maintained by the Office
of Detail.

REGISTER OF OFFICERS ACKNOWLEDGING ORDERS AND REPORTING ("Officers Avail-
     able"). Mar. 1862 - Dec. 1863. 1 vol. 1 in. Arranged by rank
     and thereunder chronologically, Mar.-Oct. 1862; by chronology
     alone thereafter. Indexed.   135
  Gives name of officer, date of acknowledging orders, and date of
reporting.

REGISTER OF ORDERS ISSUED BY THE SECRETARY OF THE NAVY. Aug. 1862 -
     Aug. 1865. 1 vol. 2½ in. Arranged by ships' names.   136
  Includes description of vessel, name of recipient of order, rank,
date of order, from what vessel ordered, when detached, whither ordered,
and remarks.

REGISTER OF ORDERS AND DETACHMENTS ISSUED TO OFFICERS OF THE MISSISSIPPI
     SQUADRON. Oct. 1864 - July 1865. 1 vol. 1 in. Arranged
     chronologically.   137

REGISTER OF ORDERS ISSUED TO OFFICERS. Jan. 1872 - Aug. 1873. 1 vol.
     1 in. Arranged chronologically.   138
  Rough and barely legible, with irrelevant scribblings at front and
back.

                      E. Legal Records, 1807-1876

     The records described below resulted from the administration by the
Office of the Secretary of the Navy of certain legal and regulatory functions, particularly those relating to contracts, claims, prize vessels and
their cargoes, prisoners, courts martial and courts of inquiry, and the
examination, promotion, and retirement of officers of the Navy and the
Marine Corps. As explained in Section III-G, these and other legal functions of the Office of the Secretary were transferred to the Office of the
Judge Advocate General when it was established in 1880. In that section
are described certain series of records begun in the Office of the Secretary
of the Navy and continued in the Office of the Judge Advocate General.

LETTERS FROM THE ATTORNEY GENERAL. June 1807 - Nov. 1825. 1 vol.
     2 in. Arranged chronologically. Registered.   139
  Replies to questions submitted by the Secretary of the Navy.   M1029

NOTES AND EXTRACTS OF DECISIONS ON CASES REFERRED TO AND FROM THE SECRE-
TARY OF THE NAVY, Feb. 1834 - Dec. 1848, AND NOTES ON NAVY RATIONS
AND TRAVEL PAY, July 1831 - Aug. 1857 ("Claims, Travel Pay, etc.").
1 vol. 3/4 in. Arranged chronologically in each of 2 unrelated
parts. Indexed.   140
Apparently compiled by one or more clerks for their own use.

LEDGER OF CONTRACTS ENTERED INTO BY THE NAVY DEPARTMENT. Nov. 1834 -
Dec. 1856. 2 vols. 6 in. Arranged chronologically. Indexed.   141
"Contract Ledger, A, Navy Commissioners' Office," Nov. 1834 - July
1842, giving contractor's name, place of delivery, appropriation under
which made, date of making and of expiration, for what articles or services, estimated amount, agent's reports of deliveries, and amount paid;
and "Contract Ledger A, Navy Equipment," Apr. 1838 - Dec. 1856, giving
the same information for timber, hemp, supplies, copper, candles, canvas,
wood and coal, oakum, and paints. Information concerning such "equipment"
was entered in the earlier volume before 1838 but not after.

MISCELLANEOUS CASE FILES. Aug. 1846 - July 1874. 7 vols. 1 ft. 6 in.
Each volume in roughly chronological order. Indexed.   142
(1) and (2), "Claims Arising from Prize Cases and Other Prize
Matters" (2 vols., Aug. 1846 - July 1874 and Aug. 1860 - May 1873);
(3) "Miscellaneous Prize Matters" (June 1861 - Apr. 1871); (4) "Claims
Against Navy Department" (Aug. 1861 - Feb. 1874); (5) [label lost]
(Nov. 1861 - June 1867); (6) "Miscellaneous Claims" (Nov. 1861 - July
1874); and (7) "Complaints, Charges, and Courts of Inquiry" (July 1862 -
Nov. 1873). To be associated with these volumes is a volume in Record
Group 125, Records of the Office of the Judge Advocate General (Navy),
entitled "Miscellaneous Subjects: Arrests, Courts Martial, Dismissals,
Desertions, Suspensions" (Dec. 1860 - Apr. 1874). In spite of their
various labels, the eight volumes seem from the remnants of their original
binding to have been identical in format, and each is composed of papers
relating to claims and charges, not exhibiting clearly the limitations of
subject indicated by the labels, which represent only a rough classification. Most of the papers are in groups resembling dossiers, each relating
to a particular claim or charge, the subject of which is usually designated on a narrow slip attached to the top of the first sheet of the group
or dossier. The papers include letters from naval officers, United States
attorneys and marshals, the Second Comptroller and the Fourth Auditor, the
Solicitor of the Treasury, the Solicitor of the Navy, private claimants,
informers, and others, with prize lists, inventories of prizes, libels of
information, records of proceedings of courts and boards, copies of correspondence, and other documents, either as enclosures or without covering
letters. Each dossier is apparently an exhibit or a collection of exhibits or references rather than a file of all the papers relating to a
case and to the final action taken. See Entry 297 for later records of
similar character.

CONTRACTS FOR TRANSPORTATION OF MAIL AND FOR MANUFACTURE OF PARTS OF
SHIPS ("Contracts, Transportation of Mail"). Apr. 1847 - Oct. 1860.
1 vol. 1¼ in. Handwritten copies. Arranged chronologically.
Indexed.   143

REPORTS OF OFFICERS ON CORPORAL PUNISHMENT AND THE SPIRIT RATION.
("Corporal Punishment and the Spirit Ration.—Reports of Officers"). Jan.-Feb. 1850. 1 vol. 2½ in. Arranged by date of
receipt.   144

Submitted in response to a circular letter (copied in the front of
the volume) from the Secretary of the Navy, requesting the views of
officers as to whether corporal punishment and the issuance of rations
of spirits could be dispensed with, and, if so, what substitutes could
be provided.

RECORDS OF PROCEEDINGS OF COURTS OF INQUIRY CONVENED UNDER THE ACT OF
JANUARY 16, 1847 ("Courts of Inquiry, Act, January 16, 1857").
Feb. 1857 – Feb. 1859. 24 vols. 8 ft. 4 in. Arranged
chronologically.   145

An act of Feb. 28, 1855, had provided for the dropping, furloughing,
or retirement of officers of the Navy under certain conditions. Complaints resulting from its application led to the act of Jan. 16,
1857, which provided that upon written application from an officer
affected by the previous act "the said court shall in their finding
report whether the said officer, if he has been dropped from the rolls
of the navy, ought to be restored, and, if restored, whether to the
active list or the reserved list, and if to the latter, whether on
leave of absence or furlough pay; and in case the officer making the
written request . . . shall have been placed on the reserved list, then
the court, in their finding, shall report whether the said officer ought
to be restored to the active list, or, if not restored, whether he ought
to remain on the retired list on leave of absence or furlough pay."

ROUGH LISTS OF CAPTURED AND CAPTURING VESSELS. 1861-65. 5 vols. 3 in. 146
(1) "Captures by U. S. Vessels," 1861-65, alphabetical by name of
captor vessel, giving name of captor, name of prize, amount, and remarks.
(2) "Captures Made by U. S. Vessels," undated, alphabetical by name of
captor. (3) "Captures Made by U. S. Vessels," 1861-65, alphabetical
by name of captor, O–Z (A–N not being found). (4) "Record of Captures
Made by U. S. Vessels," 1863-64, alphabetical by name of captured vessel.
(5) "Prizes Captured by Vessels in the Civil War," 1864-65, alphabetical
by name of captured vessel, apparently a sequel to (4). These volumes
appear to be working papers, probably prepared by different clerks for
their own temporary use.

SUMMARIES OF PROCEEDINGS FOR THE ADJUDICATION OF PRIZES IN COURTS OF THE
DISTRICT OF NEW YORK ("Prize Adjudications in the District of New
York"). May 1861 – Jan. 1863. 1 vol. 1¼ in. Arranged by dates
of opening of cases. Indexed.   147

Presented to the Secretary of the Navy by Francis H. Upton, Counsel
for Naval Captors.

SUMMARIES OF DISTRICT-COURT PROCEEDINGS IN PRIZE CASES ("Reports of
Prize Cases"). June 1861 – July 1867. 7 vols. 2 ft. 4 in.
Arranged by districts, thereunder chronologically. Indexed.   148

A 2-page printed form, with blanks for name of vessel, type, date
of capture, captor vessel, date of libel, interlocutory sale, schedule

of cargo, hearing in district court, decree, appeal, hearing in circuit court, decree in circuit court, appeal therefrom, subsequent proceedings, venditioni exponas, total sales and disposition of money, reference before Prize Commissioners, decree as to vessels entitled to share, and remarks. Volumes for Boston and Springfield, Ill.; Key West; New York (2 vols.); Philadelphia (2 vols.); and Washington, Baltimore, and New Orleans.

REGISTER OF PRIZE CASES ("Prize Cases"). June 1861 – Dec. 1874. 14 vols.
    2 ft. 7 in. Arranged alphabetically by district courts where
    prizes were condemned; no order perceptible thereunder.   149
    Gives name of prize, when and by what vessel captured, when libeled, cargo, date of interlocutory decree, date of hearing, total sales, date of final decree of distribution, amount to be distributed, date of sending papers to Fourth Auditor, and often copy of prize list of officers and crew. Volumes for Boston (vol. 2), Key West (vols. 1-3), New Orleans (vol. 1), New York (vols. 1, 3), Philadelphia (vols. 1-3), Springfield (vol. 1), St. Augustine (vol. 1), and Washington (vols. 1-2).

INDEX TO REGISTER OF PRIZE CASES ("Index to Prize Cases"). 1861-68.
    1 vol. $2\frac{1}{2}$ in. Arranged by first letter of name of prize, there-
    under chronologically. Index to preceding series.   150

REGISTER OF PRIZES. Aug. 1861 – Dec. 1863. 1 vol. 2 in. Arranged
    chronologically. Indexed.   151
    Gives name of prize; when, where, and by what vessel captured; details of adjudication; and list of officers and crew entitled to share in proceeds.

CORRESPONDENCE WITH CONSULS RELATING TO BLOCKADE RUNNERS AND TO VESSELS
    FITTED OUT ABROAD TO SERVE THE CONFEDERATE STATES ("Department
    and Consular Letters"). Sept. 1861 – June 1863. 1 vol. 5 in.
    Arranged chronologically.   152
    Original letters from consuls to officers of the Navy, press copies and sometimes originals of letters from consuls to the Secretary of State, extracts and handwritten copies of the same, occasional copies of letters sent by the Secretary of the Navy, and other correspondence.

REGISTER OF PRIZES ("Prizes Captured by U. S. Vessels"). Sept. 1861 –
    Oct. 1864. 1 vol. $1\frac{1}{2}$ in. Arranged chronologically.   153
    Gives name of captured and captor vessels, place where captured, and how disposed of. At the end is a list of squadrons of the Civil War, with names of their commanding officers and date on which each assumed command.

LIST OF OFFICERS AND CREWS ENTITLED TO SHARE IN PROCEEDS OF PRIZES
    ("Prize Lists"). Jan. 1862 – Mar. 1866. 12 vols. 2 ft. 9 in.
    Arranged chronologically. Indexed.   154
    Submitted with covering letters to the Secretary of the Navy by commanding officers of captor vessels.

CONTRACTS FOR MANUFACTURE OF MACHINERY FOR VESSELS ("Contracts for
    Vessels, 1862"). Aug.-Dec. 1862. 1 vol. 2 in. Printed and
    handwritten copies. Arranged chronologically. Indexed.   155

REGISTER OF PRISONERS CAPTURED ON BLOCKADE-RUNNERS. Sept. 1862 -
    July 1865. 1 vol. 1 in. Arranged chronologically. Indexed.   156
    Gives name of prisoner, where captured, country of which a citizen,
where imprisoned, date of release, and occasionally other information.
Compiled in Washington from field reports, beginning with one dated
Sept. 1862, which contains information concerning previous captures of
prisoners in custody at "this port," apparently Hampton Roads.

DECREES OF DISTRIBUTION OF PRIZE MONEYS ("Final Decrees"). Sept. 1862 -
    Dec. 1869. 6 vols. 1 ft. 8 in. Arranged by district courts,
    thereunder chronologically. Indexed.   157
    Certified copies received by the Secretary of the Navy from clerks
of United States district courts, consisting of two printed forms:
final decree of distribution issued by district court, and "Clerk's
Certificate of Costs." Volumes for Key West, Sept. 1862 - May 1865
(3 vols.); New York, Springfield, and St. Augustine, Sept. 1862 -
May 1868 (1 vol.); Philadelphia, Dec. 1862 - Dec. 1867 (1 vol., in no
detectable order); and Washington, Boston, and New Orleans, Oct. 1863 -
Dec. 1869 (1 vol.).

LETTERS RECEIVED RELATING TO UNION PRISONERS OF WAR. Nov. 1862 -
    July 1865. 1 vol. 4 in. Arranged chronologically. Indexed.   158
    From officers and seamen of the United States Navy who were prisoners
of war, and from officers responsible for exchange of prisoners.

INDEX TO PRIZES ("Prize Cases"). Nov. 1862 - June 1871. 1 vol.
    1¼ in. Arranged by first letter of name of prize, thereunder
    chronologically.   159
    Gives name of prize, name of captor, gross proceeds, costs, amount
for distribution, date when case was sent to Fourth Auditor, name of
flag officer of captor, court where adjudged, case number, and remarks.

LETTERS RECEIVED RELATING TO CONFEDERATE PRISONERS OF WAR ("Letters
    From and in Relation to Blockade Runners"). Mar. 1863 -
    July 1865. 4 vols. 11 in. Arranged chronologically.   160
    From prisoners of war, Army officers in charge of prisons, United
States marshals, commandants, and other persons, enclosing lists of
prisoners of war and printed paroles of honor signed by them. The
backstrip title is apparently erroneous in indicating that all the
prisoners were blockade-runners.

LETTERS FROM SPECIAL INVESTIGATORS OF FRAUDS IN NAVAL PROCUREMENT.
    Feb.-Dec. 1864. 2 vols. 6 in. Arranged chronologically.
    Indexed.   161
    From H. S. Olcott, Special Commissioner, and William E. Chandler,
Nathaniel Wilson, and H. H. Goodman, Special Counsel for the Navy
Department.

RECORD OF PROCEEDINGS OF A GENERAL COURT MARTIAL IN THE CASE OF COMMO.
        CHARLES WILKES ("Wilkes' Trial"). Mar. 9 – Apr. 26, 1864.
        3 vols. 8 in. Arranged chronologically.   162
    The record seems incomplete, breaking off somewhat before the close
of the trial. It is not clear why this record was not bound and
numbered in the series described in Entry 294.

RECORD OF PROCEEDINGS OF A GENERAL COURT MARTIAL IN THE CASE OF
        FRANKLIN W. SMITH AND BENJAMIN G. SMITH ("Contractors' Cases,
        Smith Trial"). Sept. 15, 1864 – Jan. 30, 1865. 10 vols. 3 ft.
        4 in. Arranged chronologically.   163
    The Smiths were contractors furnishing supplies for the Navy under
the name and style of Smith Brothers & Company. The record seems complete except for the finding of the court. It is not clear why the
record was not bound and numbered in the series described in Entry 294.

LETTERS SENT BY WILLIAM E. CHANDLER, SPECIAL COUNSEL FOR THE NAVY
        DEPARTMENT, AND GEORGE H. CHANDLER, INVESTIGATING FRAUDS CONNECTED
        WITH WAR CONTRACTS. Dec. 1864 – Apr. 1865. 1 vol. 1½ in.
        Press copies. Arranged chronologically.   164
    William E. Chandler was appointed in Mar. 1865 as Solicitor and
Judge Advocate of the Navy, but no letters sent by him in that capacity
are included in the volume.

REGISTER OF LETTERS RECEIVED RELATIVE TO CLAIMS. Jan. 1865 – May 1876.
        6 vols. 8 in. Arranged in a single alphabet by first letter of
        claimants' names, thereunder chronologically.   165
    Gives only the name of the writer or claimant, the date of the
letter, and the bureau or office to which it was referred. All or most
of the letters were apparently retained by bureaus or offices, and are
not found among records of the Office of the Secretary of the Navy.

REPORT FROM THE BOARD FOR THE EXAMINATION OF VOLUNTEER OFFICERS FOR
        ADMISSION TO THE REGULAR NAVY. Dec. 5, 1867. 6 vols. 1 ft.
        2 in.   166
    The Board, with Commo. Samuel Phillips Lee as President, was appointed
by an order of Aug. 27, 1866, in compliance with an act of July 25, 1866.
The act provided that of the number of line officers on the active list,
5 lieutenant commanders, 20 lieutenants, 50 masters, and 75 ensigns might
be appointed from those officers who had served in the volunteer naval
forces for a period of not less than 2 years and who either were in the
service or had been honorably discharged from it. The records consist of
(1) "Records of the Board for the Examination of Volunteer Officers for
Admission to the Regular Navy," received by the Secretary of the Navy
Dec. 5, 1867, being a record of proceedings, Sept. 5, 1866 – Dec. 5, 1867;
(2) register of officers waiving claims to examination, Aug. 30, 1866 –
Nov. 26, 1867, numbered 1–466, with index; (3) examination papers from
volunteer officers at sea, with covering letters and reports from their
commanding officers, Jan.–June 1867 (2 vols.); (4) "Register of Volunteer
Officers with Board of Examiners," Sept. 1866 – Dec. 1867 (with additions of Apr.–May 1868), arranged alphabetically, giving rank of officer

and dates of application, summons, report, waiving of claim, withdrawal, physical disqualification, and/or examination, with remarks; and (5) "Final Merit Roll, Examination of Candidates for Admission into the United States Navy," Dec. 5, 1867, a register of examination grades, arranged from highest total numerical grade to lowest.

LETTERS FROM THE NAVAL EXAMINING BOARD AT WASHINGTON. Jan. 1870 -
        Dec. 1872. 3 vols. 4 in. Arranged chronologically.   167
    The Board, with R. A. Joseph Smith as President, was convened to consider the cases of officers who were candidates for promotion.

REPORT FROM THE BOARD APPOINTED UNDER THE RESOLUTION OF JULY 1, 1870,
        ON OFFICERS NOT PROMOTED UNDER THE ACT OF JULY 25, 1866. Dec. 21,
        1871. 2 vols. 6 in. Arranged chronologically. Indexed.   168
    See Entry 166. The President of the Board was Vice Admiral Stephen C. Rowan.

F. Other Records, 1797-1911

    The records described below relate to specific subjects other than finance, personnel, and law, and consist chiefly of 1-volume series that may be collectively described as miscellaneous.

LIST OF VESSELS OF THE UNITED STATES NAVY ("Situation of the U. S.
        Naval Force"). 1797-1816. 1 vol. 1 in. Arranged by ships'
        names.   169
    Apparently begun in 1814 as a preliminary draft, containing information from various sources, with penciled additions as new information came to hand. Gives name of each vessel, number of guns, name of commander, caliber and kind of guns, where built, when built, by whom built, length of gun deck, length of keel, breadth of beam, and remarks.

LIST OF VESSELS OF THE UNITED STATES NAVY ("List of the U. States Navy").
        1797-1850. 1 vol. 2½ in. Arranged by ships' names.   170
    Probably originated as a smooth copy of the preceding volume, with added entries for facts of later date.

REGISTER OF SHIPS AND OFFICERS ("Ships Service"). 1803-9. 1 vol.
        2 in. Indexed.   171
    Tabular description of 11 brigs and schooners built 1803-6; tabular description of 93 gunboats contracted for during the years 1803-8; details regarding various frigates, schooners, and gunboats; lists of ships and officers of squadrons of Commodores Richard Dale, Edward Preble, Samuel Barron, and John Rodgers, 1803-5; journal of occurrences during the Tripolitan War; register of ships and officers, with statements as to officers' services, 1803-9; and names of officers at naval stations, 1806-7. The origin and purpose of the volume are unknown.

LETTERS SENT RELATING TO THE BARBARY POWERS ("Barbary Powers").
        Mar. 1803 - May 1808. 1 vol. 2½ in. Handwritten copies.
        Arranged chronologically. Indexed.   172
    To merchants and naval agents concerned in procuring certain naval

supplies, and to bankers and representatives of the Department of State concerned in delivering them to the Dey of Algiers and the Bashaw of Tripoli.

LETTERS SENT RELATING TO GUNBOATS ("Officers Commanding Gunboats").
    Dec. 1803 - Dec. 1808. 1 vol. 2 in. Handwritten copies.
    Arranged chronologically. Indexed.   173
    To shipbuilders and to officers commanding gunboats, concerning chiefly the construction, equipment, and repair of such vessels.

REPORTS TO CONGRESS ("Reports of the Secretary of the Navy"). Jan.
    Jan. 1811 - Mar. 1820. 1 vol. (labeled "2"). 3½ in. Hand-
    written copies. Arranged chronologically.   174
    Reports submitted in compliance with requests from Congress. Vol. 1 is lacking, and successor volumes are not found.

REGISTER OF ALIEN ENEMIES REPORTED BY THE MARSHAL OF NEW YORK.
    Mar. 5 - July 20, [1813?]. 1 vol. 3/4 in. Arranged by date of
    reporting.   175
    Gives number of immigration permit, alien's name, height, age, description, residence, occupation, and by whom recommended for surveillance.

REGISTER OF SUSPECTED PERSONS REMOVED FROM THE ATLANTIC COAST. May-
    Sept. 1813. 1 vol. ½ in. Arranged by first letter of names
    of suspected persons, thereunder chronologically.   176
    Gives suspected person's name, residence, whether indulgence (permission to remain) was granted or refused, place to which removed, date of order for removal, and remarks. The authority responsible for the removals and for the making of this record is not named.

LETTERS RECEIVED RELATING TO LIBERIA ("African Letters"). Jan. 1819 -
    Mar. 1841. 5 vols. 10 in. Arranged chronologically (with
    papers probably overlooked in binding the earlier volumes
    brought together in the fifth volume). Indexed.   177
    Chiefly from Agents of the United States upon the Coast of Africa for the Reception of Liberated Africans and from members of the American Colonization Society. The Agents, appointed in compliance with an act of Mar. 3, 1819, were subject to instructions from the Secretary of the Navy and were under the protection of the African Squadron. The first volume is erroneously labeled "African Squadron Letters."

LETTERS SENT RELATING TO LIBERIA ("African Letters"). Jan. 1820 -
    Sept. 1858. 1 vol. 2 in. Handwritten copies. Arranged
    chronologically. Indexed.   178
    Flyleaf title: "Record of Letters to the Agents Appointed under the Act of Congress in Addition to the Acts Prohibiting the Slave Trade Passed March 3rd 1819, & Other Persons."

REGISTER OF SHIPS, CRUISES, AND OFFICERS. Nov. 1823 - Dec. 1832.
    1 vol. 3/4 in. Arranged by ships from greatest to least number
    of guns. Indexed.   179
    Names of many ships are entered on pages otherwise blank.

REGISTER OF SHIPS AND OFFICERS. Ca. 1824. 2 vols. 1 in. Arranged
    by ships from greatest to least number of guns.
  Gives only names of ships and their officers, without dates.
180

CORRESPONDENCE OF THE GENERAL LAND OFFICE RELATIVE TO NAVAL TIMBER
    RESERVATIONS. Mar. 1825 - Mar. 1843. 1 vol. 3/4 in. Hand-
    written copies. Arranged chronologically. Indexed.
  Copied at an unknown date for the use of the Navy Department.
181

REPORTS ON LIVE-OAK LANDS ADJOINING ESCAMBIA BAY AND THE ESCAMBIA
    RIVER ("Reports and Surveys--Lands & Live Oak"). June-Oct.
    1828. 1 vol. 2 in. Handwritten copies. Arranged chronologi-
    cally.
  From Charles Haire and Thomas F. Cornell, "Agents for Preservation
of Timber in East Florida," reporting to the Secretary of the Navy.
182

REPORT OF J. N. REYNOLDS ON THE PACIFIC OCEAN AND ITS ISLANDS AND
    COASTS. Sept. 24, 1828. 1 vol. $\frac{1}{4}$ in.
  Facts assembled in Nantucket from whalers and other residents, by
request of the Secretary of the Navy, in preparation for a contemplated
naval expedition to the Pacific.
183

EXTRACTS AND SUMMARIES OF LETTERS RECEIVED RELATIVE TO LIVE OAK
    ("Treasury"). Apr. 1831 - Apr. 1835. 1 vol. 2 in. Arranged
    by regions, thereunder chronologically. Indexed.
  Compiled at an unknown date, perhaps after the administration of
naval timber reservations was transferred in 1843 to the Bureau of Yards
and Docks.
184

LETTERS SENT RELATING TO THE NAVAL ASYLUM AND THE NAVY HOSPITAL FUND
    ("Navy Hospital"). July 1834 - Sept. 1840. 1 vol. (labeled "2").
    2 in. Handwritten copies. Arranged chronologically. Indexed.
  To the Governor of the Naval Asylum, commandants of navy yards and
naval stations, commanding officers of vessels, the Commandant of the
Marine Corps, and applicants for admission to the Naval Asylum. The
latter part of the volume is blank, suggesting that the series was
discontinued.
185

RECORDS RELATING TO THE SERVICE OF THE NAVY AND THE MARINE CORPS ON THE
    COAST OF FLORIDA ("Florida-Indian War"). 1835-42. 1 vol. 1$\frac{1}{4}$ in.
    Typed copies. Arranged chronologically.
  Letter of transmittal to the Commissioner of Pensions, December 19,
1853, enclosing copies of and extracts from instructions to officers of
the Navy cooperating with the Army during the Florida War, 1835-42;
copies of and extracts from reports of naval officers during the war,
1836-42; and extracts from logs of vessels operating off the coast of
Florida, 1836-42.
186

REPORTS DESCRIBING EXPERIMENTS OFF SANDY HOOK WITH BOMB GUNS AND HOLLOW
    SHOT. Oct. 12, 1839, and Jan. 4 and 25, 1841. 2 vols.
    (duplicates). 2$\frac{1}{2}$ in. Table of contents.
  From Capt. Matthew C. Perry, Inspector of Ordnance for the Navy.
187

LETTERS FROM ENGINEERS IN CHIEF ("Engineer in Chief Letters"). Jan. 1847 –
Dec. 1850. 1 vol. 2 in. Arranged chronologically. Indexed.   188
   From Charles H. Haswell (till December 1850) and B. F. Sherwood and
Charles B. Stuart (December 1850), addressed for the most part to the
Chief of the Bureau of Construction, Equipment, and Repairs, and relat-
ing to experiments and tests, inventions, engineer personnel, and other
matters. The letters were apparently forwarded to the Secretary of the
Navy. See Entry 278 for letters of similar character.

LETTERS RECEIVED RELATING TO THE NAVAL ASYLUM ("Naval Asylum Letters").
Feb. 1848 – Dec. 1850. 1 vol. 3/4 in. Arranged chronologically.
Indexed.   189
   From Commo. Jacob Jones, Governor of the Naval Asylum, and from
inmates, physicians, and applicants for admission and those testifying
in their behalf. See Entries 185 and 231 for other letters relating to
the Naval Asylum.

RECORDS RELATING TO THE UNITED STATES REVENUE CUTTER SERVICE. June 1860 –
Dec. 1865. 2 vols. (one a carbon copy, one a press copy). 2 in.
Arranged chronologically. Indexed.   190
   Chiefly copies of correspondence of the Secretary of the Navy with
the Secretary of the Treasury. The ribbon copy, with a covering letter,
was transmitted to the Secretary of the Interior Aug. 7, 1905.

REGISTER OF TELEGRAPHIC DESPATCHES OF THE NAVY DEPARTMENT. June 1861 –
Apr. 1865. 1 vol. 1 in. Arranged chronologically, with
despatches sent and despatches received on facing pages.   191
   Gives date of despatch, person from whom received or to whom sent,
address, and number of words.

REPORTS FROM THE NAVAL EXAMINING BOARD. Jan.–July 1862. 1 vol. 2 in.
Arranged chronologically. Indexed.   192
   Reports on inventions and other scientific projects referred to the
Board by the Secretary of the Navy for examination. See Entry 361 for
records of the Board.

REPORTS FROM THE PERMANENT COMMISSION. Mar. 1863 – Sept. 1865. 1 vol.
3 in. Arranged chronologically. Indexed.   193
   The Commission inherited the functions of the Naval Examining Board.
See Entry 363 for records of the Commission.

TELEGRAMS SENT THROUGH THE TELEGRAPHIC OFFICE OF THE WAR DEPARTMENT.
Sept. 1869 – Sept. 1871. 2 adhesive binders. 9 in. Handwritten
copies. Arranged chronologically.   194
From the Secretary of the Navy and heads of bureaus.

REPORT ON BRITISH DOCKYARDS. Nov. 16, 1870. 1 vol. 2 in.   195
   The writer, Theodore D. Wilson, Assistant Naval Constructor, was
ordered on May 12, 1870, to inspect the dockyards of France and England.
Failing to obtain permission from French authorities to examine dockyards in France, he reported in great detail on a number of public and
private dockyards in England and Ireland.

LETTERS TO NEWSPAPERS RELATING TO ADVERTISEMENTS FOR THE NAVY DEPARTMENT.
    May 1873 - Sept. 1876. 1 vol. 1½ in. Press copies. Arranged
    chronologically. Indexed by names of newspapers.   <u>196</u>

LETTERS FROM THE PERMANENT SENIOR NAVAL OFFICER OF THE PORT OF PORT
    ROYAL, S. C. ("Senior Officer's Letters"). Feb.-Dec. 1876.
    1 vol. 1 in. Arranged chronologically. Table of contents.   <u>197</u>
  From Commo. John M. B. Clitz. This volume resembles the "Commandants'
Letters" (Entry 34), but no other organized on the same basis is known
to exist.

REPORTS ON THE SALE OF NAVY YARDS. Dec. 1876, Feb.-Dec. 1883. 1 vol.
    1 in.   <u>198</u>
  (a) "Proceedings of the Board of Officers Convened by Authority of
Congress for the Examination of Navy Yards," addressed to the Secretary
of the Navy Dec. 5, 1876, recording meetings from Oct. 3 to Dec. 5, 1876.
Admiral David D. Porter was Senior Member of the Board. The report includes a copy of "Report of the Board of Officers Appointed To Consider
the Propriety of Accepting League Island, &c., for Naval Purposes,"
addressed to the Secretary Apr. 11, 1867. The earlier board had been
appointed in compliance with an act of Feb. 18, 1867, with R. A. Charles
H. Davis as Senior Member. (b) Reports of the Commission on Navy Yards
to Congress, Feb. 27 and Dec. 1, 1883, and to the Secretary, June 6 and
Oct. 11, 1883 (the last 3 reports printed). The Commission, with Commo.
Stephen B. Luce as President, had been appointed in compliance with an
act of Feb. 27, 1883, to report "upon the question whether it is advisable
to sell any of the Navy Yards, and if so, which," and to furnish certain
data pertaining to the several yards.

REPORT FROM THE NAVAL ADVISORY BOARD. Nov. 1881. 1 vol. 2½ in.
    Indexed.   <u>199</u>
  Printed report, November 7, 1881, including journal of proceedings,
July 11 - November 7; manuscript minority report and endorsements
thereon; and correspondence. The Board, meeting at Washington
with R. A. John Rodgers as President, had been appointed by an
order of June 29, 1881, to examine "the number and class of such
vessels as should be constructed, and to unite in recommending
such as Congress would be most likely to approve."

CORRESPONDENCE CONCERNING CONSTRUCTION OF NEW VESSELS ("Memoranda
    Concerning Construction of New Vessels"). Apr. 1882 - Jan. 1888.
    1 vol. 1 in. Arranged chronologically.   <u>200</u>
  Letters from Congress, chiefs of bureaus, and officers, with enclosures,
chiefly statistical; and copies and drafts of letters sent.

REPORTS ON INSPECTION AND SURVEY OF NAVAL VESSELS ("Inspection Reports").
    Jan. 1883 - Dec. 1884. 2 vols. 3 in. Arranged chronologically.
    Indexed by ships.   <u>201</u>
  Chiefly reports from the Board of Inspection and Survey to Admiral
David D. Porter, forwarded by him with endorsements to the Secretary of
the Navy. Some reports from chiefs of bureaus are included.

REPORTS FROM THE GUN FOUNDRY BOARD. Feb. and Dec. 1884. 1 vol. 1 in.   202
    Printed report, Feb. 16, 1884, including record of proceedings,
Apr. 10, 1883 - Feb. 8, 1884; and 2-page supplementary report, Dec. 20,
1884. The Board, known also as "The Board of Army and Navy Officers
Relative to the Best Location for Establishing a Government Foundry,"
appointed in compliance with an act of Mar. 3, 1883, met at League
Island with R. A. Edward Simpson as President, and afterward visited
Europe.

MONTHLY REPORTS OF THE NUMBER AND CONDITION OF VESSELS IN NAVY YARDS.
    Jan.-Nov. 1885. 1 vol. 3/4 in. Arranged chronologically.   203
    Form G-3, submitted by commandants.

MATERIALS RELATING TO THE POLICIES AND ADMINISTRATION OF THE NAVY
    DEPARTMENT. 1886-92. 1 vol. 2 in. Arranged by document
    numbers, 1-242. Indexed.   204
    Notes, originals and copies of letters, circulars, and other materials
relating particularly to precedents and legal matters affecting the Navy.
Assembled by John D. Hogg, Chief Clerk of the Navy Department.

LETTERS RECEIVED RELATING TO GIFTS PRESENTED TO SHIPS OF THE NAVY BY
    CITIZENS OF THE UNITED STATES. Nov. 1888 - Nov. 1899. 1 vol.
    2½ in. Arranged chronologically. Table of contents.   205
    Includes schedules of the articles composing the gifts.

SUMMARIES OF CORRESPONDENCE RELATIVE TO ESTIMATES OF REPAIRS ON NAVAL
    VESSELS. June 1889 - Dec. 1891. 3 vols. 2½ in. Each volume
    arranged chronologically. Table of contents.   206
    One volume for third-rate and one for fourth-rate vessels, 1889-90;
one general volume, 1891.

REPORT FROM THE STEEL INSPECTION BOARD. Jan. 1890. 1 vol. 4 in.   207
    No. 11722 of the general file of the Secretary's Office. The Board,
established Sept. 1, 1886, with Capt. Robert L. Phythian (succeeded by
Capt. Henry L. Howison) as President, was instructed to visit manufactur-
ing plants and inspect all steel materials for hulls and machinery of
new vessels.

MEMORANDA ISSUED AND RECEIVED BY AIDES ("Miscellaneous Memoranda").
    Oct. 1910-Dec. 1911. 1 vol. 1¼ in. Arranged chronologically.   208
    Carbon copies of memoranda issued, and originals and carbon copies of
memoranda received, by the Aides for Operations, Material, Personnel,
and Inspections. The "Aide System" began when the Secretary of the
Navy, in Changes in Navy Regulations No. 6, Nov. 18, 1909, announced
the appointment of four aides to assist the Secretary "in efficiently
administering the affairs of the Navy Department." Four divisions—of
Operations of the Fleet, Personnel, Material, and Inspections—were
established, one under each of the aides; and each division was given
cognizance over a number of bureaus, offices, or other units of the Navy
Department. The positions of Aide for Personnel and Aide for Inspections
became vacant in 1913 and 1914 respectively, and were allowed to lapse.
The functions of the other two aides were transferred to the Chief of

Naval Operations in May 1915, and the "Aide System" was discontinued by order of the Secretary of the Navy on June 24, 1915. The origin of this volume is not clear; it would not have originated naturally in the office of any one of the aides.

II. BOARD OF NAVY COMMISSIONERS, 1815-1842

The Board of Navy Commissioners was established by an act of February 7, 1815. The act provided that the Commissioners should be three officers of the Navy, with a rank not lower than that of post captain, who "shall be attached to the office of the Secretary of the Navy, and under his superintendence shall discharge all the ministerial duties of said office." The Commissioners were authorized to appoint their own secretary, who was to keep "a fair record of their proceedings" (Entry 209); to prepare "such rules and regulations, as shall be necessary for securing an uniformity in the several classes of vessels and their equipments, and for repairing and refitting them, and for securing responsibility in the subordinate officers and agents"; and at the Secretary's request to report to him on estimates of expenditure and such other matters as he might deem necessary. Nothing in the act was to be construed "to take from the Secretary of the Navy his control and direction of the naval forces of the United States, as now by law possessed."

The act did not explicitly define a division of powers between the Secretary and the Commissioners. On June 15, 1815, the Board issued a circular ordering that all correspondence with the Navy Department relating to matters within the province of the Board be addressed directly to the Board. Uncertainty as to the extent of this province was never entirely removed; but after early disagreements between the Secretary and the Board the authority of the Board came to be confined in general to the civil functions of the Department, relative to procurement of stores and materials and the construction, armament, and equipment of vessels of war, while the Secretary retained immediate supervision over matters of naval personnel and naval discipline, appointments of both civil and naval personnel, the detailing of officers, and the movements of vessels.

The members of the Board, all of whom were captains with the honorary title of commodore, were the following:

John Rodgers, 1815-24, 1827-37
Isaac Hull, 1815
David Porter, 1815-22
Stephen Decatur, 1815-20
Isaac Chauncey, 1822-24, 1833-40
Charles Morris, 1823-25, 1826-27, 1832-41
William Bainbridge, 1824-27
Jacob Jones, 1824-26

Lewis Warrington, 1827-30, 1840-42
Thomas Tingey, 1827
Daniel T. Patterson, 1828-32
Charles Stewart, 1830-33
Alexander S. Wadsworth, 1837-40
John B. Nicolson, 1840-41
William M. Crane, 1841-42
David Conner, 1841-42

The secretaries of the Board, whose duties included that of maintaining its records, were James K. Paulding, 1815-23, and Charles W. Goldsborough,

1823-42. The Presidents of the Board were Rodgers, 1815-24, 1827-37; Bainbridge, 1824-27; Chauncey, 1837-40; Morris, 1840-41; and Warrington, 1841-42.

After twenty-seven years the Board was abolished by an act of August 31, 1842, which divided the powers of the Board among five bureaus and required "that the books, records, and papers, now belonging to the office of the Navy Commissioners shall be distributed among the bureaus, according to the nature of their duties respectively." The three officers who constituted the Board at the time of its dissolution were appointed chiefs of bureaus, and the secretary of the Board was appointed chief of a fourth bureau. The Board may thus be regarded as the predecessor of the bureaus. Most of its correspondence was inherited by the Bureau of Construction, Equipment, and Repairs (later the Bureau of Construction and Repair) and was transferred by the Bureau of Construction and Repair to the Office of Naval Records and Library in July 1926.

All but a small part of the known records of the Board of Navy Commissioners are in the Naval Records Collection. Other records of the Board are in Record Group 80, General Records of the Department of the Navy.

A. Journal, 1815-1842

JOURNAL OF THE BOARD OF NAVY COMMISSIONERS. Apr. 1815 - Sept. 1852.
    19 vols. 3 ft. 1 in. Arranged chronologically.   209
    Vols. 1 and 2; an unnumbered volume succeeding them (Aug. 1821 - Nov. 1823); vol. A (Sept. 1823 - Dec. 1824); vols. 1-14 (Jan. 1825 - Aug. 1842); and "Rough Minutes," Feb. 22 - Sept. 23, 1842. Except for the last volume, the journal is the "fair record" of proceedings called for by the act of Feb. 7, 1815. The record consists largely of summaries of letters sent by the Commissioners.

REGISTER OF THE NAVY COMMISSIONERS' JOURNAL ("Key to Journal").
    Jan. 1825 - Aug. 1842. 6 vols. 8 in. Arranged chronologically by volumes, thereunder by subjects in order of first mention. Indexed.   210
    Neither register nor index is known to have been maintained before 1825.

B. Copies of Letters Sent, 1815-1842

LETTERS SENT. Apr. 1815 - Aug. 1842. Loose papers. 8 ft. Press copies. Arranged and labeled by subject according to the system applied by the Office of Naval Records and Library to the papers forming the series described in Entries 463 and 464; original order unknown.   211

    These papers were mounted on white backsheets by the Office of Naval Records and Library with a view to their eventual insertion into the "Area File" and the "Subject File." They are duplicated in the various series of handwritten copies described below.

CIRCULARS ISSUED. 1815-42. 2 vols. 7 in. Arranged chronologically.
        Handwritten copies. Registered.   212
    Chiefly to commandants of navy yards and shore stations and to navy
agents in the United States and abroad. Not numbered.

LETTERS TO THE SECRETARY OF THE NAVY. Apr. 1815 - Aug. 1842. 7 vols.
        2 ft. Handwritten copies. Arranged chronclogically. Registered.   213
    Letters relative to the building, equipment, and repair of naval
vessels; timber, ordnance, and other materials; provisions, clothing,
and other supplies; inventions and scientific projects; civil employees
in navy yards; and contracts, bonds, appropriations, estimates, and
accounts. For the original letters received by the Secretary of the
Navy from the Commissioners, 1827-42, see Entry 28.

LETTERS TO OFFICERS. Apr. 1815 - July 1842. 2 vols. 7 in. Handwritten
        copies. Arranged chronologically. Indexed.   214
    Chiefly to officers commanding ships and squadrons, to inspectors of
ordnance, and to the officer in command of the Dépôt of Charts and Instruments. Concerned with supplies, stores, and accounts, the inspection and distribution of ordnance, and the purchase and distribution of
maps, charts, chronometers, and other hydrographic supplies and equipment.

LETTERS TO NAVY AGENTS. Apr. 1815 - Feb. 1842. 5 vols. 1 ft. 6 in.
        Handwritten copies. Arranged chronologically. Indexed.   215
    To agents in navy yards or foreign ports and to timber agents. Con-
cerned with supplies, stores, and accounts, the purchase and sale of
naval property, repairs of vessels, and newspaper advertisements.

LETTERS TO COMMANDANTS. Apr. 1815 - Aug. 1842. 14 vols. 5 ft. 9 in.
        Handwritten copies. Arranged chronologically. Indexed.   216
    Concerned with contracts and expenditures, buildings and other naval
property, ordnance and other materials, supplies (including timber), the
building and repair of vessels, and civil personnel. Copies of circulars
are included.

MISCELLANEOUS LETTERS SENT ("Miscellaneous Letters"). May 1815 - Aug.
        1842. 8 vols. 2 ft. 6 in. Handwritten copies. Arranged
        chronologically. Indexed.   217
    To contractors, merchants and manufacturers, naval constructors,
editors of newspapers, and other persons, chiefly outside the Navy
Department.

LETTERS TO NAVAL CONSTRUCTORS, STEAM ENGINEERS, AND CIVIL ENGINEERS
        ("Naval Constructors"). Jan. 1838 - Aug. 1842. 1 vol. 3½ in.
        Handwritten copies. Arranged chronologically.   218
    Before 1838 such letters were copied in the preceding series.

C. Letters Received, 1814-1842

    The first five series described below begin in 1814 either because of
the inclusion of letters addressed to the Secretary of the Navy but presumably referred at a later date to the Navy Commissioners, or because of the
faulty placing of enclosures.

MISCELLANEOUS LETTERS RECEIVED. Feb. 1814 - Aug. 1842. 77 vols. 12 ft.
    Arranged chronologically. Indexed.   219
    Includes such letters as were not bound in other series, chiefly
letters from correspondents outside the Navy Department, particularly
contractors, merchants, and manufacturers.

LETTERS FROM COMMANDANTS. Mar. 1814 - July 1842. 101 vols. and 126
    adhesive binders. 36 ft. Arranged by yards and stations, there-
    under chronologically. Some volumes indexed.   220
    From commandants of several stations, 1815-20, 1833 (2 vols.);
Baltimore, 1830-41 (3 vols.); Charleston and Baltimore, 1815-29 (1 vol.);
Charlestown (Boston), 1817-42 (42 vols.); Gosport (Norfolk), 1815-42
(40 vols.); New Orleans, 1815-26 (2 vols.); New York, 1815-42 (46 vols.);
Pensacola, 1826-42 (17 vols.); Philadelphia, 1815-42 (24 vols.); Sackett's
Harbor, 1837 (1 vol.); Sackett's Harbor and Charleston, 1838-39 (1 vol.);
Sackett's Harbor, Whitehall, and Erie, 1815-33 (1 vol.); and Washington,
1814-42 (47 vols.). These letters relate to the civil as distinguished
from the strictly military activities of yards and stations, and concern
the building, equipment, and repair of naval vessels; the purchase,
storage, and expenditure of supplies and materials; the purchase of land
for naval purposes; the erection and repair of naval buildings; the appointment, supervision, and retirement of civil personnel; the preparation
of estimates for necessary funds and supplies; and the keeping of accounts.

LETTERS FROM OFFICERS. Apr. 1814 - Jan. 1815, Jan. 1819 - July 1842.
    22 vols. 3 ft. 8 in. Arranged chronologically. Some volumes
    indexed.   221
    From officers other than commandants. Concerned chiefly with
supplies, equipment, and repairs for naval vessels.

LETTERS FROM THE SECRETARY OF THE NAVY. Apr. 1814 - July 1842. 11 vols.
    and 10 adhesive binders. 3 ft. 4 in. Arranged chronologically.
    Indexed.   222
    For copies of these letters, maintained in the Secretary's Office,
see Entry 8.

LETTERS FROM NAVY AGENTS. Sept. 1814 - July 1842. 33 vols. and 33
    adhesive binders. 10 ft. 3 in. Arranged by place, thereunder
    chronologically. Some volumes indexed.   223
    Letters from navy agents in general, 1815-36 (20 vols.); reports,
estimates, and surveys from agents, 1814-34 (6 vols.); and letters from
agents in Baltimore, 1837-42 (5 vols.), Charlestown (Boston), 1837-42
(6 vols.), foreign stations, 1837-42 (2 vols.), Gosport (Norfolk), 1815-
20, 1837-42 (6 vols.), New York, 1815-20, 1837-42 (7 vols.), Pensacola,
1837-42 (4 vols.), Philadelphia, 1815-20, 1837-42 (5 vols.), Portsmouth,
1839-42 (1 vol.), Valparaiso, Chile (Agent Michael Hogan), 1822-34 (1 vol.),
and Washington, 1837-42 (3 vols.). The letters relate chiefly to the
purchase, storage, and expenditure of supplies and the preparation of
estimates and accounts.

LETTERS FROM NAVAL CONSTRUCTORS AND ENGINEERS. May 1815 - July 1842.
     10 vols. 1 ft. 8 in. Some volumes indexed.   <u>224</u>
    From Naval Constructors William Doughty, Henry Eckford, John Floyd,
and Francis Grice, 1815-25 (1 vol.); from Naval Constructor Samuel
Humphreys, appointed Chief Naval Constructor in November 1826, 1815-38
(4 vols.); from Humphreys, Steam Engineer Charles W. Copeland, Chief
Engineer Charles H. Haswell, and Naval Constructor John Lenthall,
1838-42 ("Superintendents & Engineers," 4 vols.); and from Civil
Engineer Edward H. Courtenay, New York Navy Yard, 1841-42 (1 vol.).

REGISTER OF LETTERS RECEIVED. Jan. 1820 - Dec. 1837. 5 vols. 7 in.
     Arranged by date of first letter from each correspondent, later
     letters from the same correspondent immediately following.
     Indexed.   <u>225</u>
    Since vol. 2 begins in Jan. 1823, it is presumed that the previous
volume, 1820-22, with no volume number, was the first of the series.
Vol. 3, July 1825 - June 1827, is lacking; but since entries for particular correspondents in it are continued in vol. 4, the period is not
entirely blank. The book that was labeled for use as vol. 7, which would
have begun with Jan. 1838, was inherited blank by the Bureau of Yards
and Docks, which entered in it a register of letters received beginning
in Jan. 1845 (Entry 265).

LETTERS FROM INSPECTORS AND ASSISTANT INSPECTORS OF ORDNANCE ("Ordnance").
     July 1820 - Oct. 1840, June-Aug. 1842. 4 vols. 8 in. Arranged
     chronologically. Indexed.   <u>226</u>
    From Capt. John Cassin (1820-27), Capt. Alexander S. Wadsworth
(1827-29, 1842), Capt. Thomas ap Catesby Jones (1831-33), Capt. William
Branford Shubrick (1834-38), Capt. Edmund P. Kennedy (1839), Comdr.
John L. Chauncey (1839-40), and Capt. Matthew C. Perry (1840). These
officers had the title of Inspector (or Ass't Inspector) of Ordnance and
Ammunition Belonging to the Navy. A volume for 1840-42 is in Record
Group 80, General Records of the Department of the Navy.

REPORTS OF THE CHIEF NAVAL CONSTRUCTOR ("Reports of Naval Constructor,
     Navy Commissioners Office"). Mar. 1827 - Apr. 1834. 1 vol.
     1¼ in. Handwritten copies. Arranged chronologically. Indexed.   <u>227</u>
    From Samuel Humphreys, chiefly to the Board of Navy Commissioners.
Originals of some of the reports are in the series described in Entry
224.

LETTERS FROM THE DÉPÔT OF CHARTS AND INSTRUMENTS. June 1831 - May 1857,
     Jan. 1838 - May 1839, Jan. 1840 - Aug. 1842. 7 vols. 1 ft. 2 in.
     Arranged chronologically. Some volumes indexed.   <u>228</u>
    From Lt. Louis M. Goldsborough (1831-33), Lt. Charles Wilkes, Jr.
(1833-37), Passed Mdn. W. Ward (1836), Lt. Robert B. Hitchcock (1836-37),
Lt. James Melville Gilliss (1837-42), and Lt. Matthew Fontaine Maury
(1842). Two volumes are lacking. The Dépôt of Charts and Instruments,
predecessor of the Hydrographic Office and the Naval Observatory, was
under the cognizance of the Board of Navy Commissioners. Its duty was
to procure, store, and distribute maps, charts, books, chronometers, and
other navigational equipment.

LETTERS FROM THE AMERICAN CONSUL IN LONDON ("Letters, London Consuls").
        Oct. 1831 - Apr. 1835. 1 vol. 2 in. Arranged chronologically.
        Indexed.   229
    From Thomas Aspinwall, concerning the purchase of scientific books
and instruments in Great Britain for the use of the Navy.

REPORT ON THE NAVAL ORDNANCE OF THE UNITED STATES. Jan. 20, 1834.
        1½ in. Arranged by navy yards, with an inventory of, and remarks
        on, the ordnance in each.   230
    By Capt. Thomas ap Catesby Jones, Inspector of Ordnance.

LETTERS RECEIVED RELATING TO THE NAVAL ASYLUM ("Asylum"). Aug. 1838 -
        May 1842. 1 adhesive binder. 2 in. Arranged chronologically.   231
    Chiefly from Capt. James Biddle, Governor of the Naval Asylum, con-
cerning supplies and accounts or transmitting monthly reports. The
reports themselves are not included and have not been found.

LETTERS REFERRED BY THE SECRETARY OF THE NAVY TO THE NAVY COMMISSIONERS
        ("Reference from Secretary"). Nov. 1838 - June 1842. 5 adhesive
        binders. 10 in. Arranged chronologically. Indexed.   232

LETTERS OF APPLICATION FOR OFFICE AND ACCOMPANYING RECOMMENDATIONS.
        Dec. 1839 - June 1841. 2 adhesive binders. 4 in. Arranged
        chronologically.   233
    For civil appointments, such as ropemaker, painter, blacksmith,
joiner, timber inspector, and clerk.

LETTERS FROM CONTRACTORS AND OTHERS RELATIVE TO MATERIALS AND SUPPLIES
        ("Contractors & Others, Relative to Timber at Navy Yards").
        Dec. 1841 - June 1842. 3 vols. 6 in. Arranged chronologically.   234
    In spite of the title, the letters concern provisions, metal goods,
and other supplies in addition to timber.

D. Other Records, 1794-1842

CONTRACTS. June 1794 - Dec. 1842. 15 vols. 3 ft. 3 in. Handwritten
        copies. Arranged chronologically. Indexed.   235
    Vols. 1-4 (June 1794 - Aug. 1823) and 1-11 (June 1815 - Dec. 1842).
The earliest contracts were made by the War Department before the establishment of the Navy Department. In and after 1815 nearly all the
contracts in both subseries were made by the Navy Commissioners. The
subseries of 1794-1823 is labeled "Navy Department" but appears to have
been bound or rebound much more recently than 1823; the 1815-42 subseries
is labeled "Navy Commissioners." For the years 1815-23 no difference in
nature, purpose, or origin between the two subseries is perceptible; and
it is not at present possible to discover why the two were maintained
concurrently.

INVENTORIES OF STORES IN NAVY YARDS ("Naval Stores"). Jan. 1814 -
        Jan. 1816. 1 vol. 2 in. Arranged chronologically.   236

REGISTER OF OFFICERS OF THE NAVY ("Register, U. S. Navy Commissioners'
    Office"). May 1815 - June 1821. 1 vol. 2½ in. Arranged by
    first letter of officers' names, thereunder chronologically.   257
    Gives officer's name, rank, date of appointment to the rank, age,
and tenor of superior officers' comments regarding his fitness for
promotion.

ESTIMATES AND OTHER STATISTICS RECEIVED OR COMPILED. 1815-57. 2 vols.
    and 2 adhesive binders. 10 in. Arranged chronologically.
    Indexed.   238
    Labeled "Estimates" (2 vols. and 1 binder) and "Navy Yard Estimate for
1838" (1 binder). The two volumes (1815-36) consist of handwritten copies
of exhibits of actual and estimated expenses of navy yards and single
projects, schedules of materials, tables indicating costs of sustenance
for officers and crews, and many other kinds of statistics, some compiled
by the Navy Commissioners and others received by them. The first binder
apparently contains only appendixes or exhibits of a budget report of the
Commissioners, numbered from D through M. The second binder contains
estimates submitted by navy yards and is presumed to be an enclosure to
the missing main report.

SUMMARY OF INFORMATION RESPECTING THE LIVE-OAK TIMBER OF THE CAROLINAS
    AND GEORGIA. Oct. 1815 - Nov. 1817. 1 vol. ½ in. Arranged by
    States, thereunder chronologically.   239
    Prepared by the Navy Commissioners from reports of Agents Nathaniel
Hutton, Thomas M. Newell, and Abraham Thomas.

SCALE OF OFFERS FROM BIDDERS. Apr. 1816 - Oct. 1823, Jan. 1827 -
    Aug. 1842. 6 vols. 7 in. Arranged by dates of bidding, there-
    under from lowest bid to highest. First 2 vols. indexed.   240
    The first volume, "Proposals for Contracts," tells only what articles
are offered, by whom, and when and where deliverable.

GENERAL ESTIMATES OF MATERIALS REQUIRED FOR BUILDING NAVAL VESSELS.
    1817. 1 vol. ½ in.   241
    Wood, iron, copper, lead, and other materials.

JOURNAL OF JAMES KEEN ON AN EXPEDITION FROM PHILADELPHIA TO BLACKBEARD
    (SAPELO) ISLAND, GA. Nov. 27, 1817 - Apr. 5, 1818. 1 vol. ½ in.   242
    George Harrison, Navy Agent at Philadelphia, chartered the schooner
Twins (Edward Lafferty, Master) to transport workmen in charge of Keen
to cut timber in Georgia, where Keen supervised their labor under the
general direction of Lt. Thomas M. Newell.

JOURNAL OF JOHN LANDRETH ON AN EXPEDITION TO THE GULF COAST. Nov. 15,
    1818 - May 19, 1819. 1 vol. 1¼ in.   243
    John Landreth, Timber Agent, was appointed as surveyor in the expedi-
tion of James Cathcart and James Hutton, Timber Agents, to the coasts of
Louisiana, Mississippi, and Alabama to select unappropriated lands pro-
ducing live oak and red cedar suitable for naval use. The party sailed
from Norfolk to New Orleans on the USS Nonsuch, commanded by Lt. Alexander
Claxton, and made extensive surveys of timber-bearing lands on and near
the coast, particularly in Louisiana. The volume contains maps in water
color.

BILLS APPROVED BY THE NAVY COMMISSIONERS ("Account Book"). June 1819 -
    Feb. 1845. 4 vols. 7 in. Handwritten copies. Arranged
    chronologically. Indexed.   244
    Each bill is signed in autograph by a member of the Board, and the
date of payment is indicated. After Aug. 1842 the series consists of
bills against the former Board, approved by the Chief of the Bureau of
Yards and Docks, Capt. Lewis Warrington, formerly one of the Commissioners.

CONTRACTORS' BONDS. Apr. 1820 - Mar. 1842. 5 vols. 10 in. Handwritten
    copies. Arranged chronologically. Indexed.   245

DATA RELATIVE TO CONTRACTS ("Abstracts of Contracts"). July 1820 -
    Nov. 1821, Nov. 1836 - May 1839. 1 vol. 1 in. Indexed.   246
    Abstracts of contracts, July 1820 - Nov. 1821, giving name of con-
tractor, date of contract, articles contracted for, agreed place of
delivery, agreed date of completion, and amount paid; "Accepted Offers
Under Different Scales & Shewing Contracts Have Been Executed in Compliance Therewith," Nov. 1836 - June 1838; and "Memorandum of Contracts
and Bonds Drawn and Forwarded for Execution," Sept. 1838 - May 1839.

INVENTORIES OF STORES IN NAVY YARDS. Jan. 1825 - Dec. 1843. 11 vols.
    1 ft. 5 in.   247
    Submitted from Boston, Jan. 1825 - Sept. 1826, Oct. 1837 - Aug. 1843
(3 vols.); Norfolk, Nov. 1830 - Dec. 1843 (4 vols.); Pensacola, Oct. 1840 -
Dec. 1843 (1 vol.); Philadelphia, Oct. 1840 - Dec. 1843 (1 vol.);
Washington, Oct. 1840 - Dec. 1843 (1 vol.); and Boston, Norfolk,
Pensacola, Philadelphia, Portsmouth, Washington, and New York, 1834-37
(1 vol.). Inventories after Aug. 1842 were submitted to the Bureau of
Yards and Docks. Other volumes of inventories of navy-yard stores are
among the records of the Board of Navy Commissioners in Record Group 80,
General Records of the Department of the Navy.

ADVERTISEMENTS. Mar. 1827 - June 1833. 1 vol. ("2"). 3/4 in. Hand-
    written and printed copies. Arranged chronologically. Indexed.   248
    Chiefly advertisements cut from newspapers, announcing classes of
materials upon which the Navy Department desired to receive bids.

MONEY REQUISITIONS FROM NAVY AGENTS AND PURSERS ("Requisitions from
    Navy Agents"). Jan. 1828 - Dec. 1841. 21 adhesive binders. 3 ft.
    4 in. Arranged chronologically by volumes, thereunder by navy
    yards.   249
    Signed as approved by the Navy Commissioners.

ABSTRACT OF RECEIPTS AND EXPENDITURES UNDER APPROPRIATIONS FOR "ORDNANCE,
    GRADUAL INCREASE" AND "ORDNANCE, REPAIRS." Jan. 1829 - Oct. 1837.
    2 vols. 1 in. Arranged chronologically by volumes, thereunder by
    type of ordnance.   250

REGISTER OF IMPROVEMENTS AND REPAIRS IN NAVY YARDS ("Improvements &
    Repaires in Navy Yards"). Apr. 1830 - June 1836. 1 vol. 1 3/4 in.
    Arranged by navy yards.   251
    Gives date of estimate for each improvement or repair, object for
which estimated, estimated cost, date of authorization, appropriation,
date of completion, final cost, and remarks.

REGISTER OF REQUISITIONS FROM NAVY YARDS. Apr. 1830 - Dec. 1835.
    1 vol. 1½ in. Arranged chronologically.   252

ANNUAL CONTRACTS MADE BY THE NAVY COMMISSIONERS. Dec. 1835 - Jan. 1837,
    Jan.-Dec. 1841. 3 vols. 8 in. Each volume arranged chronologi-
    cally under each article contracted for. Indexed.   253
    (1) "Contracts, Vol. 10, Copper, Iron, Paints, &c.," Dec. 1835 -
Jan. 1837; (2) "Contracts, Vol. 11, Flour, Biscuit, Whiskey," Dec. 1835 -
Dec. 1836; and (3) "Annual Contracts," Jan.-Dec. 1841. All these contracts are handwritten copies on printed forms. The articles contracted
for in 1841 were ship biscuit, butter, cheese, bolt and sheet copper,
spermaceti candles, superfine flour, groceries, iron, raw linseed oil,
spermaceti oil, paints, and whisky. The three volumes are probably fragments of a large series.

INVENTORY OF MISCELLANEOUS STORES IN NAVY YARDS. Oct. 1837 - Oct. 1840.
    1 vol. 1½ in. Arranged by types of stores.   254
The volume is considerably damaged by fire.

INVOICES OF STORES SHIPPED BY NAVAL STOREKEEPERS. Jan. 1838 - Sept.
    1842. 4 adhesive binders. 7 in. Arranged chronologically.   255
Received by the Navy Commissioners and bound without covering letters.

REGISTER OF LIABILITIES OF THE NAVY COMMISSIONERS UNDER PURCHASES AND
    AGREEMENTS. Dec. 1838 - July 1842. 1 vol. 1 in. Arranged
    chronologically. Indexed.   256

MONTHLY EXHIBITS OF MONEY REQUISITIONS MADE BY NAVY AGENTS UPON THE
    NAVY COMMISSIONERS. Jan.-Nov. 1841. 1 vol. 2 in. Arranged
    chronologically.   257
Printed forms submitted by navy agents.

III. BUREAUS OF THE NAVY DEPARTMENT, 1799-1914

The act of August 31, 1842, which abolished the Board of Navy Commissioners, established five bureaus—Navy Yards and Docks; Construction,
Equipment, and Repairs; Provisions and Clothing; Ordnance and Hydrography;
and Medicine and Surgery. An act of July 5, 1862, expanded these to eight—
Yards and Docks, Equipment and Recruiting, Navigation, Ordnance, Construction and Repair, Steam Engineering, Provisions and Clothing (renamed the
Bureau of Supplies and Accounts by an act of July 19, 1892), and Medicine
and Surgery.

In addition to the bureaus, a number of more or less autonomous
offices have been established from time to time. These include the Dépôt
of Charts and Instruments, created by a circular of the Board of Navy Commissioners, December 6, 1830, and continued under various names until by
an act of June 21, 1866, it was divided into the Hydrographic Office and
the Naval Observatory; the Nautical Almanac Office, created by an act of
March 3, 1849, and eventually incorporated into the Naval Observatory; the

Nautical Almanac Office, created by an act of March 3, 1849, and eventually incorporated into the Naval Observatory; the Office of the Judge Advocate General, created by an act of June 8, 1880; the Office of Naval Intelligence, created by an order of the Secretary of the Navy, March 23, 1882; and the Office of the Chief of Naval Operations, created by an act of March 3, 1915. These units have been subject to the authority either of various bureaus or of the Office of the Secretary of the Navy, but have functioned with such a degree of independence that, with respect to their records, they differ only nominally from bureaus and need not be classified separately from bureaus.

Several of the bureaus and offices mentioned above are entirely unrepresented in the Naval Records Collection. Records in the Collection that were created by bureaus and offices of the Navy Department are described below. The records consist largely of isolated 1-volume series.

A. Bureau of Yards and Docks, 1811-1879

The Bureau of Navy Yards and Docks was created by the act of 1842, which provided that the Chief of the Bureau should be a captain in the naval service. The name of the Bureau was changed to the Bureau of Yards and Docks by an act of 1862. Its agents in the navy yards were civil engineers.

The province of the Bureau was first defined in a regulation issued November 26, 1842:

> The Navy Yard proper, the Docks & wharves thereof; all buildings thereon or appertaining thereto, including the magazine & hospital buildings; all machinery attached to the yard or ordinarily used in its operations; all vessels in ordinary; all boats, watertanks, buoys &c. used for the purposes of the yard; all carts or other vehicles; all horses, oxen used in the yard, & all other labour therein, and belonging to the objects of this Bureau; the police of the yard; all persons belonging to the yard or ordinary; all contracts & all accounts, returns &c embracing these objects or such as shall, from time to time be assigned to this Bureau.

A regulation of April 14, 1845, placed vessels in navy yards, whether in ordinary (that is, not in commission) or under repair, under the cognizance of the Bureau of Construction, Equipment, and Repairs, and placed all timber in navy yards under the cognizance of the Bureau of Navy Yards and Docks.

Cognizance over timber in navy yards entailed control over the timber agents and timber reservations of the Navy Department, a function previously exercised by the Office of the Secretary of the Navy and, to some extent, by the Board of Navy Commissioners. An act of March 1, 1817, had required the Secretary

> to cause such vacant and unappropriated lands of the United States as produce the live oak and red cedar timbers to be

explored, and selection to be made of such tracts or portions thereof, where the principal growth is of either of the said timbers, as in his judgment may be necessary to furnish for the navy a sufficient supply of the said timbers. The said Secretary shall have power to employ such agent or agents and surveyor as he may deem necessary for the aforesaid purpose.
. . .

Various records relating to the procurement of timber for naval use are described above in Entries 181, 182, 184, 234, 239, 242, and 243. Of the related series described below, some were begun in the Office of the Secretary of the Navy and continued by the Bureau of Navy Yards and Docks; others were begun and maintained entirely in the Bureau.

Other records created by the Bureau are in Record Group 71, Records of the Bureau of Yards and Docks.

PAY ROLLS OF CIVIL PERSONNEL IN SHORE ESTABLISHMENTS. 1811-79. Loose sheets and booklets in 12 labeled wrappers. 1 ft. 6 in. Arranged alphabetically by shore establishments, thereunder chronologically. 258
Charlestown (Mass.) Naval Station, 1819-33; Gosport Navy Yard, 1819-22; Jeannette (Arctic steamer constructed at Mare Island Navy Yard), 1879; Mound City Navy Yard, 1868-72; New Orleans Navy Yard, 1821-65; New York Navy Yard, 1819-64; Pensacola Navy Yard, 1829-63; Philadelphia Navy Yard, 1822-23; Portsmouth (N. H.) Navy Yard, 1821-24; and Washington Navy Yard, 1811-55. The pay rolls are few and scattered between the dates cited for each yard and station. The rolls previous to 1842 were maintained by the Office of the Secretary of the Navy and were presumably transferred in 1842 to the Bureau of Navy Yards and Docks, which continued the series. Other pay rolls and lists of civil personnel in shore establishments, combined with those for naval personnel, are described in Entries 92 and 95.

LETTERS FROM TIMBER AGENTS ("Live Oak Letters," later "Letters from Timber Agents"). June 1828 - Feb. 1836, June 1839 - Dec. 1859. 16 vols. 2 ft. 11 in. Arranged chronologically. Indexed. 259
Addressed to the Secretary of the Navy till 1845, thereafter to the Chief of the Bureau of Navy Yards and Docks. The chief sources of naval timber were Georgia, Florida, Alabama, Mississippi, and Louisiana.

REGISTER OF LETTERS FROM TIMBER AGENTS. Apr. 1845 - Dec. 1860. 2 vols. 1¼ in. Arranged chronologically. Indexed. 260
Gives date of letter, name of writer, and abstract.

LETTERS RECEIVED RELATING TO LIVE OAK ("Letters & Papers Relating to Live Oak Plantations"). Oct. 1829 - Apr. 1861. 1 vol. 2 in. Arranged chronologically. Indexed. 261
Addressed to the Secretary of the Navy till 1845, thereafter to the Chief of the Bureau of Navy Yards and Docks. Chiefly from the Commissioner of the General Land Office, timber agents, and (after 1845) the Secretary of the Navy. Lists of timber agents, with data concerning their appointments, are included. Apparently the volume was assembled by the Bureau of Navy Yards and Docks.

ANNOTATED MAPS OF TIMBER RESERVATIONS. Ca. 1831 – ca. 1857. 1 vol.
1½ in. Arranged by regions (Florida, Alabama, Mississippi,
Louisiana). Indexed.   262
    Some of the maps convey information concerning location, quantity,
and quality of timber. Most are printed maps with manuscript notes.

LETTERS TO TIMBER AGENTS. Mar. 1840 – Apr. 1861. 3 vols. 6 in. Handwritten copies. Arranged chronologically. Indexed.   263
    From the Office of the Secretary of the Navy till 1845.

SYNOPSIS OF ANNUAL EXPENSES OF TIMBER AGENCIES ("Live Oak Ledger").
1845-60. 1 vol. 3/4 in. Arranged chronologically.   264

REGISTER OF LETTERS RECEIVED ("Letters Received, No. 7, Navy Commissioners' Office"). Jan. 1845 – Mar. 1847. 1 vol. 3 in.
Arranged by classes of correspondents (Secretary of Navy, bureaus,
yards, stations, officers, navy agents, miscellaneous), thereunder
chronologically.   265
    As there exists a register of letters received by the Bureau of Yards
and Docks, Sept. 1842 – Dec. 1885, among the records of that Bureau in
Record Group 71, with no gap for 1845-47, and as this volume was originally labeled for the use of the Navy Commissioners (Entry 225), it
seems probable that the volume was a preliminary draft.

LETTERS FROM THE SECRETARY OF THE NAVY RELATIVE TO TIMBER AGENCIES.
Apr. 1845 – Mar. 1855. 1 vol. 1 in. Arranged chronologically.
Indexed.   266

BILLS SUBMITTED BY TIMBER AGENTS AND APPROVED ("Live Oak Bill Book").
Apr. 1845 – Apr. 1861. 2 vols. 3 in. Handwritten copies.
Arranged chronologically. Indexed.   267

REPORTS OF EXPERIMENTS ON PRESERVING TIMBER AGAINST MARINE WORMS.
Jan. 1850 – Jan. 1855. 1 vol. 2½ in. Arranged chronologically.   268
    Addressed by James Jarvis, Timber Inspector, Norfolk Navy Yard, to
the Chief of the Bureau of Navy Yards and Docks or to the Commandant of
the Norfolk Navy Yard, who forwarded the reports to the Bureau.

PAY ROLLS OF LABORERS AND MECHANICS IN THE NAVY YARDS AT CAIRO,
Oct. 1863, AND MOUND CITY, July 1871 – July 1873. 1 vol. 2 in.
Arranged chronologically.   269

HISTORY OF THE BOSTON NAVY YARD, 1797-1875, BY COMMO. GEORGE HENRY
PREBLE. 3 vols. 5 in. Arranged chronologically. Indexed.   270
    Preface signed at the Philadelphia Navy Yard, June 30, 1875. Commo-
dore Preble had received orders in Nov. 1873 from the Chief of the Bureau
of Yards and Docks to prepare this work. It is a handwritten original,
with various interlineations and corrections, and was evidently designed
for publication. Flyleaf title: "History of the Boston Navy Yard in
Charlestown, Mass., from 1797 to 1875, with an Historical Introduction
and Appendix. Prepared by Commodore George Henry Preble, U. S. N.,
Under the Direction of the Bureau of Yards and Docks, Navy Department."

M118

B. Bureau of Ordnance and Hydrography, 1842-1862

The Bureau of Ordnance and Hydrography was created by the act of 1842, which provided that the Chief of the Bureau should be a captain in the naval service. The province of the Bureau was first defined in a regulation of November 26, 1842, which treated the Bureau for administrative purposes as two bureaus combined under a single chief. "The Bureau of Ordnance" received cognizance over

> All ordnance & ordnance stores & the materials relating thereto; such as guns, muskets, pistols, swords, cutlasses, pikes, powder, shot, shells; cartridges, gun-carriages, battle & magazine lanterns & lamps &c &c, embracing all & every thing connected with and appertaining to Ordnance & ordnance stores; all labour employed thereon; all contracts relating thereto; all accounts & returns embracing the same.

The province of the "Bureau of Hydrography" was defined as

> All maps, charts, chronometers, spyglasses, Barometers, telescopes, quadrants, sextants & other mathematical and philosophical instruments as are used in the Navy, the building used as a Depot of charts; all persons on duty or employed therein; all books and papers relating to the subjects with which this Bureau is charged; all accounts and returns, & all contracts relating to the above objects & such others as the Bureau shall hereafter be charged with; & generally whatever relates to the subject of Hydrography.

The distinction made between the "Bureau of Ordnance" and the "Bureau of Hydrography" was purely for administrative convenience; they had no legal existence as separate entities. The act of 1862 transferred the hydrographic functions of the Bureau of Ordnance and Hydrography to the Bureau of Navigation and changed the name of the former Bureau to the Bureau of Ordnance.

Hydrographic functions had first been separately exercised by the Dépôt of Charts and Instruments, established in 1830 and placed under the control of the Board of Navy Commissioners (Entry 228). It was this agency, under a new name, that virtually constituted the "Bureau of Hydrography" mentioned in 1842. In 1854 its name was changed to the United States Naval Observatory and Hydrographical Office, which was transferred to the Bureau of Navigation in 1862 and was divided in 1866 into the Hydrographic Office and the Naval Observatory, both of which were transferred to the Bureau of Equipment by a general order of June 25, 1889. The Hydrographic Office was restored to the Bureau of Navigation by a general order of December 24, 1892, and the Naval Observatory in 1910. By an executive order of April 8, 1942, both were attached to the Office of the Chief of Naval Operations.

The only records created by the Bureau of Ordnance that are in the Naval Records Collection are nine volumes, each bearing the following note:

"Property of the Bureau of Ordnance, to be returned when no longer needed by the Navy Department Library. Not to be transferred to the National Archives." These volumes are not described below.

Other records created by the Bureau of Ordnance and Hydrography, the Bureau of Ordnance, and the Hydrographic Office are in Record Group 74, Records of the Bureau of Ordnance, and Record Group 37, Records of the Hydrographic Office.

LETTERS RECEIVED RELATING TO HYDROGRAPHY. Aug. 1842 - July 1862. 16 adhesive binders. 1 ft. 10 in. Arranged by classes of correspondents, thereunder chronologically. Indexed.

271

From (1) the Secretary of the Navy, vols. 1 (Sept. 1842 - Dec. 1845), 3 (June 1852 - Sept. 1853), and 5 (June 1856 - July 1862); (2) commandants, vols. 1-2 (Aug. 1842 - Sept. 1843), 4 (Aug. 1844 - Dec. 1846), and 13-14 (Apr. 1857 - Jan. 1859); (3) the Naval Observatory, vols. 3 (Jan. 1846 - Oct. 1848) and 9 (June 1856 - June 1858); (4) the Hydrographic Office, vol. 1 (Sept. 1842 - Jan. 1844); (5) the Naval Academy, vol. 2 (Nov. 1860 - May 1862); and (6) other correspondents ("Miscellaneous"), vols. 1-2 (Sept. 1842 - Feb. 1853) and 4-5 (Jan. 1856 - Apr. 1862). The series must originally have consisted of at least 40 binders or volumes, but only these are known to survive. The records relate chiefly to the collection and distribution of nautical information, maps and charts, books, and instruments. They are distinguished not only in subject but in binding and dimensions from the other series of letters received by the Chief of the Bureau of Ordnance and Hydrography during these years—a fact indicating an intention to file hydrographic records separately from ordnance records.

JOURNALS OF THE NORTH PACIFIC EXPLORING EXPEDITION UNDER THE COMMAND OF COMDRS. CADWALADER RINGGOLD AND JOHN RODGERS. Mar. 1853 - July 1856. 12 vols. 11 in.

272

Journals bearing file numbers beginning with "C 451.36," belonging to the "Survey File" of the Hydrographic Office but, in view of their date, most conveniently listed as records of the Bureau of Ordnance and Hydrography. They comprise the following: (1) Journal of Act'g Lt. Henry K. Stevens, commanding the Fenimore Cooper, later the John Hancock, Mar. 21, 1853 - July 10, 1855 (3 vols.). (2) Journal of Lt. Henry Rolando, commanding the Porpoise, May 31 - Sept. 7, 1853, and Mar. 25 - Aug. 16, 1854. (3) Journal of Ass't Draftsman William R. Baker on the Vincennes, June 11 - Sept. 12, 1853. (4) Journal of Act'g Master Edwin Osgood Carnes on the Porpoise and the John Hancock, June 11, 1853 - Apr. 11, 1855, with many gaps. (5) Journal of Surgeon William Grier on the Vincennes, June 11, 1853 - July 11, 1856. (6) Journal of Act'g Lt. Jonathan H. Carter on the John P. Kennedy, June 11, 1853 - July 23, 1854. (7) Journal of Act'g Lt. and Ass't Astronomer John M. Brook on the Vincennes, June 13, 1853 - Jan. 15, 1854. (8) Journal of Lewis M. Squires, translator and ass't naturalist, on the John Hancock, June 27, 1854 - May 29, 1855. (9) Journal of F. H. Bierbower, Captain's Clerk on the Vincennes, Apr. 6 - May 14, 1855. (10) Tagebuch of Arthur Witzleben, Second Hydrographer, on the Vincennes, Feb. 2 - July 14, 1856. For related records see Entries 392 (84), 392 (85), and 395 (97). Other related records are among the records of the Hydrographic Office and the Bureau of Navigation.

ABSTRACT OF BILLS APPROVED UNDER APPROPRIATIONS FOR THE NAVAL OBSERVA-
TORY, THE NAUTICAL ALMANAC OFFICE, AND THE HYDROGRAPHIC OFFICE.
Aug. 1852 - Nov. 1862. 1 vol. 1¼ in. Arranged by appropriation,
thereunder chronologically.   273
    Identified by label on binding as originally a record of the Bureau
of Ordnance and Hydrography.

STATEMENTS AND TESTIMONIALS FROM THOMAS F. WILLS, OF BOSTON, RELATING
TO THE WILLS & GOWEN SUBMARINE ARMOR. Ca. 1862. 1 vol. ½ in.   274
    Detailed description of "the Wills & Gowen Submarine Armor," with
copies of correspondence, Mar. 29, 1851 - Sept. 4, 1862, and a clipping
of Nov. 15, 1861.

C. Bureau of Construction,
Equipment, and Repairs, 1825-1858

    The Bureau of Construction, Equipment, and Repairs was created by the
act of 1842. Its functions were first defined by a regulation of November
26, 1842, which treated it for administrative purposes as two bureaus combined under a single chief. "The Bureau of Construction & Repairs" was
given cognizance over "the building & repairing of all vessels of war &
boats; all materials used therein; all labour employed thereon; all contracts & all accounts & returns relating thereto." "The Bureau of Equipments" received cognizance over

        All sails; anchors; cables; cordage, and rigging of all kinds;
        fuel, water-tanks & casks; cambouses & other implements for
        cooking; all necessary furniture for messes & for officers;
        stoves used for warming the ship; all lights, except battle
        & magazine lamps & lanterns; signals, & generally, all that
        is usually understood by the general term "equipment"; all
        labour relating thereto; all contracts, accounts, and returns
        touching the same.

A regulation of April 14, 1845, placed vessels in navy yards, whether in
ordinary (that is, not in commission) or under repair, under the cognizance
of the Bureau of Construction, Equipment, and Repairs. By the act of 1862
the Bureau was divided into a Bureau of Construction and Repair, a Bureau
of Steam Engineering, and (with certain functions transferred from the
Office of the Secretary of the Navy) a Bureau of Equipment and Recruiting.
Scanty records originally maintained by the Bureau of Construction, Equipment, and Repairs are in Record Group 19, Records of the Bureau of Ships.

ORDERS FOR AND ACKNOWLEDGMENTS OF RECEIPT OF SIGNAL BOOKS AND
TELEGRAPHIC DICTIONARIES. July 1824 - Oct. 1848. 1 vol. ("1").
2 in. Arranged chronologically. Table of contents.   275
    To the Board of Navy Commissioners, later the "Bureau of Equipments."

STATISTICS OF THE COST OF BUILDING VARIOUS NAVAL VESSELS. 1825-53.
2 vols. 3 in. Arranged by vessels.   276
    Figures for the cost of separate items of parts and equipment of each
vessel, and recapitulations. The first volume, "Cost of Vessels of the

U. S. Navy," contains statistics for the Fulton, the Saranac, the Fairfield, the John P. Kennedy, the Franklin, the Falmouth, the Susquehanna, the Grampus, and the Phoenix, 1825-53. The second, "Nautical & Mathematical Instruments &c, N° 1," contains statistics for the Somers, the Bainbridge, the Truxtun, the Congress, and the Savannah, 1841-42. The statistics before 1842 were prepared by the Board of Navy Commissioners.

REPORTS ON THE SAILING QUALITIES OF NAVAL VESSELS ("Qualities of
    Vessels"). Dec. 1826 - Feb. 1848. 1 vol. 1½ in. Handwritten
    copies. Arranged chronologically. Indexed.   277
    Copies of reports submitted to the Secretary of the Navy and other
officials, chiefly by commanding officers of ships. What seem to be
later volumes of the same series, Oct. 1874 - Aug. 1886, are among the
records of the Bureau of Construction and Repair. The copies in this
volume are presumed to have been made by the Bureau of Construction,
Equipment, and Repairs.

REPORTS OF THE ENGINEER IN CHIEF ("Reports, A, Engineer Corps").
    Oct. 1844 - Nov. 1850, Oct. 1853 - Apr. 1856. 1 vol. 2 in.
    Arranged chronologically. Indexed.   278
    From Charles H. Haswell to the Chief of the Bureau of Construction,
Equipment, and Repairs, Oct. 1844 - Nov. 1850; and from Daniel B.
Martin to the Secretary of the Navy, Oct. 1853 - Apr. 1856. See Entry
188 for letters of similar character. The volume was received by the
Office of Naval Records and Library from the Bureau of Construction
and Repair.

REPORTS OF CHIEF ENGINEERS OF NAVAL VESSELS. Nov. 1844 - July 1849.
    1 vol. 3/4 in. Handwritten copies. No arrangement perceptible.   279
    Reports to the Secretary of the Navy, to commandants of navy yards,
and to commanding officers of naval vessels, relating to experiments
and trials applying to the machinery of vessels.

LETTERS TO NAVY AGENTS. Dec. 1850 - Dec. 1858. 1 vol. ("2"). 3 in.
    Handwritten copies. Arranged chronologically. Indexed.   280

D. Bureau of Construction and Repair, 1865-1876

The Bureau of Construction and Repair was one of the three bureaus
formed by the act of 1862 from the Bureau of Construction, Equipment, and
Repairs. Its functions are indicated by its title. Its agents were naval
constructors, who formed a corps of staff officers. By an act of June 20,
1940, this Bureau and the Bureau of Engineering were abolished, and their
functions, records, property, and personnel were consolidated to form the
Bureau of Ships. Other records created by the Bureau of Construction and
Repair are in Record Group 19, Records of the Bureau of Ships.

REGISTER OF CONTRACTS ("State of Contracts, L"). Aug. 1865 - June 1876.
    1 vol. 2 in. Arrangement not obvious. Indexed.   281

E. Bureau of Steam Engineering, 1861-1886

The Bureau of Steam Engineering was one of the three bureaus formed by the act of 1862 from the Bureau of Construction, Equipment, and Repairs. It was charged with designing, constructing, maintaining, and repairing steam machinery. Its agents were steam engineers, who from 1842 to 1899 formed a corps of staff officers; and the act of 1862 required that the chief of the Bureau should be "a skilful engineer, and be selected from the list of chief engineers of the navy." In consequence of the increasing use of oil-burning machinery, the name of the Bureau was changed by an act of June 4, 1920, to the Bureau of Engineering. By an act of June 20, 1940, this Bureau and the Bureau of Construction and Repair were abolished, and their functions, records, property, and personnel were consolidated to form the Bureau of Ships. Records created by the Bureau of Engineering are in Record Group 19, Records of the Bureau of Ships.

REGISTER OF ACTING ASSISTANT ENGINEERS ("Engineer Corps, U. S. N., Acting Appointments, Bureau of Steam Engineering"). May 1861 - July 1865. 1 vol. 2 in. Arranged by first letter of names, thereunder by rank (first, second, and third ass't engineer), thereunder chronologically.   282
    Gives engineer's name, date of appointment, date of acceptance, State of residence, present duty or station, and remarks.

REPORT OF INSPECTION OF THE MACHINERY OF THE USS TRENTON. Sept. 17, 1886. 1 vol. 1½ in.   283
    Made at the Norfolk Navy Yard by Benjamin B. H. Wharton, Chief Engineer, and submitted to the Chief of the Bureau of Steam Engineering.

F. Bureau of Navigation, 1813-1911

An act of 1862 divided the Bureau of Ordnance and Hydrography into the Bureau of Ordnance and the Bureau of Navigation. During the next twenty-seven years the functions of the Bureau of Navigation were largely confined to the supervision of the Hydrographic Office and the Naval Observatory. The Bureau of Navigation was the scientific bureau of the Navy Department. According to a general order of March 30, 1882, it was the duty of the Bureau to

> furnish navigation supplies and stores of all kinds, including charts, nautical and navigating instruments and books, sailing directions and instructions, stationery and blank books for commanding and navigating officers ashore and afloat, libraries, binnacles, flags, signal lights, running lights, and standing lights on board vessels, including electrical apparatus for lighting purposes, logs, leads, lines, and glasses, log books, illuminating oil . . .
>   It shall be charged with the collection of foreign surveys, publication of charts, sailing directions and nautical works, and the dissemination of nautical and hydrographical information to the Navy and mercantile marine.

A general order of June 25, 1889, transferred the Hydrographic Office and the Naval Observatory to the Bureau of Equipment. The Hydrographic Office was restored to the Bureau of Navigation by a general order of December 24, 1892, and the Naval Observatory by a change in Navy regulations dated June 27, 1910. By Executive order of April 8, 1942, both were attached to the Office of the Chief of Naval Operations. The Office of Naval Intelligence, created in the Bureau of Navigation by a general order of March 23, 1882, was transferred to the Office of the Secretary of the Navy by an order of October 19, 1889.

The functions removed from the Bureau by these transfers were replaced by functions relating to naval personnel. The order of June 25, 1889, gave to the Bureau of Navigation all responsibility for recruiting and supervising enlisted men, formerly under the cognizance of the Bureau of Equipment and Recruiting. The latter Bureau had received these functions (from the Office of the Secretary of the Navy) at the time of its creation by the act of 1862.

The order of June 25, 1889, also transferred to the Bureau of Navigation the Office of Detail, which then became the Division of Officers and Fleet in the Bureau of Navigation. This Office had been established in the Office of the Secretary of the Navy in or before 1861 to handle the detailing of officers, and on April 28, 1865, had been placed under the charge of the Chief of the Bureau of Navigation, who thereafter served in the dual capacity of "Chief of the Bureau of Navigation" and "Chief of the Bureau of Navigation and Office of Detail," maintaining separate records for the two organizations. The "Bureau of Navigation and Office of Detail" was concerned with the detail of officers and also, after 1885, with the movements of vessels; the "Bureau of Navigation" was concerned exclusively with matters of navigation. The ambiguity in both the title and the functions of the Office of Detail was terminated by the order of 1889, by which most matters of officer personnel passed to the Bureau of Navigation.

The delayed result of these changes was that on May 3, 1942, the Bureau of Navigation was renamed the Bureau of Naval Personnel. The only relic of its original functions was its custody of logs. Records of the Bureau of Navigation are in Record Group 24, Records of the Bureau of Naval Personnel.

LETTERS SENT CONVEYING APPOINTMENTS AND ORDERS AND ACCEPTING RESIGNA-
      TIONS ("Appointments, Orders, and Resignations"). May 1813 -
      Feb. 1842. 8 vols. (labeled 11-18). 1 ft. 6 in. Handwritten
      copies. Arranged chronologically. Indexed.   284
This is part of a series, of which the preceding volumes (presumably beginning with 1798) have been retained by the Navy Department and the succeeding volumes are in the National Archives in Record Group 24, Records of the Bureau of Naval Personnel. The letters before 1889 were maintained by the Office of the Secretary of the Navy.

RESOLUTIONS OF CONFIRMATION OF OFFICERS RECEIVED FROM THE SENATE ("Con-
      firmations"). Oct. 1814 - Dec. 1842. 1 vol. $3\frac{1}{2}$ in. Arranged
      chronologically. Indexed.   285

Succeeding volumes, Jan. 1843 - Aug. 1909, are in the National Archives in Record Group 24, among the Records of the Bureau of Naval Personnel. The volumes before 1889 were maintained by the Office of the Secretary of the Navy.

REGISTER OF ENGINEER OFFICERS ("Record, N°. 1, 1843-1899, Engineer Corps"). 1843-99. 1 vol. $2\frac{1}{2}$ in. Method of arrangement not obvious. Indexed.   286
Gives name of officer, place and date of birth and of death, and record of all service and appointments. Covers the whole existence of the Engineer Corps, abolished by an act of Mar. 3, 1899.

LIST OF VESSELS SERVING IN THE UNITED STATES NAVY DURING THE CIVIL WAR. Ca. 1847 - May 1884. 1 vol. $2\frac{1}{2}$ in. Arranged chronologically. Indexed.   287
Gives name of vessel, armament, description, rate, dimensions, how acquired, when launched, when commissioned, and how disposed of. Some of the vessels were acquired as early as 1847 or disposed of as late as 1884, but apparently all served in the Civil War.

REGISTER OF ARRIVAL AND DEPARTURE OF UNITED STATES VESSELS. May 1866 - Jan. 1868, Jan. 1871 - May 1874. 2 vols. 1 in. Arranged chronologically.   288
Rough working papers, barely legible. An intervening volume is presumed to have existed.

REGISTER OF VESSELS OF THE UNITED STATES NAVY ("Ship Book"). Apr. 1876 - June 1880. 1 vol. $2\frac{1}{2}$ in. Arranged by first letter of ships' names. Indexed.   289
Gives name of vessel, rate, dates and places of arrivals and departures, and date of decommissioning.

CRUISING REPORTS OF VESSELS OF THE UNITED STATES NAVY. Jan. 1895 - June 1910. 14 vols. 2 ft. 4 in. Arranged chronologically by volumes, thereunder by ships' names. Indexed.   290
Description of each vessel; chronological list of ports visited by it, with dates of arrival at and departure from each; distance sailed; average speed; amount of coal consumed; instructions received; and remarks. These reports were submitted quarterly by each ship to the Bureau of Navigation, eventually on BuNav Form 81.

DATA RELATING TO PILOTS WHO SERVED DURING THE CIVIL WAR. Compiled ca. 1897. 3 vols. $2\frac{1}{2}$ in.   291
These records resulted from the failure of Congress to include pilots in the act of June 27, 1890, granting service pensions to naval personnel of the Civil War. The records consist of (1) typed copies of correspondence of the Secretary of the Navy and of commanding officers with and relating to pilots of the Mississippi Squadron, Oct. 6, 1864 - Mar. 3, 1897; (2) "Pilots in the Squadron," an alphabetical list of pilots in the Mississippi Squadron, with original correspondence and orders of officers of various squadrons relating to pilots, Oct. 1862 - Apr. 1865; and (3) "Pilot Book," a register of pilots in all squadrons, giving name of pilot and date of beginning service on each naval vessel, May 1861 - June 1865. The 2 registers form appendixes to the volume of copied correspondence.

DAILY REPORTS OF ARRIVALS AND DEPARTURES OF VESSELS OF THE UNITED STATES
NAVY. Sept. 1897 - Dec. 1910. 25 vols. 2 ft. 5 in. Arranged
chronologically.   292
Printed sheet entitled "Movements of Vessels," issued daily by the
Chief of the Bureau of Navigation through Dec. 3, 1909, and thereafter
by the Aide for Operations, giving date and port of each arrival or
departure and port sailed for, as reported to the Bureau of Navigation.

REGISTER OF MOVEMENTS OF VESSELS OF THE UNITED STATES NAVY (labeled
"Movements of Vessels" on backstrip, "Ship Movement Book" on
front cover). Jan. 1900 - June 1911. 11 vols. 1 ft. 4 in.
Arranged chronologically by volumes, thereunder alphabetically by
ships, thereunder chronologically. Indexed.   293
Gives name of ship, rate, and dates of arrival at and departure from
ports throughout each year, and thus summarizes a part of the information
in the series described in Entries 290 and 292.

G. Office of the Judge Advocate General, 1799-1883

Before 1865 the legal business of the Navy Department was handled in
the Office of the Secretary of the Navy. An act of March 2, 1865,
authorized the President to appoint an officer in the Navy Department to
be called the Solicitor and Naval Judge-Advocate General. This official
was transferred, with the title of the Naval Solicitor, to the Department
of Justice by the act creating that Department, June 22, 1870. The Office
of the Naval Solicitor was abolished by an act of June 19, 1878. In the
meantime a Naval Solicitor and Judge Advocate General of the Navy Department had been designated by a circular of the Secretary of the Navy dated
March 14, 1877. The title of this official was changed to Acting Judge
Advocate by a circular of July 2, 1878. An act of June 8, 1880, authorized
the President to appoint in the Navy Department a Judge Advocate General of
the Navy with the rank of a captain in the Navy or a colonel in the Marine
Crops. Since that date the continuity of the office has been unbroken.

The duties of the Judge Advocate General were defined with great full-
ness in a general order of June 25, 1889. His primary function was

> to revise, report upon, and have recorded the proceedings of
> all courts-martial, courts of inquiry, and boards for the ex-
> amination of officers for retirement and promotion in the
> naval service; to prepare the charges and specifications and
> the necessary orders convening general courts-martial in cases
> where such courts are ordered by the Secretary of the Navy;
> to prepare general orders promulgating the final action of
> the reviewing authority in general court-martial cases; to
> prepare the necessary orders convening courts of inquiry,
> boards for the examination of officers for promotion and re-
> tirement, and for the examination of candidates for appoint-
> ment in the medical corps, and to conduct all official corre-
> spondence relating to courts-martial, courts of inquiry, and
> such boards.

The Judge Advocate General was also charged with responsibility for all proceedings and correspondence relative to claims and suits of every description, contracts requiring the Department's action, naval prisons and prisoners, and all other questions of law, regulations, and discipline. From July 1, 1908, to September 1, 1921, the civil as distinguished from the military functions here listed were handled by the Office of the Solicitor of the Navy, which was independent of the Office of the Judge Advocate General; but in 1921 the two Offices were merged, and all legal functions were again under the cognizance of the Office of the Judge Advocate General. This Office has always been a part of the Office of the Secretary of the Navy.

Other records of the Office of the Judge Advocate General are in Record Group 125, Records of the Office of the Judge Advocate General (Navy).

RECORDS OF PROCEEDINGS OF GENERAL COURTS MARTIAL AND COURTS OF INQUIRY ("Court-Martial Records"). June 1799 - Nov. 1867. 167 vols. 54 ft. Arranged by case number in approximately chronological order.

294

Vols. 1-152, 158-165, 172-173, 178, and 189, containing dossiers for cases numbered from 1 through 4632, with gaps for the missing volumes, which, with successor volumes, are in Record Group 125. The volumes in the Naval Records Collection and in Record Group 125 form an unbroken series of dossiers for cases from 1799 to 1935. The records previous to 1880 were maintained by the Office of the Secretary of the Navy. Each court-martial record, when complete, contains the original precept appointing the board, copies of the charges and specifications of charges, minutes of the board including a verbatim transcript of testimony, the plea of the defendant, copies of correspondence introduced and copied as part of the testimony, the finding of the court, the sentence in case of a finding of guilt, the endorsement of the Secretary of the Navy and sometimes of the President, and exhibits (often designated by numbers or letters) at the end. The proceedings are transcribed on legal-size sheets, bound at the top. The exhibits, in the backs of the same volumes, may be almost inaccessible when written on both sides or when they are pamphlets, and are not always assembled in a definite order.

INDEX TO RECORDS OF GENERAL COURTS MARTIAL AND COURTS OF INQUIRY. June 1799 - Dec. 1860. 1 vol. 2 in. Arranged by first letter of name of defendant or of subject of investigation, thereunder chronologically.

295

Gives name, case number, rank, date of trial, substance of charges, finding of court, and action taken by the Navy Department and the President. See Entry 469 for a continuation of this series.

REGISTER OF JUDGMENTS AND SENTENCES OF COURTS MARTIAL AND COURTS OF INQUIRY. Aug. 1800 - Jan. 1822. 1 vol. 2 in. Arranged chronologically.

296

First page lost.

MISCELLANEOUS CASE FILES ("Claims"). July 1863 - Apr. 1883. 41 vols.
   13 ft. 8 in. Indexed.

   Materials similar to those forming the series described in Entry 142,
and probably assembled as a continuation of that series. The volumes
are labeled with the letters of the alphabet, no order being perceptible
within a volume beyond the fact that the names of the defendants or subjects of investigation in the cases documented in the volume begin with
the same letter. The method of binding at the tops of sheets entails the
same inconveniences as those described in Entry 294. The papers relating
to disciplinary matters are indistinguishable in character from those
bound in court-martial records of the same period, and a precise designation of the series seems impossible. Its backstrip title, "Claims," is
a misnomer. The papers were evidently assembled and bound in or after
1883 as a means of consolidating a mass of loose papers that had accumulated during many years. Most of the papers are of date subsequent to
1874. In Record Group 125 is a volume labeled "General Index to Files,"
which lists the contents of each volume of this series in the order of
binding and also, for all letters after C, lists further materials of the
same character with the penciled notation "Not bound yet." At the time
these materials were stored in boxes, cases, and packages, mentioned occasionally in the margin of the "General Index"; their present where-
abouts is unknown.

REPORT OF THE NAVAL EXAMINING BOARD CONVENED TO CONSIDER THE CASES OF
   TWENTY-THREE OFFICERS PASSED OVER IN PROMOTIONS ("Record of Find-
   ings of the Le Roy Board"). May 26, 1879. 1 vol. 3½ in.

   The Board, with R. A. William E. Le Roy as President, was appointed
in compliance with a joint resolution of Congress of Feb. 5, 1879, to
consider complaints of certain officers who deemed themselves unjustly
passed over in promotions made under an act of July 25, 1866. On this
act see Entry 166. The report is a record of proceedings, May 1-26,
1879, with a letter of transmittal dated May 26.

RECORD OF PROCEEDINGS OF THE BOARD OF EXAMINING PROFESSORS IN MATHEMATICS
   ("Examinations of Candidates for Appointment as Professors of
   Mathematics"). Feb.-May 1881. 1 vol. 3½ in.

   Minutes, correspondence, and examination papers. The Board, appointed
in compliance with an act of Congress of Jan. 20, 1881, had been convened
at the Naval Observatory, with Prof. Simon Newcomb as President. The record is stamped as received by the Office of the Judge Advocate General.

H. Office of Naval Intelligence, 1888-1914

   An "Office of Intelligence" was established in the Bureau of Navigation
by a general order of March 23, 1882, "for the purpose of collecting and
recording such naval information as may be useful to the Department in time
of war, as well as in peace." The Office of Naval Intelligence was transferred to the Office of the Assistant Secretary of the Navy in 1890, restored to the Bureau of Navigation by an order of April 26, 1898, and placed
under the Chief of Naval Operations in 1915. Records of the Office of Naval
Intelligence are in Record Group 38, Records of the Office of the Chief of
Naval Operations.

CORRESPONDENCE OF LT. NATHAN SARGENT, NAVAL ATTACHÉ OF THE UNITED STATES
    AT ROME, VIENNA, AND BERLIN. Nov. 1888 – Oct. 1893. 13 vols. and
    9 adhesive binders. 4 ft. Arranged chronologically. Some volumes
    indexed.   300
    (1) Letters received, Nov. 1888 – Oct. 1893 (9 binders); (2) letters
sent, press copies, Jan. 1889 – Aug. 1893 (12 vols.); and (3) register of
letters sent, Jan. 1889 – Apr. 1893 (1 vol.).

LETTERS SENT BY NAVAL ATTACHÉS OF THE UNITED STATES IN LONDON. Apr.–Dec.
    1889, Jan. 1893 – Sept. 1914. 37 vols. 4 ft. 1 in. Press copies.
    Arranged chronologically. Indexed.   301
    From Lt. Benjamin H. Buckingham, Lt. Comdr. William S. Cowles, Lt.
John C. Colwell, Lt. John H. Gibbons, Comdr. Richardson Clover, Capt.
Charles H. Stockton, and Capt. Edward Simpson. These volumes were
evidently records of the Office of the Naval Attaché in London.

LETTERS SENT BY LT. ALBERT P. NIBLACK, NAVAL ATTACHÉ OF THE UNITED STATES
    IN BERLIN. Sept. 1896 – May 1898. 2 vols. 3 in. Press copies.
    Arranged chronologically.   302

LETTERS FROM LT. JOHN C. COLWELL, NAVAL ATTACHÉ OF THE UNITED STATES IN
    LONDON. Apr. 1897 – June 1898. 1 vol. 4 in. Arranged chronolog-
    ically.   303
    Other volumes of this series are in the National Archives in Record
Group 38, Records of the Office of the Chief of Naval Operations.

PANAMA CORRESPONDENCE. Oct. 1903 – Apr. 1904. 2 vols. 3 in. Press
    copies. Arranged chronologically.   304
    Letters sent by the commanders in chief of the Pacific and South
Atlantic Squadrons. This series and the 6 that follow, each here designated by its backstrip title, are uniform in format and have in common
the characteristic of being series assembled or copied (presumably by the
Office of Naval Intelligence) from parts of various series according to
subject and without regard to form or origin.

SANTO DOMINGO CORRESPONDENCE. Mar. 1904 – Jan. 1907. 10 vols. 1 ft.
    1 in.   305
    Press copies of letters sent by the Secretary of the Navy, the com-
mander in chief of the Caribbean Squadron, and others, Mar. 1904 –
Jan. 1907 (4 vols.); and carbon copies of letters received and letters
sent by the commander in chief, Jan. 1905 – Dec. 1906 (6 vols.).

CORRESPONDENCE RELATING TO THE CUBAN INSURRECTION. Sept.–Oct. 1906.
    3 vols. 4 in. Carbon copies. Arranged chronologically.   306
    Copies of letters received and letters sent by the President, the
Secretary of the Navy, and others. The sources of the copies are not
indicated.

CORRESPONDENCE TO AND FROM THE DEPARTMENT RELATING TO THE KINGSTON
    DISASTER. Jan.–Feb. 1907. 1 vol. 1¼ in. Carbon copies.
    Arranged chronologically.   307
    Correspondence of R. A. C. H. Davis, commanding a squadron detached
to Kingston; of other officers of the Atlantic Fleet; and of the Secretary of the Navy. Kingston had suffered an earthquake on Jan. 14, 1907.

CORRESPONDENCE RELATING TO THE HUDSON-FULTON CELEBRATION IN NEW YORK.
Sept.-Oct. 1909. 2 vols. (duplicates). 6 in. Carbon copies.
Arranged chronologically. Indexed.   308
   Printed calendar of events; copies of orders of R. A. Seaton Schroeder,
commanding the Atlantic Fleet (flagship Connecticut); copies of newspaper
notices; and correspondence of the Hudson-Fulton Celebration Commission
and its Naval Parade Committee.

NICARAGUA CORRESPONDENCE. Oct. 1909 - Sept. 1910. 3 vols. (duplicates).
9 in. Carbon copies. Arranged chronologically.   309
   Correspondence of the Secretary of the Navy; of R. A. William W.
Kimball, commanding the Nicaraguan Expeditionary Squadron (organized
Dec. 1, 1909, and disbanded Apr. 7, 1910); and of other naval officers
at Corinto and Bluefields, where a revolution had occurred.

HONDUREAN CORRESPONDENCE. Oct. 1910 - June 1911. 2 vols. (duplicates).
1½ in. Carbon copies. Arranged chronologically.   310
   Copies of telegrams and letters of the Secretary of the Navy, the
Aide for Operations, and officers commanding U. S. vessels at Amapala
and Puerto Cortez, where an insurrection was in progress.

I. Bureau of Equipment, 1888-1908

   The Bureau of Equipment and Recruiting, created by the act of 1862,
became the Bureau of Equipment when its functions relative to enlisted men
were transferred to the Bureau of Navigation by a general order of June 25,
1889. In June 1910 it became inactive and its functions were distributed
among other bureaus, the functions relative to electrical apparatus (including wireless) being transferred to the Bureau of Steam Engineering. The
Bureau of Equipment was abolished by an act of June 30, 1914. Other records
of the Bureau are in Record Group 19, Records of the Bureau of Ships.

LETTERS SENT BY LT. ALBERT W. GRANT, RESIDENT INSPECTOR AT THE UNION
IRON WORKS, SAN FRANCISCO. Dec. 1888 - Sept. 1890. 1 vol.
1½ in. Press copies. Arranged chronologically. Indexed.   311
   Mainly to the Chief of the Bureau of Equipment and to the Naval Inspector of Electric Lighting.

DESCRIPTION OF THE INSTALLATION OF A WIRELESS TELEGRAPH AT THE PUGET
SOUND NAVY YARD, WITH PHOTOGRAPHS AND BLUEPRINTS. June 1907.
1 vol. 3/4 in.   312
   Received by the Bureau of Equipment June 11, 1907, as an enclosure of
letter 155312.

DESCRIPTION OF THE INSTALLATION OF A WIRELESS TELEGRAPH AT THE SAN JUAN
NAVAL STATION, WITH PHOTOGRAPHS AND BLUEPRINTS. Ca. 1907. 1 vol.
3/4 in.   313
   Probably received by the Bureau of Equipment as an enclosure.

REPORTS ON EXPERIMENTAL CRUISES OF THE SECOND DIVISION OF THE PACIFIC
FLEET, TOWING TORPEDO-BOAT DESTROYERS, AND CORRESPONDENCE RELATIVE
TO TOWING APPLIANCES. July-Nov. 1908. 1 vol. 1 in. Carbon
copies. Arranged chronologically.   314

Copy of enclosure 1 of letter 193633, received by the Bureau of
Equipment in Mar. 1909. Cruises from San Francisco to San Diego and
back, July 1-9, 1908, and from San Francisco to Samoa and back, Aug.-
Nov. 1908.

IV. NAVAL SHORE ESTABLISHMENTS, 1814-1911

The records described below were created and maintained by navy yards,
shore stations, and the Naval Academy, and are part of the field records
of the Navy Department.

Most are records of commandants' offices, but a few are records of
departments in navy yards. Such departments were under the cognizance of
the several bureaus of the Navy Department but under the direction of the
commandants. A regulation of November 26, 1842, which first defined the
duties of the several bureaus, directed that "All communications from the
chiefs of Bureaux to persons in ships, navy yards or navy stations, must
be made through their Commanding Officers." Similar directives were issued
frequently at later times. The status of the departments was designated
with the utmost explicitness in a general order of March 11, 1869:

> All signs that have been put up in Navy Yards, indicating
> the bureaus to which different departments belong, will be
> taken down.
> Simple signs—such as "Navigation Office" or store, "Ord-
> nance Office" or store, "Steam Office" or stores, "Medical
> Office" or stores, "Clothing Office," "Office of Docks and
> Yards," &c., &c.—will be put up in their places.
> These offices are not branches of the bureaus, but are
> departments of the yards, and are under the entire direction
> of the Commandants.

A general order of May 7, 1903, grouped all shore establishments of
the Navy in the United States into 11 naval districts, each under a commandant. As all the series here listed, with one exception, are of date
previous to 1903, they have been classified not according to naval districts but alphabetically by the names of the shore establishments from
which they came. Most of the volumes are scattered and isolated items removed from the various series of which they were originally part and added
to the Naval Records Collection because of the age or historical interest
of these particular volumes.

Other records of shore establishments are in Record Group 181, Records
of Naval Districts and Shore Establishments.

Baltimore Naval Station

ORDERS ISSUED BY THE COMMANDANT. Jan. 1863 - Mar. 1864. 1 vol. 2 in.
    Press copies. Arranged chronologically. Indexed.   315
    The Commandant was Commo. Thomas A. Dornin.

Boston Navy Yard

REGISTER OF GENERAL COURTS MARTIAL HELD AT THE YARD. June 1814 –
Sept. 1833. 1 vol. 3/4 in. Arranged chronologically.   316
Indicates where court was held, when, names of persons tried, rank,
nature of charges, how proved, and sentences, with remarks.

DRAWINGS OF UNITED STATES VESSELS, GUNS, AND OTHER PROPERTY AT THE YARD.
1817-31. 1 vol. 1¼ in. Mode of arrangement not apparent. .   317
Made by Charles Ware, Sailmaker.

LETTERS SENT BY THE COMMANDANT. May 1859 – Aug. 1867. 36 vols. 3 ft.
7 in. Press copies. Arranged chronologically.   318
(1) Letters sent to the Secretary of the Navy, May 1859 – Aug. 1867
(15 vols.); and (2) letters and orders to officers, Sept. 1859 – Aug. 1866,
with a gap for Feb.–Mar. 1863 (21 vols.).

LETTERS FROM THE SECRETARY OF THE NAVY. Oct. 1862 – May 1863,
Nov. 1863 – Dec. 1864. 3 adhesive binders. 8 in. Arranged
chronologically.   319
One binder, May–Nov. 1863, is lacking.

Gosport (Norfolk) Navy Yard

ANNUAL SURVEY OF ARTICLES ON HAND IN THE DEPARTMENTS OF THE YARD.
Oct. 1, 1840. 1 vol. 1 in. Arranged by departments.   320

Havana Naval Station

OFFICE TIME BOOK. Jan. 1899 – Oct. 1902. 1 vol. 3 in. Arranged
chronologically.   321

LETTERS SENT BY THE COMMANDANT. Mar. 1899 – Mar. 1903. 7 vols. 7 in.
Press copies. Arranged chronologically.   322
(1) Letters to the Secretary of the Navy and to chiefs of bureaus,
Mar. 1899 – Mar. 1903 (2 vols.); (2) orders issued, Mar. 1899 – Mar. 1903
(1 vol.); (3) telegrams sent, Mar. 1899 – Mar. 1903 (1 vol.); (4) miscellaneous letters sent, Mar. 1899 – Mar. 1903 (2 vols.); and (5) vouchers,
Sept. 1899 – Mar. 1903 (1 vol.).

Mare Island Navy Yard

LOG. Sept. 1854 – Mar. 1856. 1 vol. 1½ in. Arranged chronologically. 323

Mound City Naval Station

LETTERS RECEIVED BY THE COMMANDANT. July–Sept. 1864, Dec. 1864 –
Aug. 1865, Apr. 1867 – May 1868. 3 adhesive binders. 4½ in.
Arranged chronologically.   324

LETTERS SENT BY THE COMMANDANT. July 1864 - Nov. 1872, with gaps.
    7 vols. 1 ft. 5 in. Press copies. Arranged chronologically.
    Indexed.   325
    Letters to (1) the Secretary of the Navy, Dec. 1864 - Dec. 1865,
Oct. 1869 - Jan. 1871 (2 vols.); (2) officers, Dec. 1865 - Nov. 1872
(1 vol.); and (3) other persons, July-Oct. 1864, Dec. 1864 - Dec. 1867
(4 vols.).

Naval Academy

LIST OF THE BOOKS IN THE LIBRARY OF THE ACADEMY. Feb. 7-10, 1852.
    1 vol. 1½ in. Arranged chronologically.   326

New Orleans Naval Station

LETTERS SENT BY THE COMMANDANT ("Letter Book No. 1"). Oct. 1863 - Feb.
    1866. 1 vol. 1½ in. Press copies. Arranged chronologically.
    Indexed.   327
    From Act'g Master Adrian C. Starrett, officer in charge of the United
States Naval Ordnance Depot, Headquarters of the West Gulf Blockading
Squadron, till the latter part of 1865; from Lt. Comdr. William Mitchell,
Inspector of Ordnance; and from Comdr. James C. Williamson, Commandant
of the New Orleans Naval Station, Feb. 1866. Much of the volume is
illegible.

New York Navy Yard

LETTERS RECEIVED BY THE COMMANDANT. Jan.-Dec. 1817, Jan. 1819 - Apr.
    1875. 109 adhesive binders. 34 ft. 7 in. Arranged chronologi-
    cally. Indexed.   328
    The volumes are in subseries according to classes of correspondents,
including the Secretary of the Navy, the Board of Navy Commissioners,
officers, and others; but most of the binders have lost their labels,
and the subseries cannot be properly identified without a reading of the
contents of each binder.

LOG. 1834-47, with gaps. 7 vols. 10½ in. Arranged chronologically.   329
    Vols. 1 (Jan.-June 1834), 5 (Jan.-June 1836), 10 (Jan.-June 1838),
13 (July-Dec. 1839), and 17-18 (July 1841 - June 1842), and an unnumbered
volume (July-Dec. 1847).

REPORT FROM A BOARD OF SURVEY (COMDR. JOSHUA R. SANDS, SENIOR MEMBER) ON
    THE USS GRAMPUS. Aug. 6, 1842. 1 vol ½ in.   330

REPORT FROM A BOARD OF SURVEY (WILLIAM L. WERDEN, SENIOR MEMBER) ON THE
    USS CONGRESS. Aug. 1, 1853. 1 vol. ½ in.   331

LETTERS SENT BY THE COMMANDANT. June 1859 - Sept. 1864, Feb.-Aug. 1865.
    9 vols. 1 ft. 10 in. Handwritten copies. Arranged chronologically.
    Indexed.   332

Letters to (1) the Secretary of the Navy, June 1859 – Feb. 1862
(1 vol.); and (2) officers, Nov. 1859 – Sept. 1864, Feb.–Aug. 1865
(8 vols.).

AUTOGRAPH BOOK COMPILED IN THE YARD. Ca. 1861-65. 1 vol. 3/4 in.   333
     No arrangement perceptible.
     Signatures, chiefly of naval personnel, cut from letters and mounted
in a blank book. The same volume contains an unlabeled list of 527
ships.

REGISTER OF ORDERS FILLED BY THE NAVAL STOREKEEPER'S OFFICE. Mar.–Oct.
     1863. 1 vol. 3/4 in. Arranged chronologically.   334

Newport Naval Station

CLASSROOM NOTEBOOKS PREPARED FOR COURSES AT THE TORPEDO STATION, NEWPORT.
     Undated. 6 vols. 6 in.   335
     Notebooks of Master Nathan Sargent and Lt. Albert R. Couden on
electricity; of Sargent on explosives and torpedoes; of Comdr. George C.
Remey on torpedoes and electricity; and of Lt. Charles M. McCarteney on
torpedoes. The courses were probably given in the Naval War College,
established by an order of Oct. 6, 1884, and connected with the Torpedo
Station.

Pensacola Navy Yard

LOG. 1837-75, with gaps. 12 vols. 1 ft. 6 in. Arranged chronologi-
     cally.   336
     Jan.–Dec. 1837, Jan. 1865 – Dec. 1866, July 1867 – Dec. 1871, and
Jan. 1874 – Dec. 1875.

LETTERS SENT BY THE COMMANDANT. Dec. 1862 – Nov. 1863, Mar. 1864 –
     Jan. 1865, June 1865 – Apr. 1869, Oct. 1869 – June 1870, June
     1872 – Feb. 1874. 15 vols. 1 ft. 5 in. Handwritten and press
     copies. Arranged chronologically. Indexed.   337

REGISTER OF ORDERS AND DETACHMENTS OF OFFICERS STATIONED AT THE YARD.
     Dec. 1862 – Sept. 1911. 1 vol. 1 in. Arranged chronologically.   338
     Gives name of officer, rank, date of orders, date of reporting,
station from which reporting, date of orders detaching, date of detachment, and station to which detached.

LETTERS RECEIVED BY THEODORE D. WILSON, ASS'T NAVAL CONSTRUCTOR, FROM
     THE COMMANDANT. June 1866 – Dec. 1867. 1 adhesive binder.
     3½ in. Arranged chronologically. Indexed.   339

Philadelphia Navy Yard

LETTERS SENT BY THE COMMANDANT. May 1817 – Oct. 1822. 1 vol. 1¼ in.
     Handwritten copies. Arranged chronologically.   340

Sent by Commo. Alexander Murray, May 1817 - Sept. 1821, and his successor, Commo. William Bainbridge, Nov. 1821 - Oct. 1822.

REGISTER OF ARTICLES RECEIVED AND EXPENDED BY THE YARD ("Receipt
    Book"). Jan. 1823 - Nov. 1828. 1 vol. 1 in. Arranged chrono-
    logically.   341

ORDERS ISSUED BY THE COMMANDANT. June 1826 - Oct. 1831. 1 vol.
    1¼ in. Handwritten copies. Arranged chronologically.   342
    Issued by Capt. James Renshaw, Capt. William Bainbridge, Comdr.
David Conner, and Capt. James Barron.

LETTERS SENT BY THE COMMANDANT. Sept. 1859 - May 1865. 23 vols. 2 ft.
    11 in. Press copies. Arranged chronologically.   343
    (1) Miscellaneous letters, Sept. 1859 - Jan. 1862 (2 vols.);
(2) letters to the Secretary of the Navy, Sept. 1860 - Sept. 1862
(3 vols.); and (3) orders issued, May 1861 - May 1865 (18 vols.).

LETTERS SENT BY COMDR. ISAAC B. HULL. June 1861 - Sept. 1865. 2 vols.
    (one containing handwritten copies, one press copies). 2 in.
    Arranged chronologically.   344
    All the first volume and the earlier part of the second consist of
letters sent by Commander Hull while commanding the USS Savannah,
stationed at St. Louis, where he was in charge of gunboat manufacture.
From this station he was transferred to Philadelphia as Commandant.

REGISTER OF ORDERS AND DETACHMENTS OF OFFICERS STATIONED AT THE YARD.
    June 1861 - Dec. 1866. 3 vols. 3 in. Arranged chronologically.   345
    (1) Register of orders and detachments, June 1861 - Sept. 1864; (2)
register of officers detached, Dec. 1863 - Dec. 1866; and (3) list of
officers reporting to the Navy Yard, Sept. 1864 - Dec. 1866.

LETTERS RECEIVED FROM THE SECRETARY OF THE NAVY BY THE COMMANDANT.
    Jan.-Dec. 1862. 1 adhesive binder. 3½ in. Arranged chronologi-
    cally. Indexed.   346

REGISTER, MAINTAINED IN THE NAVAL CONSTRUCTOR'S OFFICE, OF VESSELS
    DOCKED AT THE YARD ("Docking Book"). June 1866 - Jan. 1876.
    1 vol. 1½ in. Arranged chronologically. Indexed.   347

Portsmouth (N. H.) Navy Yard

LOG. 1840-45, with gaps. 3 vols. 4 in. Arranged chronologically.   348

Rio Grande Station

LETTERS SENT BY OFFICERS COMMANDING THE USS RIO BRAVO, IN CHARGE OF
    NAVAL OPERATIONS ON THE RIO GRANDE. Nov. 1875 - Apr. 1879. 1 vol.
    1 in. Handwritten copies. Arranged chronologically.   349
    Operations on the Rio Grande, connected with various border troubles,

were successively under the command of Comdr. George C. Remey, Lt. Comdr.
Henry L. Johnson, Comdr. Benjamin F. Day, Comdr. Bartlett J. Cromwell,
Lt. Thomas A. De Blois, and Comdr. Charles F. Schmitz. The Rio Bravo was
stationed at Brownsville and Matamoras. The volume was received from the
Bureau of Engineering.

Washington Navy Yard

REPORTS ON REMOVAL OF POWDER FROM THE YARD AT THE TIME OF THE BRITISH
      INVASION OF WASHINGTON. Aug.-Sept. 1814. 1 vol. 3/4 in.   350
   Submitted to Commodore Thomas Tingey, Commandant, by Mordecai Booth,
clerk.

LOG. Nov. 1822 - Mar. 1830. 1 vol. 1½ in. Arranged chronologically. 351

LETTERS SENT BY CAPT. ISAAC HULL, COMMANDANT. Jan.-July 1832. 1 vol.
      ¼ in. Handwritten copies. Arranged chronologically.   352

INVENTORY OF THE PUBLIC PROPERTY IN THE YARD. Apr. 1, 1844. 1 vol.
      ½ in.   353

LETTERS SENT BY THE COMMANDANT. Nov. 1860 - Dec. 1861, Nov. 1862 -
      June 1869. 7 vols. 8 in. Arranged chronologically.   354
   (1) Orders issued, Nov. 1860 - Dec. 1861, Jan. 1864 - June 1864
(handwritten copies, 3 vols.); (2) telegrams sent, Nov. 1862 - Oct.
1863 (press copies, 1 vol.); (3) letters to the Secretary of the Navy,
Jan. 1863 - June 1868 (handwritten copies, 2 vols.); and (4) miscellaneous letters, July 1864 - June 1869 (handwritten copies, 1 vol.).

CIRCULARS AND ESTIMATES ISSUED BY THE COMMANDANT AND RECORD OF ARTICLES
      MANUFACTURED AND LABOR PERFORMED IN THE YARD. Sept. 1861 - Nov.
      1873. 1 vol. 1 in. No arrangement apparent.   355

LETTERS RECEIVED BY THE COMMANDANT. Nov. 1862 - June 1866. 1 vol. and
      3 adhesive binders. 9 in. Arranged chronologically.   356
   (1) Telegrams received, Nov. 1862 - Sept. 1863 (handwritten copies,
1 vol.); and (2) letters from the Secretary of the Navy, July 1863 -
June 1866 (3 binders).

LETTERS SENT BY OR THROUGH THE CHIEF ENGINEER OF THE YARD TO THE COM-
      MANDANT. Nov. 1874 - Feb. 1908. 2 vols. 2 in. Press copies.
      Arranged chronologically.   357
   The last pages of the second volume may bear dates subsequent to
Feb. 1908 but are illegible.

INVENTORY OF THE ORDNANCE IN THE YARD. July 1, 1886. 1 vol. 3/4 in. 358

V. BOARDS AND COMMISSIONS, 1837-1902

The records described below are records of boards and commissions of
the Navy Department, other than the Board of Navy Commissioners, and are

presumed to have been placed in storage when the boards or commissions were abolished. When records of a board or commission were transmitted with a covering letter or other evidence of transmittal to a bureau or an office, they are considered to have become part of the records of the bureau or office, exactly as did materials so received from other sources. The records here described are presumed not to have been transmitted by the units that created them to other units, and for this reason to have retained their character as records of boards and commissions. This presumption rests entirely upon the lack of evidence to the contrary.

Board for Testing Ordnance

Established by the Secretary of the Navy, July 12, 1836, with Commo. Charles Morris as President, to test the efficiency and safety of the medium and light guns of the Navy. The experiments of the Board were conducted at Old Point Comfort.

MINUTES. Aug. 1836 - Sept. 1837. 1 vol. 1 in.   359

Board To Prepare a Code of Regulations for the Government of the Navy

Established by the Secretary of the Navy, August 3, 1857, in compliance with the act of Congress making appropriations for the Navy for the fiscal year 1858, with Commo. William B. Shubrick as President.

JOURNAL. Aug. 10, 1857 - Feb. 19, 1858. 1 vol. 3/4 in.   360

Naval Examining Board

Established by an order of the Secretary of the Navy, December 27, 1861, with R. A. William B. Shubrick as Senior Member, to examine and report upon "all subjects that may be submitted to you by this Dep^t.," including particularly "plans, propositions and suggestions made by ingenious persons to the Navy Department," and to "receive whatever explanations may be offered by the parties interested." See Entry 192 for reports of the Board.

LETTERS ON INVENTIONS REFERRED TO THE BOARD. Mar. 1861 - July 1862.
    1 vol. 2½ in. Arranged chronologically. Indexed.   361
    The letters written in 1861 antedated the first meeting of the Board but had not been acted upon by the Secretary of the Navy. Various letters not considered by the Board, though referred to it, are in the series described in Entry 363.

MINUTES. Jan.-July 1862. 1 vol. 3/4 in. Indexed.   362

Permanent Commission

Established by an order of the Secretary of the Navy, February 11, 1863, with Commo. Charles H. Davis, Chief of the Bureau of Navigation, as Chairman, to examine and report upon "questions of science and art upon which the Department may require information" and which should be referred to the Commission. It inherited functions and unfinished business from the Naval Examining Board. See Entry 193 for reports of the Commission.

LETTERS REFERRED TO THE COMMISSION. Jan. 1861 - Dec. 1865. 3 vols.
    9 in. Arranged chronologically in overlapping volumes (Jan. 1861 -
    Feb. 1864, Feb. 1862 - Feb. 1864, and Jan. 1864 - Dec. 1865).
    Indexed.   363
Many of these letters, which relate chiefly to inventions, had been referred to the Naval Examining Board but not acted upon by it.

MINUTES. Feb. 1863 - Feb. 1864. 1 vol. 3 in. Arranged chronologi-
    cally.   364
A successor volume, to Sept. 1865 or later, was probably maintained.

LETTERS RECEIVED. Feb.-June 1863. 1 adhesive binder. 1 3/4 in.
    Arranged chronologically. Indexed.   365

LETTERS SENT. Mar. 1863 - Sept. 1865. 2 vols. 2½ in. Press copies.
    Arranged chronologically. Indexed.   366

Joint Army and Navy Board

Established by an order of the Secretary of the Navy, February 15, 1866, and of the Secretary of War, with R. A. Charles H. Davis as Senior Member, to consider and report upon methods of defending harbors. The Board met in Washington.

JOURNAL. Mar.-July 1866. 1 vol. 1 in. Arranged chronologically.   367
    The report of the Board, July 14, 1866, is copied in the journal.

Board for the Examination of Officers for Promotion

Appointed in compliance with an act of April 21, 1864, with Capt. William H. Macomb as President, succeeded by Commo. Thomas O. Selfridge and Commo. George F. Emmons. The Board was convened at the Philadelphia Navy Yard.

LETTERS SENT. Oct. 1868 - Apr. 1869. 1 vol. 1 in. Press copies.
    Arranged chronologically.   368
Chiefly reports on the cases of particular officers.

<u>Commission To Ascertain the Cost</u>
<u>of Removing the Naval Observatory</u>

Established in compliance with an act of Congress of June 20, 1878, with R. A. Daniel Ammen as Chairman.

JOURNAL. July-Dec. 1878. 1 vol. 1 in. Arranged chronologically. Indexed.   369
    Minutes, July 15 - Dec. 7, 1878; and copies of letters sent and received.

<u>Naval War Board</u>

This Board apparently originated in informal consultations between the Secretary of the Navy and various officers concerning matters of strategy in the war with Spain. No orders or letters of appointment are found. By the inclusion of an Army officer early in April 1898 the Board became the Army and Navy Board. After the withdrawal of this officer there is no record before April 29, when the Board, with R. A. Montgomery Sicard as President, was drafting telegrams for signature by John D. Long, Secretary of the Navy. The earliest occurrence of the name "Naval War Board" ("Office of Naval War Board" on the Board's letterhead) is found for May 2. Throughout the period of the war the Secretary's correspondence pertaining to naval operations was in large part drafted by or prepared in collaboration with the Board, of which the Secretary was virtually a member.

LETTERS SENT BY CAPT. ALBERT S. BARKER, NAVAL MEMBER OF THE ARMY AND
        NAVY BOARD. Apr. 2-18, 1898. 1 vol. $1\frac{1}{4}$ in. Press copies.
        Arranged chronologically. Indexed.   370

LETTERS AND TELEGRAMS SENT. Apr. 29 - Aug. 11, 1898. 2 vols. $2\frac{1}{2}$ in.
        Press copies. Arranged chronologically. Indexed.   371
    "A," letters and telegrams to May 31, thereafter letters only; "B," telegrams only, June-Aug. Chiefly to commanding officers in Cuban waters.

LETTERS AND TELEGRAMS SENT BY THE "STRATEGY BOARD." Apr.-Aug. 1898.
        1 vol. 1 in. Press copies. Arranged chronologically. Indexed.   372
    Chiefly from the Secretary of the Navy, John D. Long. The name "Strategy Board" is not found in the volume. Many of the letters are on stationery with the letterhead of the Naval War Board.

<u>Board of Arbitration for Army and Navy Maneuvers</u>

Appointed to report upon Army and Navy maneuvers in the New London and Narragansett Artillery Districts, September 1-6, 1902, with R. A. Stephen B. Luce as Senior Member. Meetings were held at the Naval War College.

REPORT. Oct. 30, 1902. 1 vol. $\frac{1}{2}$ in. Carbon copy.   373
    Addressed to the Secretary of the Navy.

VI. RECORDS ACQUIRED FROM SOURCES OUTSIDE THE NAVY DEPARTMENT, 1691-1908

The records described below have nothing in common beyond the fact that they are known or presumed to have been acquired by the Office of Naval Records and Library or its predecessors from sources outside the Navy Department, and thus not to have been originally records of the Department or of any of its offices or bureaus. Since the Office of Naval Records and Library did not maintain a systematic record of its accessions before 1926, the origin of a particular volume is sometimes uncertain; and it is therefore possible that a few of the volumes here described may have originated in the Navy Department without giving clear evidence of the fact in their labels or contents. Conversely, it is possible that a few volumes described in preceding sections, though in appearance records created within the Navy Department, were actually acquired from external sources.

A few of the records were transferred either to the Navy Department or specifically to the Office of Naval Records and Library from other departments of the Federal Government. Eleven volumes of records of the War Department were selected by Lt. Col. Edwin N. McClellan, USMC, from records stored in the Schuylkill Arsenal, Philadelphia, and were transmitted by him to the Office of Naval Records and Library in January 1935. Certain volumes obviously originated in the Department of State and the Treasury Department, but the dates and circumstances of their transfer are unknown.

Other records were formerly the property of the Confederate States or of citizens of the Confederate States. These records, of which the total bulk is less than twenty cubic feet, are the largest collection of manuscript records of or relating to the Confederate States Navy that is known to exist. Still other volumes are originals or copies of records of foreign states or of their citizens. No effort is made to distinguish between private and public records in the listing of these two classes. The remaining 691 volumes are originals or copies of records relating to the United States Navy and known or presumed to have been formerly the property of citizens of the United States. Most of these records are described in Entries 392 (logs, journals, and diaries of officers of the United States Navy at sea, 210 vols.) and 395 (letter books of officers of the United States Navy at sea, 365 vols.).

Private records, both originals and copies, have been acquired by the Office of Naval Records and Library and its predecessors through gift and purchase. Registers of private papers acquired between 1883 and 1913 are listed in Entries 471-474, and notations concerning the source of most bound volumes in the Collection that are of unofficial origin are entered in the card catalogue listed in Entry 465. Before 1924 a chief effort of the Office of Naval Records and Library was to obtain private records relating to the Civil War, to be printed in Official Records of the Union and Confederate Navies in the War of the Rebellion. Since that date a constant search has been made for private records relating to all periods in the history of the United States Navy.

Some of the journals, letter books, and other materials were obviously private and personal. Other records, such as logs and copies of letters

sent by commanding officers of ships and squadrons, are identical in
character with records that at a later time were required by law to be
delivered to the Navy Department to become part of its records. Such a
law could not be applied ex post facto. No disciplinary action was contemplated in the circular issued by the Secretary of the Navy on February
4, 1889, asserting that for the period of the Civil War

> The correspondence of captains of ships with each other, and
> of flagofficers with their captains, and official correspond-
> ence with outside parties, is entirely wanting.
>   The narrative of many operations of importance is therefore
> extremely incomplete.
>   In order to supply these deficiencies and to do full justice
> to the activity and zeal of the officers themselves, it is de-
> sirable that this correspondence should, as far as possible, be
> transmitted to the Department, to be embodied in the publica-
> tion now in course of preparation. In a few cases this has been
> done, and very valuable additions have thus been made to the
> record. The Department therefore requests that all officers who
> may have in their possession copies of letters, reports, returns
> or official documents of any kind whatever, relating to naval
> operations, whether in the form of press-copies, letterbooks, log-
> books or loose files, would transmit them to the Department, ad-
> dressed directly to the Office of Naval War Records, which will
> make copies and return the originals to the owners if the latter
> desire it. The Department hopes that in this matter it will meet
> with the hearty co-operation of officers, not only in the interest
> of the publication, but for the good of the naval service itself.

The archival status of documents thus acquired is nebulous. Those
published in Official Records of the Union and Confederate Navies were
evidently regarded by the Navy Department as "official records," and similar documents of date before or after the Civil War would be official records to the same degree. The documents could be regarded as "historical
manuscripts," forming a part of the Naval Records Collection only in the
sense in which the printed volumes that are attached to it, and are not
included in this inventory, are part of the Collection. Various consider-
ations could be adduced as to the record or nonrecord character of such
documents, but in the present state of archival theory no final decision
seems warranted.

For the purposes of this checklist, and with no intent to establish
a precedent applicable outside the checklist itself, the documents dis-
cussed above are treated as records of their writers, bearing the same
theoretical relation to their writers as the relation that exists between
the records of a bureau or an office and the bureau or office in which
they originated. The documents are therefore designated as records of
citizens of the United States, of the Confederate States, or of foreign
states, and are presumed to retain this character regardless of their
present custody.

Only bound records are listed in this section. Loose papers from sources outside the Navy Department have been combined by the Office of Naval Records and Library with loose papers from within the Department in such a way that all the papers have lost their identity as individual records or series of records, and have been absorbed into either the Area File or the Subject File (Entries 463 and 464). Such collections as the Guert Gansevoort Papers and the William Reynolds Papers, which existed as measurable and describable entities before 1924, have been dismembered; and the volumes and loose papers of which they consisted have been intermingled with records from other sources as parts of artificial series created, as series, incidentally to the arrangement and classification of the materials that form the Naval Records Collection.

A. Records of the Federal Government, 1790-1883

1. War Department, 1790-1831

LETTERS SENT CONCERNING NAVAL MATTERS. Oct. 1790-June 1798. 1 vol.
    2 in. Handwritten copies. Arranged chronologically. Indexed.   374
M739 From the Secretary of War to naval officers, naval constructors, shipbuilders, merchants, collectors of customs, civil employees, and others. The letters consist chiefly of orders to officers, letters of appointment, estimates of expenses for building ships and paying officers and crews, and specifications for ordnance and other materials. The first letter is dated Oct. 30, 1790, the second Nov. 15, 1791, and the third Nov. 17, 1791. No other letter is included before Jan. 4, 1794. In the earlier part of the volume are a few copies of letters received. It is uncertain whether this volume was prepared by or for the Navy Department or was currently maintained in the War Department and turned over to the Navy Department in or after 1798.

ORDERS TO DELIVER NAVAL ORDNANCE ("Correspondence on Arming and Equipping Early Frigates and Ships of War When Navy was Under War Department"). May 1795 - July 1798. 1 vol. 1½ in. Handwritten copies. Arranged chronologically. Indexed.   375
    From the Secretary of War to Samuel Hodgdon and John Harris, storekeepers at Philadelphia.

REGISTER OF ESTIMATED REQUIREMENTS FOR MILITARY SUPPLIES. Jan. 1796 - Feb. 1805. 1 vol. 1¼ in. Arranged chronologically. Indexed.   376
    Kept by Samuel Hodgdon and William Irvine, United States Arsenal, Philadelphia.

RECEIPT BOOK OF JOHN HARRIS, STOREKEEPER OF MILITARY SUPPLIES, PHILA-DELPHIA. Aug. 1796 - Apr. 1799. 4 vols. 5 in. Arranged chronologically.   377
    Contains the autograph signatures of persons receiving supplies.

DAYBOOK OF MILITARY AND NAVAL SUPPLIES RECEIVED AND DELIVERED AT PHILADELPHIA. Jan. 1797 - May 1801. 1 vol. ("A"). 3 in. Arranged chronologically.   378

LEDGER OF MILITARY AND NAVAL SUPPLIES RECEIVED AND DELIVERED AT PHILA-
DELPHIA. Jan. 1797 - May 1801, AND OF CLOTHING RECEIVED, Jan.
1826 - Sept. 1831. 1 vol. ("A"). 1 3/4 in. Arranged by types
of supplies.   379

LETTERS SENT BY THE OFFICE OF THE PURVEYOR OF PUBLIC SUPPLIES.
May 1800 - June 1802. 1 vol. ("A"). 1½ in. Handwritten copies.
Arranged chronologically.   380
Addressed from Philadelphia to the Treasurer of the United States, the
Comptroller of the Treasury, the Accountant of the War Department, the
Accountant of the Navy Department, and the Secretaries of Treasury, War,
and Navy. Successor volumes are among the records formerly stored in the
Schuylkill Arsenal, Philadelphia, and now in the National Archives in
Record Group 92, Records of the Office of the Quartermaster General.

SUMMARIES AND COPIES OF ORDERS RECEIVED BY THE OFFICE OF THE PURVEYOR
OF PUBLIC SUPPLIES ("Memorandum Book"). Jan. 1801 - May 1808.
1 vol. 1 in. Arranged chronologically.   381

RECEIPT BOOK OF ROBERT JONES, STOREKEEPER OF MILITARY SUPPLIES.
May 1801 - Feb. 1802. 1 vol. 1¼ in. Arranged chronologically.   382

REGISTER OF RECEIPTS AND DISBURSEMENTS OF POWDER FOR MILITARY AND NAVAL
USE. July 1805 - June 1814. 1 vol. 3/4 in.   383
One side of the volume ("Military Side") was used by the Military
Storekeeper at Philadelphia; the other ("Naval Side"), by the Naval
Storekeeper at Philadelphia.

2. Department of the Treasury, 1809-1865

INDEX TO OFFICIAL BONDS EXECUTED BY NAVAL PAY OFFICERS ("Paymasters of
U. S. Navy"). Mar. 1809 - June 1865. 1 vol. 2 in. Arranged
by first letter of pay officers' names, thereunder chronologically. 384
Gives date of bond, name of pay officer, office held by him, names of
sureties, and amount of bond. The officers included are pursers, naval
storekeepers, navy agents, paymasters of the Marine Corps, navy pension
agents, paymasters, and ass't paymasters. The original list was prepared
before May 1855 from data submitted by the Second Comptroller of the
Treasury to the Fourth Auditor of the Treasury, and was kept current by
additions.

NOTES ON FISCAL MATTERS AFFECTING THE NAVY. Ca. 1853 - ca. 1864. 2 vols.
4 in. Indexed.   385
Compiled by Mason Campbell and Tobias Purrington, clerks in the
Office of the Second Comptroller of the Treasury. The first volume
(ca. 1853 - ca. 1855) contains the signature of "M. Campbell"; the
second, that of "T. Purrington." Both are identified by a list of clerks
employed in the Second Comptroller's Office (1829-52), in the first volume. The volumes consist of copies of and references to official correspondence, notes of decisions and of acts of Congress, working rules, and
the like, all relating to accounts of the Army and the Navy, and were

probably assembled for reference in reviewing such accounts. The first
volume treats, in order, pensions, pension agents, teamsters, retained
pay, travel, place of enlistment, the place of residence, servants,
minors, prisoners of war, furlough, soldier detailed for hospital nurse,
hospital stewards, bounty, desertion, forage, notary public, descents,
pay before muster into service, administrators of wills, army chaplains,
recruits, and the War with Mexico. The second volume gives further information concerning the same or similar subjects. On the duties of the
Second Comptroller, see Entry 57.

REGISTER OF LETTERS SENT FROM THE WARRANT DESK, TREASURY DEPARTMENT
    ("Memo. of Letters Written from Warrant Desk"). July 1853 -
    Dec. 1861. 1 vol. 1 in. Arranged chronologically.   386
    Gives date of letter, to whom addressed, address to which sent, and
abstract. The letters are not confined or particularly devoted to naval
affairs.

INDEX TO OFFICIAL BONDS EXECUTED BY NAVAL PAY OFFICERS ("New Bond Book").
    July 1861 - Oct. 1865. 1 vol. 3/4 in. Arranged by first letter
    of pay officers' names, thereunder by rank (paymaster, ass't pay-
    master, act'g ass't paymaster), thereunder chronologically.   387
    Gives name of pay officer, date of bond, names of bondsmen, and
amount of bond. The predecessor volume may have been that described in
Entry 384.

3. Department of State, 1812-1883

LETTERS FROM COLLECTORS OF CUSTOMS RELATING TO COMMISSIONS OF PRIVATEERS
    ("Privateers, War of 1812"). 1812-15. 6 vols. 2 ft. 2 in.
    5 vols. arranged numerically, 1-780; 1 vol. arranged alphabeti-
    cally by names of States containing offices of collectors of cus-
    toms.   388
    These letters to the Secretary of State enclose abstracts of commis-
sions and requests received from owners of merchant vessels for the issuance of letters of marque and reprisal. The numbers on the collectors'
letters are in pencil and not in a chronological, an alphabetical, or a
regional order. The letters in the alphabetical volume are not numbered.
The letters in all the volumes seem identical in character and purpose.
The date and motive of transfer of the records from the Department of
State to the Department of the Navy are unknown. All the volumes have
"Navy Department" stamped on the back.

INDEX TO LETTERS FROM COLLECTORS OF CUSTOMS. 1812-15. 1 vol. 1¼ in.
    Arranged alphabetically, with names of vessels and names of owners
    and captains grouped separately under each letter.   389
    Covers the chronological volumes described above, giving name and
number only. The handwriting appears recent.

REPORT ON NAVAL EXPERIMENTS AGAINST ARMOR PLATING IN DENMARK. Apr. 30,
    1883. 1 vol. ½ in.   390
    Experiments on the Isle of Amager, Denmark, under the direction of

the Ordnance Select Committee of the Navy of Denmark. Report addressed to "the Artillery"; translation forwarded to the Department of State from the United States Consulate, Copenhagen, with Despatch 209 (May 21, 1883).

B. Records of Citizens of the United States, 1775-1908

CORRESPONDENCE OF ESEK HOPKINS, COMMANDER IN CHIEF OF THE CONTINENTAL NAVY. Oct. 1775 - Oct. 1777. 2 vols. 3 in. Photostat. Arranged chronologically. Typed index.   391
    (1) Letters received, Oct. 1775 - Oct. 1777; and (2) letters sent, handwritten copies, Feb. 1776 - Apr. 1777. The papers reproduced in the photostat are in the possession of the Rhode Island Historical Society.

LOGS, JOURNALS, AND DIARIES OF OFFICERS OF THE UNITED STATES NAVY AT SEA. Mar. 1776 - June 1908. 210 vols. (forming 160 subseries, listed in Appendix D). 16 ft. 4 in.   392
    A few of these volumes are logs in an official sense: daily records of occurrences aboard naval vessels, of the condition of vessels, and of the condition of the ambient air and water, consisting of hourly entries by watch officers and approved by the commanding officer. Other volumes are daily records confined to such data but maintained throughout by one officer; many of these were kept by midshipmen as a part of their training. Still others, containing only such information, were kept by one officer at different times on two or more naval vessels. Many volumes, on the other hand, were personal records of the experience, activity, and observation of their writers, and could not have been designed for perusal by superior officers. The personal nature of such records is suggested by drawings, scraps of verse, and scribblings on the flyleaves and the insides of the covers, and by evidences that pages have been cut or torn from the volumes. Most of the volumes are known to have been acquired by the Office of Naval Records and Library from officers of the United States Navy or their heirs; the others are presumed to have been so acquired before the Office began to keep detailed records of the sources of its acquisitions. Many volumes of similar character remain in the possession of descendants of naval officers or have been received by historical societies and other learned organizations; photostats of a number of such volumes are part of the present series.

LOGS AND JOURNALS OF AMERICAN PRIVATEERS AND MERCHANT VESSELS. Nov. 1776 - Oct. 1867. 9 vols. 9 in.   393
    (1) Log of the schooner Active, Nov.-Dec. 1776. Several pages at the beginning are damaged. (2) Excerpts from the journal of Jonathan Haskins, Jr., surgeon on the Massachusetts privateer sloop Charming Sally (photostat), Dec. 1776 - Oct. 1778. Original in possession of Maine Historical Society. The vessel was captured by the British Jan. 16, 1777. (3) Journal of the Rev. Medad Rogers on the privateer Hazard, cruising in and near Long Island Sound (photostat), July-Sept. 1778. Original in Yale University Library. (4) Log of the frigate South Carolina, on a voyage from Texel, The Netherlands, to Charleston, Aug. 1781 - May 1782. (5) Log

of the privateer Hague, on a voyage from Boston to Martinique, Sept. 1782 - Feb. 1782. The note "Dr. Barnard's Papers" appears on a flyleaf, and references to treatment of the sick suggest that a surgeon was the writer of the log. (6) Journal kept by Richard Dale on the Alliance (Thomas Read, Master), on a voyage from Philadelphia by way of the Indian Ocean to the East Indies and China (photostat), June 1787 - Oct. 1788. Original in possession of Edward C. Dale, Bryn Mawr, Pa., 1935. At the end of the volume is a fragment of the journal of an unidentified ship on a voyage from Madras to Canton, June-July 1788. (7) Journal of Jeduthun Upton, Jr., master of the privateer Polly, of Salem, Mass., on a voyage from Salem to England and back to Portland, Maine (typed copy), Dec. 1812 - June 1813. Presented by Luther H. Evans, National Supervisor, Historical Records Survey. The Polly was captured Dec. 23, 1812, by HMS Phoebe. Upton was confined on the prison ship Hector and later in England. After being exchanged he was returned to America on a cartel ship. (8) Log of the bark Tacony, on a voyage from Philadelphia to New Orleans and back, Oct. 1862 - June 1863. (9) Log of the schooner Mabel, of Baltimore (W. Donaldson, Master), on a voyage from New York to Galveston, July-Oct. 1867.

ACCOUNT BOOKS OF VESSELS OF THE UNITED STATES NAVY. Feb. 1777 - July 1879. 21 vols. 2 ft. 2 in. **394**

(1) Papers of the Continental brig Lexington, commanded by Henry Johnson (photostat), Feb. 26 - Sept. 19, 1777, containing lists of stores and expenditures, lists of the crew, and fragments of a log, with typed introduction and index. (2) Register of stores received by the Independence, June 1815 - Apr. 1817. (3) Register of stores received and expended by the Constitution, Carpenter's Department, Sept. 1824 - June 1828. (4) Accounts kept by Purser Edward N. Cox on the Brandywine, consisting of register of individual accounts by account number, 1-800, June 1826 - Oct. 1828 (2 vols.), and cashbook, Mar. 1827 - Oct. 1829 (1 vol.). (5) Register of stores received and expended by the Lexington, May 1827 - July 1828. (6) Register of stores received and expended by the Peacock, Sept. 1829 - May 1831. (7) Register of stores received and expended by the Independence, Boatswain's Department, Feb. 1837 - Feb. 1838. (8) Register of stores received and expended by the Macedonian, Carpenter's Department, June 1837 - Mar. 1838. (9) Register of stores received and expended by the Lexington, July 1837 - Nov. 1839. (10) Register of stores received and expended by the Ontario, Aug. 1837 - May 1839. (11) Register of stores received and expended by the Vincennes, Carpenter's Department, July 1838 - June 1842. (12) Register of stores received and expended by the Cyane, Aug. 1841 - June 1844. (13) Register of expenditures by the Cyane, July 1842 - Feb. 1846. (14) Register of stores received and expended by the Marion, Aug. 1842 - July 1843 (2 vols.). (15) Register of stores received and expended by the Columbus, Aug. 1842 - June 1844. (16) Daily record of expenditures by the Metacomet, renamed the Pulaski, 1858-62. (17) Receipted requisitions filled by the Brooklyn (printed forms with signatures of persons receiving the requisitioned articles), Jan. 1859 - Sept. 1861. (18) Accounts of expenses incurred in preparation for the Arctic Expedition under the command of Lt. Comdr. George W. De Long, Feb. 1878 - July 1879.

LETTER BOOKS OF OFFICERS OF THE UNITED STATES NAVY AT SEA. Mar. 1778 –
July 1908. 365 vols. and adhesive binders (forming 133 subseries,
listed in Appendix E). 46 ft. 9 in. Some volumes and binders
indexed.   395

Handwritten copies of letters sent and letters received, press copies
of letters sent, and originals of letters received. Most volumes are
confined to letters sent; but some contain copies of both letters sent
and letters received, some contain only original letters received, and a
few contain copies of letters sent bound with originals of letters received. The letters consist chiefly of orders, reports, and other official communications, but were regarded as the private property of
officers. Most of the letter books are known to have been acquired by
the Office of Naval Records and Library from officers of the United States
Navy or their heirs; the others are presumed to have been so acquired before the Office began to keep detailed records of the sources of its acqui-
sitions. No volumes of similar character previous to 1874 are known to
have been retained by the Navy Department, though 1,398 volumes and binders
of such letters, 1874-1910, are in the National Archives in Record Group 24,
Records of the Bureau of Naval Personnel, where they are arranged alphabetically by ships' names. Such an arrangement would not be feasible for
the private letter books that compose the present series, for a single letter
book may contain correspondence for a period of several years during which
an officer served on two or more ships, often with intervals of duty on
shore. Many letter books of naval officers remain in the possession of
their descendants or are in the custody of historical societies or other
learned organizations; photostats of a number of such volumes are part of
the present series. A list of the volumes, comprising 133 subseries, is
furnished in Appendix E.

ROSTERS OF OFFICERS AND CREWS OF THE BONHOMME RICHARD, THE PALLAS, AND
THE VENGEANCE. 1779. 1 vol. 1¼ in. Photostat. Typed index of
names.   396

Original in Library of Congress. The rosters were copied in 1789 and
signed by "Paul Jones," apparently in the hand of Capt. John Paul Jones.

PAY ROLL OF THE CONTINENTAL SHIP CONFEDERACY. June 1780 – Mar. 1781.
1 vol. 1 in. Arranged chronologically. Typed index of names.   397

Found at Princeton and presented to the Office of Naval Records and
Library.

LETTERS SENT BY ROBERT MORRIS AS AGENT OF MARINE. Sept. 1781 – Oct.
1784. 2 vols. 4½ in. Photostat. Arranged chronologically.
Typed index.   398

The originals, in the Naval Academy, are loose handwritten copies.

SUMMARY JOURNALS AND NOTES OF MOSES HILLARD, MERCHANT, ON VARIOUS
ATLANTIC, ARCTIC, AND PACIFIC VOYAGES. May 1796 – July 1835.
1 vol. 3/4 in. Table of contents.   399

The writer made an entry in this volume after returning from voyages
on each of the following vessels: the Harriot (to Demerara, 1801-3),
the Neptune (to Surinam, 1803), the Antelope (to Lisbon, 1804), the

Catharine (to La Guaira, 1805), the Sussex (to Puerto Rico, 1805-6), the Maria (to Bilbao and Lisbon, 1806-7), the Amiable Matilda (to Barcelona, 1807-8), the Havana Packet (to Yucatán and Montevideo, 1809-11), the Isabella (to Archangel, 1812-13), the Oneida (to Havre de Grâce, 1817-18), the Marcus (to Havre de Grâce, 1818-19), the John (to Cádiz and Vera Cruz, 1822-23), the Edgar (to La Guaira, 1824), the Laura (to Callao and Mazatlán, 1828-29), the McLellan (to Callao and Mazatlán, 1832-33), and the Pantheon (to Mazatlán, 1934-35). In the middle of the volume is a "Memorandum of Voyages & Cruises of Which I Have No Journals," 1796-1807. The entries in the volume consist chiefly of itineraries, sailing directions, and remarks on trade.

LIST OF FRENCH PRISONERS OF WAR ("French Prisoners"). Ca. 1799.
    1 vol. 1½ in. Arranged by first letter of prisoners' names.   400
  Contains no indication of place, prison, or conditions of captivity, or of date except "1799" on the backstrip. Compiler unidentified.

NOTES AND COMPILATIONS OF OFFICERS OF THE UNITED STATES NAVY. Mar. 1803 -
    1900. 12 vols. 11 in.   401
  (1) Notebook of Commo. Edward Preble (flagship Constitution), commanding the Mediterranean Squadron (typed copy), Mar. 1803 - Feb. 1806. Original in possession of Frank Littleton, Leesburg, Va., 1929. Commodore Preble arrived at New York Feb. 26, 1805, and was occupied thereafter with shore duties. (2) Notebook of Capt. Arthur Sinclair, in service on Lake Ontario (photostat), 1813. Original in possession of Mrs. George Barnett, 1926. Captain Sinclair was ordered Feb. 17, 1813, to fit out a flotilla for service on the Great Lakes. The volume contains notes, accounts, and at least parts of what may have been a connected narrative; but the sheets have apparently not been filmed in order, and the continuity of the record is lost. (3) Notebook of Lt. Charles Gauntt, ca. 1818 - ca. 1834. Apparently compiled for reference; contains directions for making and repairing naval equipment, directions for performing various naval processes, recipes, statistics, and a recapitulation of the station bill of the USS North Carolina. (4) Notebook of Lt. George S. Blake, 1822 - ca. 1831, consisting of various sailing directions, chiefly copied from printed sources; journals of voyages on the merchant vessels Sicily (Boston to Trieste and back to Boston, Sept. 1822 - Mar. 1824), Cambridge (Boston to the Florida Keys, Apr.-May 1825), and Florida (Florida Keys, May 1825); and dimensions and watch, station, and quarter bills of the USS Java (ca. 1831). (5) Notebook of Lt. Samuel Woodard Le Compt, ca. 1832, containing regulations of the USS Constellation, June 13, 1842; watch, quarter, and station bill of the same; dimensions of the USS Hudson; watch bill of the USS Brandywine; and various notes on seamanship. (6) Notebooks of Second Ass't Engineer, later First Ass't Engineer, Richard C. Potts, the first containing the steam log of the USS Saranac at Portsmouth, N. H., Apr.-May 1850, a fragment of the steam log of an unnamed vessel, May 19-24, 1853, dimensions of various steamers, drawings showing details of the coast survey steamers Walker and Water Witch, 1851, and various computations; and the second containing computations, directions, and other data relative to steam engineering, 1860-61. (7) "El Loring; or, The Return: A Poem by Chaplain Fitch W. Taylor" (2 vols.), written ca. 1854, when the author was stationed on the USS Independence, and consisting of

heroic couplets detailing the adventures of El Loring, the hero, in Rio de Janeiro, Muscat, Bombay, and New Haven. The first volume begins with Book 4, Canto 3; at least one volume must have preceded. Though there are blank pages at the end of the second volume, the poem appears not to be finished. (8) Notebook of David Howard Tribou, Chaplain, USN, on the engagement between the Alabama and the Kearsarge, June 19, 1864, consisting chiefly of penciled notes from printed sources, with page references. A list of addresses at the end of the notebook is dated 1910. (9) Rough draft of a manual of procedure for naval courts and boards, by Capt. George C. Remey, ca. 1880, in pencil, with corrections and interlineations. (10) Compilation of general orders, regulations, and procedures, by Lt. Nathan Sargent, 1897-1900, consisting of entries in no particular order, probably made for the compiler's reference.

REGISTER OF BRITISH PRISONERS OF WAR IN THE UNITED STATES. July 1812 – Mar. 1815. 2 vols. 3 in. Arranged by first letter of prisoners' names.   402

Gives date of returns or of capture, name of prisoner, where imprisoned, "quality" of prisoner, vessel to which belonging, where captured, by what or whom captured, date of capture, and where and to whom released. The compilation of the volumes apparently began with lists of May 1814, to which lists of earlier and later date were presently added. The smaller volume ("British Prisoners") is shown by cross references to be a supplement to the larger ("British Prisoners of War"). The compiler is unidentified.

REGISTER OF BRITISH PRISONERS ON THE CARTEL BRIG ANALOSTAN, COMMANDED BY MASTER WILLIAM PETERS SMITH. Nov. 1812 – July 1815. 1 vol. 1½ in. Arranged chronologically.   403

Prepared by Charles J. Deblois, Captain's Clerk. Gives name of prisoner, rank, in what vessel taken, by what vessel taken, when taken, and when delivered, with remarks.

SIGNAL BOOKS. Ca. 1813 – June 1865. 10 vols. 8 3/4 in.   404

(1) Guides to signals and maneuvers, prepared by Commo. Charles Morris, ca. 1813 and ca. 1827, consisting largely of alphabetical lists of words followed by code numbers, and lists of code numbers followed by their translations (6 vols.). (2) Signal book of the Pacific Exploring Expedition, 1838-39. (3) Rough signal log of the USS Columbus, 1845-47. (4) Signal log of the USS New Hampshire, Dec. 1864 – June 1865. (5) Undated index to signal words, prepared for an unidentified squadron. See also Entries 392 (61) and 413 (6).

JOURNAL AND ACCOUNTS OF THOMAS D. ANDERSON, UNITED STATES CONSUL AT TUNIS. Aug. 1815 – Dec. 1817. 1 vol. ½ in.   405

WATCH, QUARTER, AND STATION BILLS OF VARIOUS UNITED STATES SHIPS. 1829-96. 16 vols. 1 ft. 1½ in.   406

Lists of officers and crew, with the duties assigned to each member in the operations and maneuvers of the ship, comprising volumes for (1) the Constellation, commanded by Capt. Alexander S. Wadsworth, 1829 (prepared by Lt. William Pearson); (2) the Columbus, commanded by Capt. Thomas W. Wyman, 1846 ("Internal Rules and Regulations of the U. S. S. Columbus," to which is added "The Excellent Gunnery, Copied for Lieu^t. Guert Gansevoort, Executive Officer, U. S. Ship John Adams, by His Friend & Subordinate, G. M. [George J. Marshall, Gunner]"); (3) the Brandywine, 1847 (prepared by Lt. John Julius Guthrie at Rio de Janeiro); (4) the Wabash, commanded by Lt. Thomas G. Corbin, South Atlantic Blockading Squadron, 1861-62; (5) the Pittsburg, commanded by Comdr. Egbert Thompson, Mississippi Squadron, 1862; (6) the Constellation, Mediterranean Squadron, 1862-63; (7) the Miami, North Atlantic Blockading Squadron, 1863-64 (2 vols., index only); (8) the Susquehanna, 1864; (9) the Canandaigua, 1865-66 (prepared by Mdn. George W. De Long); (10) the Sabine, commanded by Lt. George C. Remey, 1869-70; (11) the California, commanded by Capt. John M. B. Clitz, Pacific Squadron, Dec. 1870 - July 1873; and (12) the Castine, 1894-96; and (13) watch, quarter, and station bills for a typical first-class sloop, a typical third-class sloop, and a typical first-class screw steamer (1 vol. each), undated (probably prepared as part of some course in navigation, at a time when both sailing ships and steamships were in common use in the Navy, perhaps ca. 1855).

PAPERS RELATING TO LIGHTHOUSES IN EUROPE. June 1845 - Jan. 1846. 1 vol. 1¼ in.   407
    Lts. Thornton A. Jenkins and Richard Bache were detailed to inspect lighthouses in Europe and report their findings to the Secretary of the Treasury. This volume consists of correspondence concerning their appointment and credentials, letters and pamphlets received by them, and materials illustrating their observations. Their report is not included.

LETTERS SENT BY GORDON M. NEWTON. Sept. 1858 - Aug. 1866. 1 vol. 3/4 in.
        Press copies. Arranged chronologically.   408
    The writer was apparently a merchant or timber dealer in New York. He owned timber lands in the vicinity of Pensacola and employed or corresponded with C. P. Knapp as his agent there. The volume was later in the possession of Capt. Ebenezer Farrand, CSN.

REGISTERS OF THE NORTH ATLANTIC BLOCKADING SQUADRON. Aug. 1861 - Aug. 1865.
      6 vols. 5 in.   409
    (1) Register of battery, 1861-65; (2) register of ships and officers, arranged alphabetically by ships, describing each ship and listing the officers ordered to each, with rank of officers, date of orders, places from which and to which ordered, and date when detached, with index to ships, Apr. 1861 - Sept. 1864 ("Squadron Book"); (3) list of ships and officers, apparently working papers, 1864-65 (2 vols.); (4) register of ships and officers, arranged by ships, Jan.-Apr. 1864 ("Letter Book, N. A. Blockading Squadron"); and (5) register of courts martial held by the squadron, indexed, Oct. 1864 - Aug. 1865.

REGISTERS OF OFFICERS OF THE MISSISSIPPI SQUADRON. Aug. 1861 - July 1865.
      5 vols. 7 in.   410
    (1) Register of volunteer officers, apparently working papers, 1861-65; (2) and (3), registers of volunteer officers, Aug. 1861 - June 1863 and Nov. 1862 - June 1865, each arranged by rank of officers, thereunder alphabetically by officers' names; (4) list of officers and pilots,

1864-65, arranged chronologically; and (5) register of leaves of absence granted, Oct. 1864 - July 1865.

REGISTER OF VESSELS EXAMINED AND PASSED OFF FORTRESS MONROE BY UNITED
    STATES GUARD SHIPS, May 1863 - Apr. 1865. 3 vols. 2 in.
      Arranged chronologically.   411
    Maintained by the Young Rover, May 1863 - Nov. 1864, and the Princess
Royal, Dec. 1864 - Apr. 1865.

REGISTER OF LETTERS SENT BY THE COMMANDING OFFICER OF THE ATLANTIC
    SQUADRON. May-Nov. 1866. 1 vol. 3/4 in. Arranged chronologi-
      cally.   412
    Sent by Commo. Joseph Lanman, aboard the flagships New Hampshire and
Tacony.

REGISTERS MAINTAINED BY THE SOUTH ATLANTIC SQUADRON. June 1867 - July
    1869. 16 vols. 10 in.   413
    Registers of (1) letters forwarded through Comdr. Francis M. Ramsay,
Fleet Captain (2 vols.); (2) reports forwarded through Commander Ramsay
(2 vols.); (3) surveys held (2 vols.); (4) requisitions made (3 vols.);
(5) orders issued (2 vols.); (6) signals; (7) American vessels boarded;
(8) bills for purchase of repairs; (9) monthly reports of condition, distribution, and employment of the ships of the Squadron; and (10) ships of
the Squadron, and officers on each. The Squadron was commanded by R. A.
Charles H. Davis (flagship Guerrière).

CONDUCT BOOKS OF THE NIPSIC, 1871-72, AND THE ST. MARY'S, Feb. 1871 -
    Jan. 1873. 2 vols. 1½ in. Arranged alphabetically by names of
      enlisted men.   414
    Register of offenses and punishments of enlisted men. An entry is
made for each enlisted man, regardless of whether he committed an offense.

REGISTERS MAINTAINED BY THE ASIATIC SQUADRON. Apr. 1875 - Nov. 1877.
    4 vols. 3 in.   415
    Registers of (1) letters received, Apr. 1875 - Nov. 1877; (2) reports
from officers, June 1875 - Mar. 1877; (3) orders issued, June 1875 -
Jan. 1877; and (4) surveys of personnel and material, July 1875 -
Nov. 1877. The Squadron was commanded by R. A. William Reynolds (flagship Tennessee).

REGISTERS MAINTAINED BY THE ASIATIC SQUADRON. Jan. 1900 - Feb. 1902.
    2 vols. 2 in.   416
    Registers of (1) arrivals and departures of ships of the Squadron,
arranged by rate of ships, Jan. 1900 - Feb. 1902; and (2) general courts
martial held by the Squadron, containing printed reports with MS annota-
tions, arranged chronologically, Mar. 1900 - Feb. 1902. The Squadron was
commanded by R. A. George C. Remey.

C. Records of the Confederate States of America and Its Citizens, 1861-1867

NOTES OF MDN. JOHN A. WILSON, CSN, ON HIS SERVICES DURING THE CIVIL WAR.
    1861-65. 1 vol. 1½ in.   417
    In pencil.

ACCOUNT BOOKS OF VESSELS OF THE CONFEDERATE STATES NAVY. May 1861 –
Dec. 1864. 5 vols. 5 in. 418
(1) Accounts of the Raleigh for clothing and small stores, 1861.
(2) Steward's weekly return of provisions expended on the Savannah,
May 1861 – May 1862; the Oconee, May–June 1862; the Isondiga, Jan.–May
1863; the Resolute, Dec. 1862 – June 1863; and the Firefly, Mar.–Apr.
1863. (3) Steward's weekly return of provisions expended on the Resolute,
Aug. 1861 – Apr. 1862; Gunboat No. 1, Apr.–May 1862; and the Georgia,
Oct. 1862 – May 1864. (4) General pay and receipt book of the Georgia,
kept by Ass't Paymaster Dewitt C. Seymour, Oct. 1862 – Aug. 1863. (5)
Steward's weekly return of provisions expended on the Isondiga, Apr. 1863 –
Dec. 1864.

MUSTER ROLLS AND PAY ROLLS OF VESSELS OF THE CONFEDERATE STATES NAVY.
May 1861 – Apr. 1865. Sheets and booklets in 71 labeled wrappers.
1 ft. 2 in. Arranged alphabetically by names of vessels, thereunder chronologically, with one wrapper for each of the following: 419

Albermarle, 1864
Alert, 1861
Arctic, 1864
Atlantic (Fingal), 1863
Baltic, 1862–63
Beaufort, 1862
Carondelet, no date
Caswell, 1862
Chameleon, no date
Charleston, 1863
Chattahoochee, 1862–63
Chicora, 1862–63
Columbia, 1865
Dalman, 1863
Danube, 1864
Ellis, 1861
Fanny, 1861
Firefly, 1863
Florida, 1862
Forrest, no date
Fredericksburg, 1863
General Polk, 1861
Georgia, 1863–64
Gunboat on the Pee Dee
River, 1862

Huntsville, 1863
Indian Chief, 1864
Iron King, 1864
Isondiga, 1863–64
Ivy, 1861
Jackson, 1861
James River Squadron,
1864
Jamestown, 1862
Launches 1–6, 1861–62
Livingston, 1862
McRae, 1861–62
Manassas, 1861–62
Maurepas, 1862
Missouri, 1864
Mobile, 1861–62
Morgan (with Selma
and Alert), 1862–64
Nashville, 1861–62
Neuse, 1864
New Orleans, 1861–62
North Carolina, 1864
Oconee, 1863–65
Olustee, 1864

Palmetto State,
1862–63
Pamlico, 1861
Patrick Henry,
1861–64
Pickens, 1861–62
Pontchartrain, 1862
Raleigh, 1861
Rappahannock, 1861–62
Red Rover, 1862
Resolute, 1863
Richmond, 1861–63
Roanoke, 1863
Sampson, 1863
Savannah, 1862–63
Sea Bird, 1861–62
Spray, 1863–64
Stono, 1863
Sumter, 1861
Tallahassee, 1864
Talomico, 1862
Torch, 1864
Torpedo, 1864
Tuscaloosa, 1863
Tuscarora, 1861–62
United States, 1862
Winslow, 1861

SHIPPING ARTICLES OF THE CONFEDERATE STATES NAVY. May 1861 – Feb. 1865.
1 vol. 4 in. No order apparent beyond grouping of documents by
stations. Typed index of names and typed table of contents. 420
A printed form, "Shipping Articles for the Naval Service, for Persons
to Serve Not Exceeding Three Years," giving date of enlistment, signature
or mark of recruit in his own hand, name of recruit written by recruiting

officer, rating of recruit, wages monthly, wages advanced, bounty paid, signature of surety for advance wages and bounty, and witness to signature of recruit.

INDEX TO NAMES IN THE SHIPPING ARTICLES OF THE CONFEDERATE STATES NAVY. 1861-65. 1 folder. 1/3 in. Carbon copy. Arranged alphabetically.   421
  For ribbon copy, see Entry 420.

PAY ROLLS OF CIVIL PERSONNEL IN SHORE ESTABLISHMENTS OF THE CONFEDERATE STATES NAVY. May 1861 - Dec. 1864. Sheets and booklets in 47 labeled wrappers. 1 ft. 5 in. Arranged alphabetically by names of shore establishments, thereunder chronologically, with one wrapper for each of the following except as otherwise indicated: 422

Albany (Ga.) Naval Station, 1864
Atlanta Naval Station, 1862-64
  (3 wrappers)
Botetourt Co. (Va.) Coal Mines, 1864
Charleston Naval Station, 1862-64
  (6 wrappers)
Charlotte (N. C.) Naval Station, 1863
Columbus (S. C.) Naval Powder Works, 1862-63
Columbus (Ga.) Naval Station, 1863-64
  (4 wrappers)
Fluvanna Co. (Va.) Naval Station, 1863-64
Halifax (N. C.) Naval Station, 1864
Jackson (Miss.) Naval Station, 1863
Keswick (Powhatan Co., Va.) Naval Station, 1862-63
Kinston (N. C.) Naval Station, 1863-64
Little Rock Naval Station, 1863
Marion Court House (S. C.) Naval Station, 1863-64

McIntosh Bluff (Ala.), construction of Ironclads, 1864
Memphis Naval Station, 1862
Mobile Naval Station, 1864
Montgomery Naval Station, 1864
New Orleans Naval Station, 1861-62
  (3 wrappers)
Norfolk Naval Station, 1861-62
Pee Dee Naval Station, 1864
Pensacola Navy Yard, 1861
Petersburg (Va.) Naval Station, 1861-64
Prattsville (Ala.) Naval Station, 1863-64
Richmond Naval Station, 1861-63
  (6 wrappers)
Savannah Naval Station, 1862-63
Selma Naval Gun Foundry, 1863-64
Shreveport Naval Station, 1863-64
Wilmington (N. C.) Naval Station, 1862-64
Yazoo City Naval Station, 1862

CERTIFICATIONS OF NAVAL ACCOUNTS BY THE FIRST AUDITOR OF THE CONFEDERATE STATES TREASURY DEPARTMENT. May 1861 - Dec. 1864. 1 vol. 3/4 in. Arranged chronologically. Indexed.   423

LOGS OF CONFEDERATE PRIVATEERS. June-Nov. 1861. 5 vols. 5 in.   424
  (1) Log kept by R. F. Stuart on the Jeff Davis, cruising off the Carolinas, June-Aug. 1861. (2) Steam log of the North Carolina Steamer Beaufort, commanded by Lt. Robert C. Duvall, cruising in and near Chesapeake Bay, July-Aug. 1861. (3) Log of the Gordon (T. J. Lockwood, Master), on a cruise from Charleston to Hatteras Inlet, July-Aug. 1861. (4) Log of the Dixie (Francis J. Moore, Master), on a cruise beginning and ending at Charleston, July-Aug. 1861. (5) Log of the Sallie (A. S. Lebby, Master), cruising off the east coast of Florida, Oct.-Nov. 1861.

MUSTER ROLLS AND PAY ROLLS OF CONFEDERATE STATES NAVAL STATIONS.
June 1861 - Sept. 1864. 7 vols. 1 ft. 9 in. Each volume ar-
ranged chronologically.   **425**
A volume each for Charleston Station and Fleet, Nov. 1862 - Sept. 1864;
Mobile and Jackson Stations, Mar. 1862 - Sept. 1864; New Orleans Station
and Fleet, June 1861 - Sept. 1863; North Carolina Station, Dec. 1861 -
Dec. 1862; Richmond Station and James River Squadron, Nov. 1861 - Mar.
1864; Savannah Station and Fleet, Dec. 1861 - June 1864; and Wilmington
Station, Marine Corps, and miscellaneous, Dec. 1861 - June 1864.

MUSTER ROLLS AND PAY ROLLS OF MARINE DETACHMENTS OF THE CONFEDERATE
STATES NAVY. July 1861 - Dec. 1864. Sheets and booklets in 9
labeled wrappers. 2½ in.   **426**
One wrapper each for marines at Mobile, Aug.-Dec. 1862; Company B,
Dec. 1862 - Dec. 1864; Company C, Dec. 1861 - Dec. 1864; marines transferred from the Army to the Marine Corps at Drewry's Bluff, Va., May-
June 1863; marines in the Georgia and South Carolina Station, Dec. 1861 -
Mar. 1862; marines in and near Richmond, Dec. 1862 - Dec. 1864; marines
at Savannah, July 1863 - Oct. 1864; marines at Wilmington Station, June
1864; and marines who served under Capt. George Holmes at different
places, July 1861 - Dec. 1864. Muster and pay rolls usually occupy the
left and the right side of the same printed form. The records include
many receipt rolls for issues of clothing to noncommissioned officers,
artificers, musicians, and privates.

REGISTER OF PAYMENTS MADE TO OFFICERS AND ENLISTED MEN OF THE CONFEDERATE
STATES NAVY. Aug. 1861 - Oct. 1864. 1 vol. 1¼ in. Arranged
alphabetically.   **427**
Gives name of recipient, rank, by whom registered, name of vessel,
date of first payment, number of months for which paid, person designated
to receive payment, where payable, monthly sum allotted, and remarks.
This register probably applies only to payments made at a particular unnamed station.

LOGS AND JOURNALS OF VESSELS OF THE CONFEDERATE STATES NAVY. Aug. 1861 -
Apr. 1865. 8 vols. 7 in.   **428**
(1) Log of the Ellis, commanded by Comdr. William T. Muse, Aug. 1861 -
Feb. 1862. This volume was captured Feb. 10, 1862. (2) Abstract, by Mdn.
George D. Bryan, of the log of the Florida, commanded by Comdr. John
Newland Maffitt, cruising in and near the Bahama Islands, Aug. 1862 -
May 1863. (3) Journal of J. T. Gordon on the Cornubia, cruising off
Wilmington, Sept.-Nov. 1863. In pencil. (4) Log of the Florida, commanded
by Lt. Charles Manigault Morris, on a cruise from Brest to Bermuda, Jan.-
Sept. 1864. (5) Log of the Ram Tennessee, commanded by Comdr. James D.
Johnstone, on a voyage from Mobile to Spanish River and Fort Morgan, Feb.-
July 1864. (6) Journal kept by Mdn. Clarence Cary on the Chickamauga,
serving as a blockade-runner, Sept. 1864 - Mar. 1865. (7) Abstract of the
log of Battery Brooke, on James River, commanded by Lts. John H. Ingraham
and Charles Borum, Oct. 1864 - Apr. 1865 (2 vols., original and typed copy;
original sent by Act'g Volunteer Lt. Henry H. Gorringe, commanding the USS
Monticello, to R. A. David D. Porter, commanding the North Atlantic Blockading Squadron, Apr. 4, 1865).

REGISTER OF MONEY, CLOTHING, AND SMALL STORES ISSUED BY THE PAYMASTER
OF THE CONFEDERATE STATES NAVY ("Confederate Paymaster's Accounts"). Nov. 1861 - Feb. 1862. 2 vols. 2½ in. Arranged by
issuance number.   429

LETTERS SENT BY COMDR. JOSEPH NICHOLSON BARNEY, CSN. Dec. 1861 - Apr.
1863. 1 vol. 3/4 in. Handwritten copies. Indexed.   430
   The writer commanded the Jamestown in Chesapeake Bay and the Harriet
Lane off Galveston Bay.

REGISTER OF LETTERS RECEIVED BY AN UNNAMED FINANCIAL OFFICER OF THE CON-
FEDERATE STATES NAVY. Feb. 1862 - July 1864. 1 vol. 3/4 in.
Arranged chronologically.   431

REGISTER OF REQUISITIONS OF AN UNNAMED OFFICE OF THE CONFEDERATE STATES
NAVY DEPARTMENT ("Requisition Book"). Mar. 1862 - Mar. 1865.
1 vol. 3/4 in. Arranged chronologically. Indexed.   432

RECORDS OF THE CONFEDERATE STATES NAVAL GUN FOUNDRY AT SELMA, ALA.
June 1862 - Mar. 1865. 7 vols. 1 ft.   433
   (1) Letters sent by C. J. McRae, Agent, June-Aug. 1862, and cost records of work and materials, July 1863 - Dec. 1864 (handwritten copies,
1 vol.). (2) Letters sent by Comdr. Catesby ap R. Jones, Commandant, and
by others connected with the Naval Gun Foundry, Dec. 1862 - Mar. 1864
(press copies, indexed, 4 vols.). (3) Detailed record of guns manufac-
tured, with a full description of each gun, July 1863 - Jan. 1865 (2 vols.).

LETTERS SENT BY THE PAYMASTER OF THE CONFEDERATE STATES NAVY AT MOBILE.
June 1862 - Oct. 1864. 2 vols. 3½ in. Press copies. Arranged
chronologically. First volume indexed.   434
   Sent by Thomas R. Ware.

LEDGER AND CASHBOOK OF THE PAYMASTER AT MOBILE ("Cash"). July 1862 -
Feb. 1865. 1 vol. 2 in. Arranged chronologically.   435
   The earlier part of the volume is apparently designed as a ledger.
The latter part consists chiefly of lists of names of persons receiving
payment.

LIST OF NEGROES RECEIVED BY THE CONFEDERATE STATES ENGINEER OFFICE,
CHARLESTON ("Georgetown Harbor"). Aug. 1862 - Sept. 1863. 1 vol.
1¼ in. Arranged chronologically.   436
   Gives date when Negro was received, owner's name, and first name only
of Negro. The Negroes were employed on fortifications.

REGISTER OF PAYMENTS MADE AT THE CONFEDERATE STATES NAVAL STATION,
SAVANNAH. Nov. 1862 - Mar. 1863. 1 vol. 1 3/4 in. Arranged
chronologically. Indexed.   437
   Chiefly names of officers and enlisted men, with sums paid to each.

INVOICES OF PROVISIONS, CLOTHING, SMALL STORES, AND CONTINGENT EXPENDI-
TURES ISSUED BY THE NAVAL STOREKEEPER AT SAVANNAH. Nov. 1862 -
Dec. 1864. 2 vols. 1 in. Arranged by ships, thereunder chronolog-
ically.   438

Issued by James E. Godfrey to the _Georgia,_ Nov. 1862 - Dec. 1864; the _Savannah,_ Nov. 1862 - June 1863; and the _Isondiga,_ Dec. 1862 - Oct. 1864.

LETTERS SENT BY LT. JONATHAN H. CARTER, CSN. Feb. 1863 - Apr. 1865, July-Nov. 1867. 1 vol. 3/4 in. Handwritten copies. Arranged chronologically. Indexed.   439
The writer commanded the CSS _Missouri,_ stationed at Shreveport and on the Red River, and had charge of the naval defenses of western Louisiana. The letters of 1867 are private. Notes and accounts are in the back of the volume.

LETTERS RECEIVED BY THE CONFEDERATE STATES DEPOSITORY AT KNOXVILLE, TENN. ("Letter Book B"). Apr. 1863 - Aug. 1864. 1 vol. 1 in. Arranged chronologically.   440
A printed summary of the Census of 1840, from which the earlier leaves have been cut about an inch from the binding, leaving stubs to which the letters received are glued.

DIARY KEPT BY R. A. RAPHAEL SEMMES, CSN, IN THE OLD CAPITAL PRISON, WASHINGTON. Dec. 1865 - Mar. 1866. 1 vol. $\frac{1}{4}$ in. Typed copy.   441

D. Records of Foreign States and of Their Citizens, 1691-1908

ROUGH DRAFT OF A BIOGRAPHY OF ADMIRAL SIR GEORGE BYNG, FIRST VISCOUNT TORRINGTON ("Materials Collected for Lord Torrington's Memoirs"). Jan. 1691 - Dec. 1702. 1 vol. 3/4 in.   442
This volume, of unknown authorship, is apparently a fragment of a more extensive narrative. It may be related to British Museum Additional MS 31958. Corrections and interlineations indicate that it is not a smooth copy.

COLLECTION OF AUTOGRAPHS, LETTERS, AND MISCELLANY PERTAINING TO THE BRITISH NAVY. Oct. 1719 - Aug. 1849. 1 vol. $4\frac{1}{2}$ in. Arranged chronologically. Indexed.   443
Chiefly requisitions and other routine documents signed by personnel of the British Navy and Admiralty, and mounted on large sheets.

LOGS AND JOURNALS OF BRITISH VESSELS. May 1775 - Mar. 1899. 25 vols., and loose papers in 1 box. 1 ft. 7 in.   444
(1) Excerpts of logs of His Majesty's Ships _Fowey,_ May 1775 - Jan. 1777; _Liverpool,_ July 1775 - Feb. 1777; _Roebuck,_ Jan.-Mar. 1776; _Kingfisher,_ Feb. 1776 - Feb. 1777; and _Orpheus,_ May-Aug. 1776 (photostat). Folded or flat papers. Originals in Public Record Office. (2) _Seven Log-Books Concerning the Arctic Voyages of Captain William Scoresby, Senior, of Whitby, England, Issued in Fac-Simile by the Explorers Club of New York_ (New York, 8 vols., 1916-17), edited by Frederick S. Dellenbaugh. The first volume is introductory; the others reproduce 7 logs of 14 voyages made to the vicinity of Spitzbergen and Greenland by Capt. William Scoresby, Sr., Apr. 1786 - Sept. 1822. The publication was received by the Hydrographic Office May 26, 1925, and was filed in a cardboard box labeled with the library number VK211.Sco 1786-1822. (3) Journal and log of HMS _Ceres,_ commanded by Capt. George Stevens, on a voyage from London to Madras,

Manila, and Canton and back to London, Feb. 1797 - Oct. 1798. The log proper is preceded by a narrative of the voyage, with observations on manners and customs and with illustrations in water color. At the end is a list of officers and crew. (4) Log kept by J. Baker aboard HMS Calypso, commanded by Capt. Henry Garrett, on a cruise from England to Jamaica, Sept. 1799 - Nov. 1800. At the beginning of the cruise the writer, "Josh Baker," received an unnamed commission from the Admiralty. (5) Log kept by Mdn. Thomas Henderson aboard HMS Furieuse, commanded by Capt. William Mouncey, on a cruise in the Mediterranean, Jan.-Oct. 1812 (with gaps). (6) Log kept by Thomas Cooper, mate of the British packet brig Duke of Montrose, June 10-28, 1813. This vessel was captured by the USS President June 10, 1813. (7) Log of HMS Wolfe, flagship of Sir James Yeo on Lake Ontario, June-Dec. 1813. (8) Log of HMS Magicienne, cruising between India, Madagascar, and Mauritius, Aug. 1817 - Apr. 1819. (9) Log of the British whaling vessel Surprise (Balfour Miller, Master), on a voyage from Sydney, Australia, to London, Oct. 1844 - Aug. 1846. (10) Log of the British barque Sophia, of Liverpool (James Forbes, Master), on a voyage from Liverpool to Nassau and Baltimore, June-Nov. 1862. (11) Log of the British merchant vessel Pevensey (William H. Hawks and Caleb Collins, Masters), on a voyage from London to Bermuda, Mar.-June 1864 (2 vols.). (12) Logs of the British merchant vessel Luciline on several voyages between Great Britain, France, the Black Sea, the West Indies, and the United States, Oct. 1893 - Mar. 1899 (7 vols., chiefly in pencil).

LETTERS AND DOCUMENTS FORMERLY AT ST. MARY'S ISLE, SCOTLAND, RELATING TO
    CAPT. PAUL JONES. Apr. 1778 - Apr. 1791. 1 vol. 1¼ in. Typed
    copies.   445
    Letters and reminiscences of persons concerned in a raid on St. Mary's Isle, and extracts from the logs of the Ranger and the Bonhomme Richard. Copies were transmitted by the naval attaché, London, to the Secretary of the Navy. The originals were destroyed in a fire in 1938.

SELECTED LETTERS SENT BY THE COMMISSIONERS OF THE BRITISH NAVY.
    Nov. 1784 - June 1790. 1 vol. 2 in. Handwritten copies. Ar-
    ranged chronologically.   446
    The copies appear to be in an early hand. By whom they were made, and for what purpose, cannot be determined.

LEGAL DOCUMENTS RELATING TO CAPT. JOHN PAUL JONES ("Pièces Justifica-
    tives"). Mar. 1788 - July 1789. 1 vol. 1 in. Photostat.
    Arranged by document number, 1-93.   447
    Original volume in Library of the Masonic Temple, Boston.

ORDERS AND ACCOUNTS OF CAPT. FRANK SOTHERON, RN. Mar. 1793 - Aug. 1799,
    Oct. 1806 - Jan. 1824. 3 vols. 2 in.   448
    (1) Handwritten copies of orders received and issued, entered separately in different parts of each of 2 vols., Mar. 1793 - Aug. 1799, when the writer commanded His Majesty's Ships Fury, Monarch, and Romney, with 1 letter of appointment, Aug. 1782; and (2) an account book, kept apparently after the writer's retirement to private life, Oct. 1806 - Jan. 1824.

REGISTERS OF UNITED STATES PRISONERS IN HALIFAX, BARBADOS, AND JAMAICA.
Nov. 1805 - Mar. 1815. 3 vols. 4 in. Each volume arranged by
date of arrival of prisoner.   449
(1) "Americans Imprisoned in Halifax, N. S.," Nov. 1805 - Sept. 1814;
(2) "Americans Imprisoned in Barbados, W. I.," Aug. 1812 - Mar. 1815; and
(3) "Americans Imprisoned in Jamaica, W. I.," Aug. 1812 - Mar. 1815. All
three volumes consist of entries made by British jailers on a printed
form labeled "General Entry Book of Americans Prisoners of War," giving
name of prisoner, date and place of capture, ship on which captured, ship
by which captured, rank or rate of prisoner, and date and conditions of
beginning and end of imprisonment. How the Navy Department acquired these
originals is not clear.

NAVAL MANUSCRIPTS COPIED FOR CAPT. ALFRED T. MAHAN. Dec. 1807 - 1815.
5 vols. 7 in. No arrangement apparent. Tables of contents.   450
"Miscellaneous Naval MSS," Dec. 1807 - June 1814, probably copied in
the Canadian Archives (1 vol.); and "British Naval MSS, War of 1812,"
probably copied in the Public Record Office, containing data concerning
courts martial of officers and crew of the Macedonian, the Guerrière, and
vessels on Lakes Erie and Champlain and concerning the expedition against
New Orleans and various other matters. The sources and nature of the documents are not clearly indicated, and their contents could be described only
by a calendar.

NOTEBOOK OF HEINRICH CHRISTIAN SCHUMACHER, MATHEMATICIAN AND ASTRONOMER
("Excerpta"). 1809 et seqq. 1 vol. 1 in.   451
On the flyleaf is written "Göttingen, 1809." The volume consists of
quotations and summaries of Professor Schumacher's reading on biographical,
mathematical, and astronomical subjects. He gave it to his student Sonntag,
who later came to the United States, accompanied Dr. Elisha Kent Kane as
astronomer in the Arctic Expedition of 1853-55, and entered on page 64 of
the volume the highest and lowest temperatures and barometric readings for
each month in the Arctic quarters of the party, June 1853 - April 1855.

REGISTER OF UNITED STATES PRISONERS OF WAR AT QUEBEC ("General Entry
Book of American Prisoners of War at Quebec"). June 1813 - Mar.
1815. 1 vol. 2 in. Typed copy. Arranged by date of arrival of
prisoner.   452
Original in Canadian Archives; copy presented to the Navy Department
by the National Society of United States Daughters of 1812. Gives
prisoner's number, by what ship or how taken, when and where taken, vessel on which taken, type of vessel (man of war, privateer, merchant vessel), prisoner's name, "quality" of prisoner, when received into custody,
from what ship or whence received, place of birth, age, stature, person
(stout, middle, thin), visage and complexion, hair, eyes, marks or wounds,
supplies of bedding and clothing furnished, cause of leaving prison (exchange, discharge, death, escape), date of leaving prison, and, if discharged, by what order and to what place.

JOURNAL OF ASTRONOMICAL EXPERIMENTS AND OBSERVATIONS MADE BY SIR WILLIAM
BURROUGHS, JUDGE OF THE SUPREME COURT OF BENGAL. Apr.-June 1816,
Oct. 1818. 1 vol. 3/4 in.   453
Contains an amendment to La Lande's method of finding longitude at sea,
and rules for the safekeeping of chronometers on ships.

LOGS OF THE GERMAN MERCHANT VESSEL RHAETIA, OF HAMBURG, IN VOYAGES
        BETWEEN EUROPE AND AMERICA. Apr. 1883 - May 1884, May 1889 -
        May 1898. 21 vols. 1 ft. 4 in. Arranged chronologically.   454
    (1) Engine log ("Maschinen-Journal") of a voyage from Hamburg to New
York and back to Hamburg, Apr. 1883 - May 1884 (1 vol.); and (2) navigation logs of various voyages, May 1889 - May 1898 (20 vols.). The Rhaetia
was taken over by the United States in 1917 and renamed the Black Arrow.

COMBINED CREW LISTS AND CRUISING REPORTS OF SPANISH VESSELS. 1887-98.
        10 vols. 8 in.   455
    One volume each for the ships Ventura (1887-98), Paz (1891-98),
Isabel (1892-98), Dichosa (1894-98), Guadalupe (1894-98), Julia (1896-98),
Paquete de Arecibo (1896-98), Joven Clara (1897-98), Beatriz (1897-98),
and Aquidillana (1897-98). Each volume is a printed form in two parts.
The first part is ruled for entries giving an enlisted man's name, date of
enlistment, place of birth, age, physical description (usually left blank),
nature of services, and date of landing after each cruise. The second part
is ruled for entries giving dates of arrival and departure of the vessel at
each port that it entered. The record was carried with the ship; the entries were made by port officials. All the ships were in the West Indies
in 1898.

ACTS, DECISIONS, ORDERS, AND CIRCULAR LETTERS OF THE AUGUSTINIAN PROVINCE
        OF SAN NICOLÁS DE TOLENTINO, PHILLIPINE ISLANDS ("Libra de Actas y
        Determinaciones de la Provincia de Sn. Nicolás de Tolentino de P. P.
        Recoletos del G[ran] P. Sn. Agustín, Convento Misión de Ynaganan").
        Aug. 1887 - May 1897. 1 vol. 1 in. Handwritten copies.   456
    The preface, Nov. 15, 1887, refers to an "Ynventario" of the Convent
of Ynaganan as complementary to this volume. Entries were apparently made
in the volume during a period of 10 years, not copied at a later time.

LOG OF THE SPANISH CRUISER CRISTÓBAL COLÓN, ON A VOYAGE FROM GENOA TO
        SANTIAGO DE CUBA ("Cuaderno de Bitácora"). June 1897 - July 1898.
        2 vols. 3 in. Arranged chronologically.   457
    The Cristóbal Colón was destroyed in the Battle of Santiago.

LOG OF THE SPANISH TRANSPORT MANILA, CRUISING NEAR CAVITE. July 1897 -
        Apr. 1898. 1 vol. 1½ in. Arranged chronologically.   458
    The Manila was captured at Cavite May 4, 1898.

PROCEEDINGS, ACTS, OFFICIAL LETTERS, AND CIRCULARS OF THE PROVISIONAL
        GOVERNMENT AT PUERTO PRINCESA, PHILIPPINE ISLANDS. Dec. 1898 -
        Mar. 1901. 2 vols. 3 in. Arranged chronologically.   459
    (1) Copies of proceedings, Dec. 9, 1898 - Oct. 1, 1900 (1 vol.); and
(2) copies of acts, official letters, and circulars, May 2, 1899 - Mar. 8,
1901 (1 vol.).

CASHBOOK OF AN UNNAMED PROVINCE OF THE PHILIPPINE ISLANDS ("Libro de Caja,
        Gobierno Provincial"). July 1899 - Apr. 1901. 1 vol. 1 in.   460

FISCAL RECORDS OF THE PROVINCE OF PARAGUA, PHILLIPINE ISLANDS. Aug. 1899 -
        Apr. 1901. 4 vols. 3 in.   461
    (1) Register of payments of tax moneys made by the Treasury, Aug. 1899 -
Apr. 1901; (2) register of tax moneys received by the Treasury, same dates;

(3) general census of citizens who had made extraordinary contributions
to expenses of war, 1901; and (4) list of residents whose industrial tax
had been paid, ca. 1901.

LOG OF THE GERMAN MERCHANT VESSEL NICARIA, OF HAMBURG, ON A VOYAGE FROM
    HAMBURG TO VARIOUS PORTS IN AMERICA. May 24, 1907 - Jan. 19, 1908.
    1 vol. 3/4 in. Arranged chronologically.   462
    The Nicaria was later taken over by the United States and renamed the
Pensacola.

VII. LOOSE PAPERS ASSEMBLED FROM BOTH OFFICIAL AND PRIVATE SOURCES AND COMBINED TO FORM NEW SERIES, 1648-1910

        The chief sources of these records are loose papers removed from files
of the Office of the Secretary of the Navy, the Office of Detail, and the
Bureau of Navigation; loose papers received from private donors, chiefly
naval officers and their heirs; and papers obtained by dismantling various
dilapidated or poorly assembled volumes and binders. These materials were
augmented with photographs, drawings, maps, broadsides, clippings, pamphlets,
and occasional cross-reference sheets—in short, whatever might be expected
to increase the value of the collection. The arranging of the collection
was begun in January 1924. The insertion of the papers from the Office of
Detail and the Bureau of Navigation was undertaken as recently as 1942.
The arrangement and labeling of the collection has no relation to that of
either the various series of Navy Department records or the groups of
private papers from which the collection was derived. Documents of the
most diverse origin and character, connected with one another only in subject, may be found side by side. The source of a document may sometimes be
determined by an original stamp or file number affixed to it; and registers
and indexes of Navy Department records may include dates and abstracts by
which it is possible to seek a particular document that has been removed
from a series. Often, however, there is no means of ascertaining the office,
bureau, or family of whose records a document was formerly a part, or of
discovering what other documents it was associated with before the file to
which it originally belonged was depleted or broken up.

AREA FILE. Aug. 1648 - Dec. 1910. Loose papers in labeled folders 9 x 15
    in., in 371 cardboard boxes. Ca. 123 ft. Arranged by regions,
    thereunder chronologically.   463
        The papers in this file relate chiefly to occurrences and conditions in
definite places for periods of not more than a few days. Most of the records are single papers of small bulk. They are filed by regions, defined
as follows in a typed manual of the Office of Naval Records and Library:

    4. Atlantic Ocean (North and South) excluding Areas 7 and 8. Eastern
        boundary south of the African Continent is Longitude 20° E; eastern
        boundary north of Siberia is Longitude 80° E. Tributary waters
        such as Amazon River, Mediterranean Sea, Black Sea, Baltic Sea, etc.,
        are included. [Aug. 1648 - Dec. 1910; 45 boxes.]
    7. North Atlantic Ocean west of Longitude 50° and north of line Cape
        Lookout - Bermuda - Latitude 32° N; and tributary waters. [Mar.
        1709 - Sept. 1908; 118 boxes.]

M625

94

8. North Atlantic Ocean west of Longitude 50° and south of Area 7; with
   tributary waters. [Dec. 1775 - Dec. 1910; 79 boxes.] For the period of the Civil War the two areas hereafter listed were separated
   from Area 8.

5. The Mississippi River and all its tributaries. [Jan. 1861 - Dec.
   1865; 7 boxes.]

6. The Gulf of Mexico, limited on the southeast by a line from Key West
   due south to Cuba and a line from the northeast extremity of
   Yucatán Peninsula to Cape San Antonio, Cuba. Key West itself is in
   Area 6. [Jan. 1861 - Aug. 1864; 5 boxes.]

9. The Pacific Ocean east of Longitude 180° with tributary waters. Also
   Arctic Ocean, tributary to Bering Strait. [Apr. 1814 - Dec. 1910;
   50 boxes.]

10. Pacific Ocean west of Longitude 180° and the Indian Ocean east of
    Longitude 20° E; with tributary waters. [Sept. 1798 - Dec. 1909;
    60 boxes.]

11. United States Navy and other Executive Departments including White
    House, or its corresponding antecedent administrative office. [Oct.
    1775 - Dec. 1909; 7 boxes.]

Areas 1-3, not distinguished in this file, were broken off from Area 4 for
purposes of classifying records of World War I.

SUBJECT FILE. Ca. 1775-1910. Loose papers in labeled envelopes 10 x 15
   in. in 814 cardboard boxes. Ca. 271 ft. Arranged by subjects,
   thereunder by divisions of subjects, thereunder by subdivisions of
   divisions.   464
   Consists chiefly of papers that are of considerable bulk or are
accompanied by several enclosures and that relate to occurrences and conditions extending over considerable areas for considerable periods of
time and to matters having little connection with a time and a place. The
subjects and divisions of subjects are listed in Appendix F. No list of
the subdivisions of divisions is available.

VIII.   INDEXES AND REGISTERS PREPARED BY THE OFFICE OF NAVAL RECORDS
        AND LIBRARY FOR RECORDS IN THE NAVAL RECORDS COLLECTION

      The ten series described below are indexes and registers prepared to
facilitate the use of records in the Naval Records Collection. Since, in
a strict sense, the Collection consists only of materials brought together
by the Office of Naval Records and Library from sources outside itself,
these indexes and registers should perhaps be regarded as external to the
Collection. They are, however, physically a part of the Collection and
have no relevance apart from it. Other records created by the Office of
Naval Records and Library are in Record Group 38, Records of the Office of
the Chief of Naval Operations.

CARD CATALOGUE OF TITLES AND DATES OF VOLUMES AND BINDERS IN THE NAVAL
   RECORDS COLLECTION. Mar. 1775 - Dec. 1910. 5 x 3 in. cards.
   11 ft. 8 in.   465
   (1) "Chronological Arrangement," including a card for each bound

volume, the cards being arranged in strictly chronological order; and
(2) "Subject Arrangement," including carbon copies of the same cards,
arranged according to the several recognized series under Class 1 (logs
and journals; watch, station, and quarter bills), Class 2 (indexes and
keys; matériel; miscellaneous; personnel; signals; uniforms), and Class
3 (operations). A card gives only the backstrip title of a volume, its
date (in years only, in months and years, or in days, months, and years),
and occasionally the office, bureau, or private donor from whom it was
received, the date of its accession, and whether it has been microfilmed.

INDEX TO THE AREA FILE. Ca. 1775 – ca. 1815. 5 x 3 in. cards. 4 ft.
    10 in. Arranged alphabetically, chiefly by names of persons and
    ships.   **466**
    The index includes all records in the Area File (Entry 463) before the
War of 1812, all records relating to that war, and a few cards for records
in the Subject File, the last chiefly as cross references.

LIST OF AMERICAN VESSELS CAPTURED DURING THE AMERICAN REVOLUTION. 1775-85.
    5 x 3 in. cards. 7 in. Arranged alphabetically by names of cap-
    tured vessels.   **467**
    Penciled entries from both printed and manuscript sources, giving name
of ship, description, date of capture, by what vessel captured, and place
of capture.

REGISTERS OF VESSELS OF THE UNITED STATES AND CONFEDERATE STATES NAVIES
    DURING THE CIVIL WAR. 1861-65. 3 vols. 7½ in. Register of United
    States vessels (2 vols., "Ships of the Navy, Civil War") arranged
    alphabetically by names of vessels; register of Confederate States
    vessels ("Confederate Vessels") arranged chronologically. Latter
    register indexed.   **468**
    Gives name of vessel, class, rate, construction, propulsion, length,
beam, depth, tons, rig, acquisition, disposition, builder and cost of hull,
builder and cost of engines, total cost, coal consumed per hour, speed,
draft, engines, boilers, battery, remarks, and source of each item of information (designated by a code number). The information in the Confederate volume is far less complete, from lack of data, than that in the
United States volumes.

INDEX TO GENERAL COURTS MARTIAL. 1861-67. 5 x 3 in. cards. 1 ft. 2 in.
    Arranged alphabetically. Index to court-martial records of date
    subsequent to those indexed in the series described in Entry 295.   **469**

INDEX TO PRIZES ("Prizes"). 1861-68. 1 vol. 2½ in. Arranged alphabeti-
    cally by names of prizes.   **470**
    Undertaken as a systematic compilation of information concerning
prize vessels, but left unfinished, the names of most of the prizes being
followed by blanks.

REGISTER OF RECORDS RELATING TO THE CIVIL WAR. Jan. 1861 – Dec. 1865.
    15 vols. 8¼ in.   **471**
    (1) "Index to Naval War Records," printed, with manuscript notations,
12 copies, listing records relating to the Civil War transferred to the

Naval War Records Office from the Office of the Secretary of the Navy;
and (2) "Index to Miscellaneous Files, Naval War Records," manuscript,
3 copies, listing Civil War papers received from naval officers or their
heirs. Both contain notations as to what records were printed in Official Records of the Union and Confederate Navies in the War of the Rebellion, with remarks on verification of copied passages, parts of records
copied, and suitability of records for copying, and with initials of
various clerks engaged in compiling the Official Records. Though undated,
the registers were begun as early as ca. 1885 and were maintained as late
as 1908.

REGISTER OF OFFICERS' PRIVATE PAPERS RECEIVED IN THE OFFICE OF NAVAL WAR
  RECORDS. Apr. 1883 - Apr. 1890. 1 vol. 3/4 in. Arranged
  alphabetically by officers' names.   472
 Gives name and rank of officer whose papers were received, date of
receipt, by whom delivered or file number of covering letter, date of
return and file number of covering letter (if papers were not retained),
and page in "index book" in which letter is entered. Most of the papers
were received in 1889.

REGISTER OF LETTERS RECEIVED BY THE NAVAL WAR RECORDS OFFICE IN REPLY TO
  A CIRCULAR OF DECEMBER 1, 1904, REQUESTING GIFTS OR LOANS OF
  PRIVATE PAPERS OF NAVAL OFFICERS. 1 vol. 1 in. Arranged alphabeti-
  cally by officers' names.   473
 Contains lists of the records received.

REGISTER OF NAVAL RECORDS PRESENTED TO THE LIBRARY AND NAVAL WAR RECORDS
  OFFICE. 1907-13. 1 vol. 1 in. Arranged chronologically. 474

APPENDIXES

APPENDIX A

LIST OF SUBSERIES OF "LETTERS FROM OFFICERS COMMANDING EXPEDITIONS"
(Entry 25)

(1) Correspondence Relating to Cruises of the Cyane, the Franklin,
the Ontario, the Peacock, and the United States, January 1818 - May 1827.
1 vol. 3 3/4 in. (a) Copy of a letter from Capt. Jesse D. Elliott, commanding the Cyane, to the Military Chief of Buenos Aires concerning exchange of salutes, April 5, 1826. (b) Correspondence (both copies and
originals) between Commo. Charles Stewart, commanding the Franklin, J. B.
Prevost and Jeremy Robinson, agents of the Department of State, and John
Quincy Adams, Secretary of State, concerning affairs in Chile and Peru,
October 1821 - May 1824. (c) Copies of correspondence between Capt. James
Biddle, commanding the Ontario, and Chilean authorities, January-December
1818. (d) Report from Capt. Thomas ap Catesby Jones, commanding the Pea-
cock, May 14, 1827, with enclosures dated May 1826 - May 1827, relating to
commercial agreements between the rulers of the Sandwich Islands and of
Tahiti and himself as representing the United States. (e) Copies of correspondence between Commo. Isaac Hull, commanding the United States, and
Peruvian authorities, April-September 1825. Some of the materials in this
"Five Cruises Volume" would normally have been bound in "Captain's Letters";
others are records that would normally have been retained by the Department
of State but were perhaps lent to the Navy Department and not returned.

(2) Letters from Comdr. William B. Finch, Commanding the Vincennes on
a Voyage to Tahiti, Honolulu, Canton, and Manila, July 1829 - April 1830.
1 vol. 2½ in. Table of contents. The purpose of the voyage was to make
commercial agreements with rulers of Pacific islands. The first document
in the volume is a copy, in the handwriting of Commander Finch, of an agree-
ment between Capt. Thomas ap Catesby Jones, commanding the Peacock, and
Pomene, King of Otaheite (Tahiti), September 1826.

(3) Letters Received Relating to Preparations for the Pacific Exploring Expedition, May 1836 - August 1838 ("Exploring Expedition Letters").
4 vols. 9 in. Letters from Capt. Thomas ap Catesby Jones, appointed to
command the expedition; from Lt. Charles Wilkes, appointed to the command
after the resignation of Captain Jones; from applicants for employment in
the expedition; from employees discharged before it sailed; and from other
interested persons.

(4) Letters Received Relating to the Pacific Exploring Expedition
under the Command of Lt. Charles Wilkes (Flagship Vincennes), November
1837 - July 1842 ("Wilkes Exploring Expedition"). 2 vols. 8 in. Chiefly
reports from Lieutenant Wilkes, with a few letters from other members of
the expedition and from persons who were not members.

(5) Letters and Report from Lt. William F. Lynch, Commanding an Expedition to the Dead Sea (Flagship Supply), December 1847 - February 1849
("Exped'n to the Dead Sea"). 1 vol. 3/4 in. The final reports summariz-
ing the expedition are dated February 3 and 28, 1849.

98

(6) Letters from Capt. Hiram Paulding, Commanding the St. Lawrence on a Cruise from Hampton Roads to Bremen, Naples, and Intervening Ports, September 1848 – November 1850 ("Cruise of the St. Law."). 1 vol. 3/4 in. Indexed. Captain Paulding was charged with a mission to various European capitals.

(7) Letters from Comdrs. Cadwalader Ringgold and John Rodgers (Flagship Vincennes), Commanding the North Pacific Exploring Expedition, October 1852 – July 1856. 5 vols. 11 in. (a) "Surveying Expedition, Bering Strait, North Pacific and China Seas, Commo. Cadwallader Ringgold" (letters from Ringgold, October 1852 – January 1855); (b) letters from Rodgers, succeeding Ringgold in command (2 vols., indexed, August 1854 – July 1856); (c) "Report of Com. C. Ringgold, Movements & Operations of Surveying Exp. under His Com. & Circumstances Attendant upon His Removal by Commodore Perry" (reports dated February 25 and April 6, 1855); and (d) "Addendum" to the preceding (December 21, 1855).

(8) Letters from Lt. Thomas J. Page (Flagship Water Witch), Commanding an Expedition to Survey the Rio de la Plata and the Rio Paraguay, January 1853 – August 1856. 1 vol. 2 3/4 in.

(9) Papers Relating to the Exploration of the Coast of Darien (handwritten copies), April 1854 – August 1858 ("Exploration of Coast of Darien, U. S. S. Preble, T. A. Jenkins, Com'dr"). 1 vol. 3/4 in. Table of contents. Consists of a letter from Ass't Surgeon Henry C. Caldwell to the Secretary of the Navy, May 8, 1857; a report of an exploration under Comdr. J. C. Prevost of HMS Virago, April 24, 1854; and letters from Lt. Tunis Augustus M. Craven, May 17 and August 14, 1858. The backstrip title is misleading, and the origin of the volume is not clear.

(10) Letters from Comdr. Daniel L. Braine, Commanding the Juniata on a Mission to Santiago de Cuba to Investigate the Seizure of the American Merchant Vessel Virginius (Joseph Fry, Master) and the Imprisonment and Mistreatment of Her Officers and Crew, November–December 1873. 1 vol. 1½ in. The Virginius had been seized on the high seas by the Spanish war steamer Tornado, on suspicion that she was carrying arms and ammunition to insurgents in Cuba.

(11) Letters from Commo. Robert W. Shufeldt, Commanding the Flagship Ticonderoga on a Cruise along the Coasts of Africa and Asia and through the Indian Ocean, October 1878 – November 1880. 2 vols. 5½ in. Commodore Shufeldt was under instructions to visit ports of Africa, Asia, and Oceania where no representatives of the United States Government were stationed, and to take measures to promote commercial relations.

(12) Letters and Telegrams Received concerning the Loss of the Jeannette and the Rodgers in the Arctic Expedition under the Command of Lt. Comdr. George W. De Long, July 1881 – Dec. 1883. 1 vol. 2½ in. Table of contents. Among the papers bound in this volume are "bottle papers" committed to the sea by survivors of the wreck of the 2 vessels, and papers left in cairns.

(13) Correspondence of the Secretary of the Navy Relating to Disorders in Panama, February–June 1885. 1 vol. 4 in. Chiefly letters from Comdr. Bowman H. McCalla, commanding the United States Naval Force on the Isthmus of Panama, ending with his report dated June 8, 1885. Also bound in the volume are copies of letters sent by the Secretary, and letters received by him from the Secretary of State and others.

(14) Letters from Comdr. Purnell F. Harrington, Commanding the Juniata, Relating to an Investigation of Difficulties between the Sultan of the Island of Johanna and Dr. B. F. Wilson, an American Citizen, September–December 1885. 1 vol. $3\frac{1}{4}$ in.

APPENDIX B

LIST OF VOLUMES OF THE "SQUADRON LETTERS"
(Entry 30)

Vol.	Dates	Commanding Officers	Flagships

(1) EAST INDIA SQUADRON

[1]	Feb41-Jan44	Commo. Lawrence Kearny	Constellation
[2]	Feb43-Sept45	Commo. Foxhall A. Parker	Brandywine
[3]	Aug45-May47	Commo. James Biddle	Columbus
[4]	Feb48-June50	Commo. David Geisinger	Plymouth
[5]	Mar49-Feb51	Commo. Philip F. Voorhees	Plymouth
[6]	May51-Mar53	Commo. John H. Aulick	Susquehanna
[7]	Dec52-Dec53	Commo. Matthew C. Perry	Susquehanna
[8]	Jan54-May55	Commo. Matthew C. Perry	Susquehanna, Mississippi
[9]	Sept54-Aug56	Commo. Joel Abbot	Macedonian
		Commo. John Pope	Macedonian
[10]	Sept55-Dec56	Commo. James Armstrong	San Jacinto
[11]	Jan57-Jan58	Flag Off. James Armstrong	San Jacinto
[12]	Feb58-Dec59	Flag Off. Josiah Tattnall	San Jacinto, Powhatan
[13]	May59-Dec61	Flag Off. Cornelius K. Stribling	Hartford
		Flag Off. Frederick Engle	Hartford

(2) PACIFIC SQUADRON

[1]	Dec41-Feb45	Commo. Thomas ap Catesby Jones	United States
		Commo. Alexander J. Dallas	Savannah
		Capt. James Armstrong	Savannah
[2]	Oct44-Oct46	Commo. John D. Sloat	Levant
[3]	June46-Feb47	Commo. Robert F. Stockton	Congress
[4]	Nov47-July50	Commo. Thomas ap Catesby Jones	Ohio, Savannah
[5]	July50-Jan53	Commo. Charles S. McCauley	Savannah, Raritan
[6]	Nov52-Apr55	Commo. Bladen Dulany	St. Lawrence
[7]	Sept54-June56	Commo. William Mervine	Independence
[8]	July56-Nov57	Commo. William Mervine	Independence
[9]	Sept57-Aug59	Flag Off. John C. Long	Merrimack
[10]	May59-Oct60	Flag Off. John B. Montgomery	Lancaster
[11]	Nov60-Dec61	Flag Off. John B. Montgomery	Lancaster
[12]	Dec61-Oct64	Act'g R. A. Charles H. Bell	Lancaster
[13]	Oct64-Dec65	Act'g R. A. George F. Pearson	Lancaster

(During most of the period covered by Volumes [14]-[38], the Pacific Squadron was divided into a North Pacific Squadron and a South Pacific Squadron. In the listing of these volumes an effort is made to distribute them in sequences on this basis. "P" designates the Pacific Squadron, "N" the North Pacific Squadron, and "S" the South Pacific Squadron.)

Vol.	Dates	Commanding Officers	Flagships
[14]	Jan66-Dec66	Act'g R. A. George F. Pearson (P Jan-June66; S June-Dec66)	Lancaster, Powhatan
[15]	Dec66-Dec67	R. A. John A. Dahlgren (S)	Powhatan
[16]	Jan68-Dec68	R. A. John A. Dahlgren (S)	Powhatan
		R. A. Thomas Turner (S)	Powhatan
[17]	July68-May69	R. A. Thomas Turner (S)	Powhatan
[18]	June69-Dec69	R. A. Thomas Turner (P)	Pensacola, Mohican
[19]	Jan70-Sept70	R. A. Thomas Turner (P)	Mohican, Saranac
[20]	Aug70-Feb72	Commo. David McDougal (S)	Ossipee
[21]	May66-Dec66	R. A. Henry K. Thatcher (N)	Vanderbilt
[22]	Jan67-Dec68	R. A. Henry K. Thatcher (N)	Vanderbilt, Saranac, Pensacola
[23]	Aug68-June69	R. A. Thomas T. Craven (N)	Ossipee, Independence
[24]	July69-Oct70	Commo. William Rogers Taylor (N)	Ossipee
[25]	July70-Jan71	R. A. John A. Winslow (P)	Ossipee, Saranac, Pensacola
[26]	Feb71-July72	R. A. John A. Winslow (P)	Pensacola, Saranac, California
[27]	May71-Oct72	Commo. Roger N. Stembel (N Mar71-Mar72; S May72-Aug72; P Aug72-Oct72)	Pensacola
[28]	Sept72-Nov73	R. A. Charles Steedman (S)	Pensacola
		R. A. John J. Almy (S)	Pensacola
[29]	Jan74-Nov74	R. A. John J. Almy (S)	Pensacola, Omaha
		R. A. Napoleon Collins (S)	Richmond
[30]	Jan75-Dec75	R. A. Napoleon Collins (S)	Richmond
		Capt. Edward Simpson (S)	Omaha
		R. A. Reed Werden (S)	Richmond
[31]	Jan76-Nov76	R. A. Reed Werden (S)	Richmond
		Capt. Edward Simpson (S)	Omaha
		Commo. C. H. B. Caldwell (S)	Richmond
[32]	Feb77-Dec77	R. A. George Henry Preble (S)	Omaha
[33]	Sept72-Nov73	R. A. Alexander M. Pennock (N)	California, Saranac
[34]	Jan74-Dec74	R. A. Alexander M. Pennock (N)	Saranac
		R. A. John J. Almy (N)	Saranac, Pensacola
[35]	Jan75-Dec75	R. A. John J. Almy (N)	Pensacola
[36]	Jan76-Dec76	R. A. John J. Almy (N)	Pensacola
		R. A. Alexander Murray (N)	Pensacola
[37]	Jan77-Dec77	R. A. Alexander Murray (N)	Pensacola
[38]	Jan78-Apr78	R. A. Alexander Murray (N)	Pensacola
		R. A. George Henry Preble (S)	Omaha
[39]	July78-Dec78	R. A. C. R. Perry Rodgers	Pensacola
[40]	Jan79-Dec79	R. A. C. R. Perry Rodgers	Pensacola
[41]	Jan80-Dec80	R. A. C. R. Perry Rodgers	Pensacola
		R. A. Thomas H. Stevens	Pensacola
[42]	Jan81-Dec81	R. A. Thomas H. Stevens	Pensacola
		R. A. George B. Balch	Pensacola
[43]	Jan82-Dec82	R. A. George B. Balch	Pensacola
[44]	Jan83-Dec83	R. A. George B. Balch	Pensacola
		R. A. Aaron K. Hughes	Hartford

Vol.	Dates	Commanding Officers	Flagships
[45]	Jan84-Dec84	R. A. Aaron K. Hughes	Hartford
[46]	Jan85-Dec85	R. A. John H. Upshur	Hartford
[47]	Jan86-Nov86	R. A. John H. Upshur	Hartford
		R. A. Edward Y. McCauley	Hartford

(3) BRAZIL SQUADRON

Vol.	Dates	Commanding Officers	Flagships
[1]	Dec41-Nov42	Commo. Charles Morris	Delaware
[2]	Nov42-June43	Commo. Charles Morris	Delaware
		Capt. Edward R. Shubrick	Columbia
[3]	July43-Apr44	Commo. Daniel Turner	Columbia, Columbus, Raritan
[4]	Apr44-Apr45	Commo. Daniel Turner	Raritan
[5]	May45-Jan46	Commo. Daniel Turner	Raritan
[6]	Oct45-Oct47	Commo. Lawrence Rousseau	Columbia
[7]	June47-Aug48	Commo. George W. Storer	Brandywine
[8]	Sept48-Dec48	Commo. George W. Storer	Brandywine
[9]	Jan49-Sept49	Commo. George W. Storer	Brandywine
[10]	Oct49-Dec50	Commo. George W. Storer	Brandywine
[11]	June50-July53	Commo. Isaac McKeever	Congress
[12]	Aug53-Sept54	Capt. Samuel W. Downing	Jamestown
[13]	Sept54-Apr56	Commo. William D. Salter	Savannah
[14]	Apr56-Dec56	Commo. William D. Salter	Savannah
[15]	Oct56-May59	Commo. Samuel Mecer	Savannah
[16]	Sept58-May59	Flag Off. French Forrest	St. Lawrence
		Flag Off. William Branford Shubrick	Sabine
[17]	Apr59-Aug61	Comdr. Charles Steedman	Dolphin
		Flag Off. Joshua R. Sands	Congress

(4) MEDITERRANEAN SQUADRON

Vol.	Dates	Commanding Officers	Flagships
[1]	Jan42-Aug43	Commo. Charles W. Morgan	Brandywine, Fairfield, Columbus
[2]	Apr43-Mar44	Commo. Charles Morris	Delaware
[3]	Nov43-Nov45	Commo. Joseph Smith	Cumberland
[4]	Aug47-June49	Commo. William C. Bolton	Jamestown
		Capt. Frederick Engle	Princeton
		Capt. John Gwinn	Constitution
[5]	June49-June52	Commo. Charles W. Morgan	Independence
[6]	May52-July55	Commo. Silas H. Stringham	Cumberland
[7]	June55-Jan58	Flag Off. Samuel L. Breese	Congress
[8]	May58-July61	Flag Off. Elie A. F. La Vallette	Wabash
		Flag Off. Uriah P. Levy	Macedonian
		Flag Off. Charles H. Bell	Richmond

Vol.	Dates	Commanding Officers	Flagships

(5) HOME SQUADRON

[1]	Jan42-Dec43	Commo. Charles Stewart	Independence
[2]	Jan44-Dec45	Commo. David Conner	Potomac, Falmouth
[3]	Jan46-Apr47	Commo. David Conner	Cumberland, Raritan
[4]	Mar47-July47	Commo. Matthew C. Perry	Mississippi
[5]	July47-Dec47	Commo. Matthew C. Perry	Mississippi
[6]	Jan48-May48	Commo. Matthew C. Perry	Cumberland
[7]	June48-Nov48	Commo. Matthew C. Perry	Cumberland
[8]	Nov48-Mar49	Commo. Jesse Wilkinson	Raritan
[9]	Apr49-Jan51	Commo. Foxhall A. Parker	Raritan, Saranac
[10]	Jan51-June52	Commo. Foxhall A. Parker	Saranac
[11]	July52-Dec53	Commo. John Thomas Newton	Powhatan, Albany, Columbia
[12]	Jan54-Apr55	Commo. John Thomas Newton	Columbia
[13]	Apr55-July55	Commo. Charles S. McCauley	San Jacinto
[14]	June55-Dec56	Commo. Hiram Paulding	Potomac, Wabash
[15]	Jan57-Mar58	Flag Off. Hiram Paulding	Wabash
[16]	Mar58-Jan59	Flag Off. James Mc. McIntosh	Colorado, Roanoke
[17]	Feb59-May60	Flag Off. William J. McCluny	Roanoke
[18]	June60-Sept61	Flag Off. Joseph R. Jarvis	Savannah
		Flag Off. Garrett J. Pendergrast	Powhatan, Cumberland, Roanoke

(Letters on and after 14May1861 are from West India Squadron)

(6) AFRICAN SQUADRON

[1]	Apr43-Apr45	Commo. Matthew C. Perry	Macedonian
[2]	Jan45-Aug46	Commo. Charles William Skinner	Jamestown
[3]	May46-Feb49	Commo. George C. Read	United States

(Commodore Read was transferred in Oct47 to command the Mediterranean Squadron, and the letters in the latter part of the volume are from that Squadron. His successor in the African Squadron was Commo. William C. Bolton, whose letters to the Secretary have not been found. See Entries 395 (23) and 395 (18).)

[4]	Nov48-Sept49	Commo. Benjamin Cooper	Portsmouth
[5]	Oct49-June51	Commo. Francis H. Gregory	Portsmouth
[6]	Jan51-Mar53	Commo. Elie A. F. La Vallette	Germantown
[7]	Jan53-June55	Commo. Isaac Mayo	Constitution
[8]	Nov54-Nov58	Commo. Thomas Crabbe	Jamestown
		Commo. Thomas A. Conover	Cumberland
[9]	Jan55-June57	Commo. Thomas Crabbe	Jamestown
[10]	June57-Aug59	Flag Off. Thomas A. Conover	Cumberland
[11]	May59-Feb60	Flag Off. William Inman	Constellation
[12]	Mar60-Sept60	Flag Off. William Inman	Constellation
[13]	Oct60-Sept61	Flag Off. William Inman	Constellation

Vol.	Dates	Commanding Officers	Flagships

(7) EASTERN SQUADRON

[-]	July53-Sept53	Commo. William B. Shubrick	Princeton

(8) POTOMAC FLOTILLA

[1]	Apr61-Aug62	Comdr. John A. Dahlgren	[Washington Navy Yard]
		Comdr. Stephen C. Rowan	Pawnee
		Comdr. Thomas T. Craven	Yankee
		Lt. Robert H. Wyman	Harriet Lane
[2]	July62-Sept62	Act'g R. A. Charles Wilkes	Wachuset

(This volume includes letters from Wilkes as commanding officer of the James River Flotilla, the Potomac Flotilla, and the West India Squadron.)

[3]	Jan64-Dec64	Comdr. Foxhall A. Parker	Ella, Don
[4]	Jan65-July65	Commo. Foxhall A. Parker	Don

(9) ATLANTIC BLOCKADING SQUADRON

[-]	Apr61-Sept61	Flag Off. Silas H. Stringham	Minnesota

(10) GULF BLOCKADING SQUADRON

[1]	May61-Sept61	Flag Off. William Mervine	Mississippi, Colorado
[2]	Sept61-Dec61	Flag Off. William W. McKean	Niagara
[3]	Jan62-June62	Flag Off. William W. McKean	Niagara

(The letters in the latter part of the volume are from Flag Officer McKean as commanding officer of the East Gulf Blockading Squadron.)

(11) MISSISSIPPI SQUADRON

[1]	May61-June62	Comdr. John Rodgers	Taylor
		Commo. Andrew H. Foote	Benton
[2]	May62-Oct62	Act'g R. A. Charles H. Davis	Benton, Eastport
[3]	Oct62-Dec62	Act'g R. A. David D. Porter	Black Hawk
[4]	Jan63-Feb63	Act'g R. A. David D. Porter	Black Hawk
[5]	Mar63-Apr63	Act'g R. A. David D. Porter	Black Hawk
[6]	May63-June63	Act'g R. A. David D. Porter	Black Hawk
[7]	July63-Aug63	Act'g R. A. David D. Porter	Black Hawk
[8]	Sept63-Oct63	Act'g R. A. David D. Porter	Black Hawk
[9]	Nov63-Dec63	Act'g R. A. David D. Porter	Black Hawk
[10]	Jan64-May64	Act'g R. A. David D. Porter	Black Hawk
[11]	June64-Oct64	Act'g R. A. David D. Porter	Black Hawk
		Capt. Alexander M. Pennock	Black Hawk
[12]	Oct64-Dec64	Act'g R. A. Samuel Phillips Lee	Black Hawk
[13]	Jan64-Mar65	Act'g R. A. Samuel Phillips Lee	Black Hawk
[14]	Apr65-Aug65	Act'g R. A. Samuel Phillips Lee	Black Hawk, Tempest

Vol.	Dates	Commanding Officers	Flagships

(12) NORTH ATLANTIC BLOCKADING SQUADRON

Vol.	Dates	Commanding Officers	Flagships
[1]	Sept61-Dec61	Act'g R. A. Louis M. Goldsborough	Minnesota
[2]	Jan62-Feb62	Act'g R. A. Louis M. Goldsborough	Minnesota, Philadelphia
[3]	Mar62-Apr62	Act'g R. A. Louis M. Goldsborough	Philadelphia, Minnesota
[4]	May62-June62	Act'g R. A. Louis M. Goldsborough	Minnesota
[5]	June62-Sept62	Act'g R. A. Louis M. Goldsborough	Minnesota
[6]	July62-Sept62	Act'g R. A. Louis M. Goldsborough	Minnesota
[7]	Sept62-Oct62	Act'g R. A. Samuel Phillips Lee	Minnesota, Philadelphia
[8]	Nov62	Act'g R. A. Samuel Phillips Lee	Philadelphia
[9]	Dec62	Act'g R. A. Samuel Phillips Lee	Philadelphia
[10]	Jan63	Act'g R. A. Samuel Phillips Lee	Philadelphia, Minnesota
[11]	Feb63	Act'g R. A. Samuel Phillips Lee	Minnesota
[12]	Mar63	Act'g R. A. Samuel Phillips Lee	Minnesota
[13]	Apr63	Act'g R. A. Samuel Phillips Lee	Minnesota
[14]	May63	Act'g R. A. Samuel Phillips Lee	Minnesota
[15]	June63	Act'g R. A. Samuel Phillips Lee	Minnesota
[16]	July63	Act'g R. A. Samuel Phillips Lee	Minnesota
[17]	Aug63	Act'g R. A. Samuel Phillips Lee	Minnesota
[18]	Sept63	Act'g R. A. Samuel Phillips Lee	Minnesota
[19]	Oct63	Act'g R. A. Samuel Phillips Lee	Minnesota
[20]	Nov63	Act'g R. A. Samuel Phillips Lee	Minnesota
[21]	Dec63	Act'g R. A. Samuel Phillips Lee	Minnesota
[22]	Jan64-Mar64	Act'g R. A. Samuel Phillips Lee	Minnesota
[23]	Apr64-May64	Act'g R. A. Samuel Phillips Lee	Minnesota, Agawam
[24]	June64	Act'g R. A. Samuel Phillips Lee	Agawam
[25]	July64	Act'g R. A. Samuel Phillips Lee	Malvern
[26]	Aug64	Act'g R. A. Samuel Phillips Lee	Malvern
[27]	Sept64-Oct64	Act'g R. A. Samuel Phillips Lee	Malvern
[28]	Oct64-Nov64	Act'g R. A. David D. Porter	Malvern
[29]	Dec64	Act'g R. A. David D. Porter	Malvern
[30]	Jan64	Act'g R. A. David D. Porter	Malvern
[31]	Feb65-Apr65	Act'g R. A. David D. Porter	Malvern
[32]	Apr65-Oct65	Act'g R. A. William Radford	Malvern

(13) SOUTH ATLANTIC BLOCKADING SQUADRON

Vol.	Dates	Commanding Officers	Flagships
[1]	Sept61-Dec61	R. A. Samuel F. Du Pont	Wabash
[2]	Jan62-Mar62	R. A. Samuel F. Du Pont	Wabash
[3]	Apr62-June62	R. A. Samuel F. Du Pont	Wabash
[4]	July62-Sept62	R. A. Samuel F. Du Pont	Wabash
[5]	Oct62-Dec62	R. A. Samuel F. Du Pont	Wabash
[6]	Jan63-Mar63	R. A. Samuel F. Du Pont	Wabash
[7]	Apr63-July63	R. A. Samuel F. Du Pont	Wabash
[8]	June63-Sept63	R. A. John A. Dahlgren	Dinsmore, Philadelphia
[9]	Oct63-Nov63	R. A. John A. Dahlgren	Philadelphia
[10]	Dec63	R. A. John A. Dahlgren	Philadelphia
[11]	Jan64-Mar64	R. A. John A. Dahlgren	Philadelphia, New Ironsides
[12]	Apr64-June64	R. A. John A. Dahlgren	Philadelphia
[13]	July64-Sept64	R. A. John A. Dahlgren	Philadelphia
[14]	Oct64-Dec64	R. A. John A. Dahlgren	Philadelphia
[15]	Jan65-Feb65	R. A. John A. Dahlgren	Philadelphia
[16]	Mar65-May65	R. A. John A. Dahlgren	Philadelphia
[17]	June65-July65	R. A. John A. Dahlgren	Philadelphia
		Commo. William Reynolds	New Hampshire

Vol.	Dates	Commanding Officers	Flagships

(14) WEST GULF BLOCKADING SQUADRON AND GULF SQUADRON

[1]	Jan62-July62	R. A. David G. Farragut	Hartford
[2]	July62-Dec62	R. A. David G. Farragut	Hartford
[3]	Jan63-Apr63	R. A. David G. Farragut	Hartford
[4]	Apr63-Dec63	R. A. David G. Farragut	Hartford, Pensacola, Monongahela
[5]	Aug63-Sept63	Commo. Henry H. Bell	Pensacola
[6]	Oct63-Dec63	Commo. Henry H. Bell	Pensacola
[7]	Jan64-July64	Commo. Henry H. Bell	Pensacola
		R. A. David G. Farragut	Hartford
[8]	May64-July64	R. A. David G. Farragut	Hartford
[9]	Aug64	R. A. David G. Farragut	Hartford
[10]	Sept64-Dec64	R. A. David G. Farragut	Hartford
[11]	Dec64-Feb65	Commo. James S. Palmer	Richmond
[12]	Mar65-June65	Act'g R. A. Henry K. Thatcher	Portsmouth, Stockdale
[13]	July65-Dec65	Act'g R. A. Henry K. Thatcher	Estrella

(The later letters in this volume, and all those in the
following volumes, are from the Gulf Squadron.)

[14]	Jan66-May66	Act'g R. A. Henry K. Thatcher	Estrella
[15]	Apr66-Dec66	Commo. John A. Winslow	Estrella
[16]	Jan67-May67	Commo. John A. Winslow	Estrella

(15) MORTAR FLOTILLA

[-]	Mar62-July62	Comdr. David D. Porter	Harriet Lane, Octarara

(16) EAST GULF BLOCKADING SQUADRON

[1]	May62-Dec62	Act'g R. A. James L. Lardner	San Jacinto, St. Lawrence
[2]	Dec62-May63	Act'g R. A. Theodorus Bailey	St. Lawrence
[3]	May63-Aug63	Act'g R. A. Theodorus Bailey	St. Lawrence, Magnolia, San Jacinto
[4]	Aug63-Dec63	Act'g R. A. Theodorus Bailey	San Jacinto
[5]	Jan64-Oct64	Act'g R. A. Theodorus Bailey	San Jacinto, Dale
		Capt. Theodore P. Greene	[Key West]
[6]	Oct64-Feb65	Act'g R. A. Cornelius K. Stribling	[Key West]
[7]	Mar65-July65	Act'g R. A. Cornelius K. Stribling	[Key West]

(17) WEST INDIA SQUADRON

[1]	Sept62-July63	R. A. Charles Wilkes	Wachuset, Vanderbilt, Alabama
[2]	May63-Oct64	Commo. James L. Lardner	Ticonderoga, Powhatan

(18) SOUTH ATLANTIC SQUADRON

[1]	Apr65-July67	R. A. Sylvanus W. Godon	Brooklyn
[2]	June67-Sept68	R. A. Charles H. Davis	Guerrière

(18) SOUTH ATLANTIC SQUADRON (continued)

[3]	Oct68-July69	R. A. Charles H. Davis	Guerrière
[4]	July69-Dec69	Capt. Melancthon B. Woolsey	Portsmouth
[5]	Sept69-June70	R. A. Joseph Lanman	Lancaster
[6]	July70-Dec70	R. A. Joseph Lanman	Lancaster
[7]	Jan71-Aug71	R. A. Joseph Lanman	Lancaster
[8]	Sept71-May72	R. A. Joseph Lanman	Lancaster
[9]	May72-Dec72	R. A. William Rogers Taylor	Lancaster
[10]	Jan73-Oct73	R. A. William Rogers Taylor	Lancaster
[11]	Jan74-Dec74	R. A. James H. Strong	Lancaster
		R. A. William E. Le Roy	Lancaster
[12]	Jan75-Dec75	R. A. William E. Le Roy	Lancaster, Brooklyn
[13]	Jan76-Dec76	Comdr. William A. Kirkland	Frolic
		Commo. C. H. B. Caldwell	Richmond
[14]	Jan77-Dec77	Commo. C. H. B. Caldwell	Richmond
		Commo. Edward T. Nichols	Hartford
[15]	Jan78-Dec78	Commo. Edward T. Nichols	Hartford
[16]	Jan79-Dec79	Commo. Edward T. Nichols	Hartford
		Commo. Andrew Bryson	Shenandoah
[17]	Jan80-Dec80	R. A. Andrew Bryson	Shenandoah
[18]	Jan81-Dec81	R. A. Andrew Bryson	Shenandoah
		R. A. James H. Spotts	Shenandoah
[19]	Jan82-Dec82	R. A. James H. Spotts	Shenandoah
		R. A. Pierce Crosby	Brooklyn, Galena
[20]	Jan83-Dec83	R. A. Pierce Crosby	Galena
		R. A. Thomas S. Phelps	Brooklyn
[21]	Jan84-Nov84	R. A. Thomas S. Phelps	Brooklyn
[22]	Sept85-Oct85	R. A. Earl English	Lancaster

(19) EUROPEAN SQUADRON

[1]	June65-Aug67	R. A. Louis M. Goldsborough	Colorado, Frolic
[2]	Dec67-Dec68	R. A. David G. Farragut	Franklin
		Commo. Alexander M. Pennock	Ticonderoga
[3]	Jan69-Feb69	Commo. Alexander M. Pennock	Frolic
[4]	Feb69-Aug70	R. A. William Radford	Franklin
[5]	Aug70-Jan71	R. A. Oliver S. Glisson	Franklin
[6]	Jan71-Sept71	R. A. Charles S. Boggs	Franklin, Plymouth
[7]	Jan71-Jan72	R. A. Oliver S. Glisson	Franklin
		R. A. Charles S. Boggs	Brooklyn
[8]	Nov71-Dec72	R. A. James Alden	Wabash
[9]	Jan73-Dec73	R. A. James Alden	Wabash
		R. A. Augustus Ludlow Case	Wabash
[10]	July73-July74	R. A. Augustus Ludlow Case	Wabash, Franklin
[11]	May74-Dec74	R. A. Augustus Ludlow Case	Franklin
[12]	Jan75-Dec75	R. A. John L. Worden	Franklin
[13]	Jan76-Dec76	R. A. John L. Worden	Franklin, Marion
[14]	Jan77-Dec77	R. A. John L. Worden	Marion
		R. A. William E. Le Roy	Marion, Trenton
[15]	Jan78-Dec78	R. A. William E. Le Roy	Trenton

Vol.	Dates	Commanding Officers	Flagships

(19) EUROPEAN SQUADRON (continued)

[16] Jan79-Dec79	R. A. William E. Le Roy	Trenton
	R. A. John C. Howell	Trenton
[17] Jan80-Dec80	R. A. John C. Howell	Trenton
[18] Jan81-Dec81	R. A. John C. Howell	Trenton
	R. A. James W. A. Nicholson	Lancaster
[19] Jan82-Dec82	R. A. James W. A. Nicholson	Lancaster
[20] Jan83-Dec83	R. A. James W. A. Nicholson	Lancaster
	R. A. Charles H. Baldwin	Lancaster
[21] Jan84-Dec84	R. A. Charles H. Baldwin	Lancaster
	R. A. Earl English	Lancaster
[22] Jan85-Nov85	R. A. Earl English	Lancaster
	R. A. Samuel R. Franklin	Pensacola

(20) ASIATIC SQUADRON

[1] Aug65-Dec66	R. A. Henry H. Bell	Hartford
[2] Jan67-Apr68	R. A. Henry H. Bell	Hartford
[3] Oct67-Dec68	R. A. Stephen C. Rowan	Piscataqua
[4] Jan69-Dec69	R. A. Stephen C. Rowan	Piscataqua, Delaware
[5] Jan70-Nov70	R. A. Stephen C. Rowan	Delaware
[6] Mar70-July71	R. A. John Rodgers	Colorado
[7] July71-Nov72	R. A. John Rodgers	Colorado
[8] May72-Dec72	R. A. Thornton A. Jenkins	Colorado, Lackawanna
[9] Jan73-Dec73	R. A. Thornton A. Jenkins	Lackawanna, Hartford
[10] Jan74-Dec74	R. A. Enoch G. Parrott	Hartford
	Capt. Edmund R. Colhoun	Hartford
	R. A. Alexander M. Pennock	Hartford
[11] Jan75-Dec75	R. A. Alexander M. Pennock	Hartford, Saco
	R. A. William Reynolds	Tennessee
[12] Jan76-Dec76	R. A. William Reynolds	Tennessee
[13] Jan77-Dec77	R. A. William Reynolds	Tennessee
	R. A. Thomas H. Patterson	Tennessee
[14] Jan78-Dec78	R. A. Thomas H. Patterson	Tennessee, Monocacy
[15] Jan79-Dec79	R. A. Thomas H. Patterson	Monongahela, Richmond
[16] Jan80-Dec80	R. A. Thomas H. Patterson	Richmond
	R. A. John M. B. Clitz	Richmond
[17] Jan81-Dec81	R. A. John M. B. Clitz	Richmond, Monocacy
[18] Jan82-Dec82	R. A. John M. B. Clitz	Monocacy, Richmond
[19] Jan83-Dec83	R. A. John M. B. Clitz	Richmond
	R. A. Pierce Crosby	Richmond
	R. A. John Lee Davis	Richmond
[20] Jan84-Dec84	R. A. John Lee Davis	Richmond, Trenton
[21] Jan85-Nov85	R. A. John Lee Davis	Trenton

(21) ATLANTIC SQUADRON

[-] Oct65-Nov66	Commo. Joseph Lanman	New Hampshire, Tacony

Vol.	Dates	Commanding Officers	Flagships

(22) SPECIAL SQUADRON

[-] Oct65–Dec65   Commo. John Rodgers   Vanderbilt

(23) NORTH ATLANTIC SQUADRON

[1] Jan66–Dec66   R. A. James S. Palmer   Rhode Island
       (The earlier letters are from Admiral Palmer as commanding
        officer of the West India Squadron; those on and after 11May
        are from the North Atlantic Squadron.)
[2] Jan67–Nov67   R. A. James S. Palmer   Susquehanna
[3] Nov67–Dec68   R. A. Henry K. Hoff   Wampanoag, Contoocook
[4] Jan69–Aug69   R. A. Henry K. Hoff   Contoocook, Albany
[5] Aug69–Aug70   R. A. Charles H. Poor   Tuscarora, Severn
[6] Jan70–June71   Commo. Joseph F. Green   Congress
[7] Aug70–Apr71   R. A. Samuel Phillips Lee   Severn
[8] May71–Dec71   R. A. Samuel Phillips Lee   Severn
[9] Jan72–Aug72   R. A. Samuel Phillips Lee   Worcester
[10] Aug72–Dec73   R. A. Joseph F. Green   Worcester
                    R. A. Gustavus H. Scott   Worcester
[11] Jan74–Apr74   R. A. Augustus Ludlow Case   Wabash, Franklin
                    R. A. Gustavus H. Scott   Worcester
[12] May74–Dec74   R. A. Gustavus H. Scott   Worcester
                    R. A. J. R. Madison Mullany Worcester
[13] Jan75–June75   R. A. J. R. Madison Mullany Worcester, Colorado
[14] July75–Dec75   R. A. J. R. Madison Mullany Worcester
[15] Jan76–Dec76   R. A. J. R. Madison Mullany Hartford
                    R. A. William E. Le Roy   Hartford
                    R. A. Stephen D. Trenchard   Hartford
[16] Jan77–Dec77   R. A. Stephen D. Trenchard   Hartford, Powhatan
[17] Jan78–Dec78   R. A. Stephen D. Trenchard   Powhatan
                    R. A. John C. Howell   Powhatan
[18] Jan79–Dec79   R. A. John C. Howell   Powhatan
                    R. A. Robert H. Wyman   Powhatan, Tennessee
[19] Jan80–Dec80   R. A. Robert H. Wyman   Tennessee
[20] Jan81–Dec81   R. A. Robert H. Wyman   Tennessee
[21] Jan82–Dec82   R. A. Robert H. Wyman   Tennessee
                    R. A. George H. Cooper   Tennessee
[22] Jan83–Dec83   R. A. George H. Cooper   Tennessee
[23] Jan84–Dec84   R. A. George H. Cooper   Tennessee
                    R. A. James E. Jouett   Tennessee
[24] Jan85–Dec85   R. A. James E. Jouett   Tennessee

(24) TRAINING SQUADRON

[1] Jan82–Dec82   Commo. Stephen B. Luce   New Hampshire, Portsmouth
[2] Feb83–Dec83   Commo. Stephen B. Luce   New Hampshire
       (This volume contains letters also from the Naval Stations at
        Newport, New London, and Key West.)
[3] Jan84–Dec84   Commo. Stephen B. Luce   New Hampshire
                    Capt. Philip C. Johnson, Jr. New Hampshire
                    Capt. Arthur Yates   New Hampshire
[4] Mar85–Dec85   Comdr. Silas W. Terry   Pensacola

APPENDIX C

LIST OF VESSELS OF THE UNITED STATES NAVY
FOR WHICH MUSTER ROLLS AND PAY ROLLS ARE AVAILABLE (Entry 90)

(1) Bound Records, 1798-1847

("m" refers to muster rolls; "p," to pay rolls.)

Adams, 1802-15 (m),
  with Constellation,
  1802
Alert, 1813-29 (p)
        1815-30 (m)
Alligator, 1813-22 (p)
Argus, 1803-13 (mp)
Boston, 1826-36 (mp)
Boxer, 1813-35 (p)
        1815-40 (m)
Brandywine, 1825-37 (p),
  with Vincennes, 1824
Brandywine, 1825-36 (m)
Chesapeake, 1799-1813
  (mp)
Columbus, 1819-39 (m)
          1819-39 (p)
          1830-43 (mp)
Concord, 1830-38 (mp)
Congress, 1799-1847 (m)
          1803-30 (p),
  with Constitution,
  1804-06
Connecticut, 1799-1801
  (m)
Consort, 1836-39 (mp)
Constellation, 1812-38
  (p), with Alert, Flam-
  beau, and Nonsuch
Constellation, 1798-1838 (m)
Constitution, 1798-1838 (m)
Constitution, 1803-38 (p)
Cyane, 1818-27 (mp)
Delaware, 1827-35 (m)

Delaware, 1827-41 (p)
Dolphin, 1821-35 (mp)
Enterprise, 1800-35 (m),
  with Chesapeake, 1800
Enterprise, 1809-39 (p)
Epervier, 1814-15 (mp)
Erie, 1815-40 (m)
      1815-39 (p)
Essex, 1801-14 (mp),
  with President, 1804-
  05
Fairfield, 1828-39 (mp)
Falmouth, 1828-43 (mp)
Franklin, 1805-24 (m),
  with Despatch, Hornet,
  and various gunboats
Franklin, 1815-24 (p)
          1832-33 (mp)
Fulton, 1820-38 (m)
        1827-29 (p)
Grampus, 1821-38 (p)
          1821-40 (m)
Guerrière, 1813-31 (m)
          1818-31 (p)
Gunboats, 1811-14
Hornet, 1805-28 (m)
        1805-29 (p)
Hudson, 1828-39 (mp)
Independence, 1814-28 (m)
              1815-40 (p)
Java, 1815-39 (mp)
John Adams 1, 1804-27 (m)
              1809-27 (p)
John Adams 2, 1834-40 (p)

Lexington and Lynx,
  1816-39 (mp)
Macedonian, 1815-38 (m)
            1813-42 (p)
Natchez, 1827-39 (m)
          1827-39 (p)
North Carolina, 1820-39 (m)
                1813-39 (p)
Ontario, 1813-40 (p)
Peacock, 1813-40 (m)
          1830-37 (p)
Potomac, 1831-36 (mp)
President, 1800-13 (m)
Prometheus, 1815-18 (mp)
Ranger, 1800-01
Saranac, 1814-17 (mp)
St. Louis, 1828-40 (mp)
Shark, 1821-35 (m)
        1823-37 (p)
Spark, 1811-25 (p)
        1814-25 (m)
United States, 1809-44 (m)
              1800-01 (p)
              1809-40 (p)
Vandalia, 1828-39 (p)
          1828-45 (m)
Vincennes, 1826-36 (p)
          1826-36 (m)
Vixen, Warren, Wasp,
  1806-36 (mp)
Washington, 1803-22 (m),
  with Chesapeake, 1802-03
Washington, 1815-25 (mp)
West India Squadron,
  1822-26 (mp)

Flying Squadrons (Firefly, Flambeau, Spark, Torch, D. D. Porter), 1814-16
Miscellaneous (p): Dale (1839), Experiment (1832-39), Falmouth (before
  1830), Everglades (1837-38)
Miscellaneous (mp): Superior, Lady of the Lake, Tom Bowline, 1814-17

(1) Bound Records, 1798-1847 (continued)

Miscellaneous Rolls of Ships, vol. 1, 1798-1844: Columbia, Comet, Consort,
Florida, Frolic, George Washington, Kensington, Lawrence, Louisiana,
Patapsco, Pioneer, Relief, Richmond, Troup
Miscellaneous Rolls of Ships, vol. 2, 1809-42: Jefferson, Levant, Marion,
Monroe, Nautilus, Nonsuch, Porpoise
Miscellaneous Rolls of Ships, vol. 3, 1799-1828: Rattlesnake, Revenge,
Sea Gull, Siren, Spitfire 2, Trumbull, Gunboats 1, 4, 5, 10, 58-69

(2) Bound Records, 1813-60

(Cited in order in which bound.)

Active, 1837-56	Ewing, 1855-56	Nautilus, 1856
Albany, 1846-52	Falcon, 1848	Niagara, 1857
Alleghany, 1848-56	Falmouth, 1849-57	North Carolina, 1853-60
Alligator, 1822	Fredonia, 1847-54	Ohio, 1853-56
Arctic Expedition, 1851	Fulton, 1852-57	On-ka-hy-e, 1846-48
Arctic, 1858	Fenimore Cooper, 1853	Hecla, 1848
Arago, 1854-56	Gallatin, 1856	Ontario, 1853
Arago and Belle, 1854	Germantown, 1847-54	Peacock, 1822
Atalanta, 1858-59	Graham and Hetzel,	Pensacola, 1859
Bainbridge, 1844-58	1852-53	Pennsylvania, 1854-56
Bibb, 1854-56	Hartford, 1859	Perry, 1847-58
Bonito, 1846-48	Harriet Lane, 1858	Petrel, 1846
Boston, 1846	Hetzel, 1852-57	Plymouth, 1851-59
Boxer, 1846-48	Hornet, 1822	Preble, 1853-59
Brandywine, 1834	Hunter, 1847	Pioneer, 1837
Brooklyn, 1859	Independence, 1846-57	Porpoise, 1846-53
Caledonia, 1858	Iris, 1848	Portsmouth, 1846-59
Chesapeake, 1813	Jamestown, 1851-58	Potomac, 1846-56
Columbia, 1845-55	John Adams, 1822-59	Princeton, 1845-55
Columbus, 1845-48	John Hancock, 1853	Powhatan, 1852-57
Colorado, 1858	John Y. Mason, 1852-53	Raritan, 1847-52
Concord, 1830	Lancaster, 1859	Reefer, 1846-47
Congress, 1846-59	Legaré, 1854	Release, 1856-59
Constitution, 1851-54	Levant, 1847-59	Relief, 1837-59
Constellation, 1855-59	Lexington, 1846-55	Resolute, 1856
Consort, 1837	Macedonian, 1822-59	Roanoke, 1857-59
Corwin, 1854	Graham, 1854	Sabine, 1858-59
Crusader, 1859	Massachusetts, 1850-57	San Jacinto, 1852-59
Cumberland, 1846-57	Marion, 1845-59	Saranac, 1852-59
Cyane, 1822-58	Memphis, 1858-59	Saratoga, 1847-58
Dale, 1846-59	Merrimack, 1856-60	Savannah, 1845-59
Decatur, 1847-59	Michigan, 1845	Scorpion, 1847-49
Dolphin, 1822-60	Minnesota, 1857	Somers, 1846
Electra, 1847	Mississippi, 1846-55	Southern Star, 1858
Enterprise, 1833-58	Mohawk, 1859	Spark, 1822
Erie, 1845-48	Morris, undated	Spitfire, 1848
Etna, 1847-48	Mystic, 1859	St. Lawrence, 1851-59

(2) Bound Records, 1813-60 (continued)

St. Louis, 1852-59
St. Mary's, 1846-59
Sumter, 1859
Supply, 1847-59
John P. Kennedy, 1850
Saranac, 1850
Susquehanna, 1851-58
Tampico, 1846

Taney, 1849
Union, 1847-56
United States, 1846
Vandalia, 1850-56
Varina, 1854-57
Vesuvius, 1849
Vincennes, 1846-57
Vixen, 1848-51

Wabash, 1856-58
Walker, 1854-56
Warren, 1850
Washington, 1846-47
Westernport, 1858
Wyandotte, 1859
Water Witch, 1847-59
Wyoming, 1859
Polk, 1847

(3) Loose Records, 1803-85

Agawam, 1865
Alligator, 1815
Argus, 1808-09
Asp, 1813
Bainbridge, 1843
Bonhomme Richard, 1779
   (photostat)
Boston, 1828-52
Boxer, 1832-43
Brandywine, 1826-42
Chesapeake Flotilla,
   1813-14
Chippewa, 1815-18
Columbia, 1842
Columbus, 1830
Concord, 1832-45
Congress, 1818-42
Conquest, 1812-13
Consort, 1837-43
Constellation, 1799-
   1832 (roll for 1799
   photostat)
Constitution, 1813-41
Cyane, 1824-44
Dale, 1841-57
Daylight, 1862-64
Decatur, 1840-47
Delaware, 1834-43
Dolphin, 1822-43
Dove, 1861
Enterprise, 1842
Epervier, 1815
Erie, 1809-40
Fair American, 1813-14
Fairfield, 1830-41
Falmouth, 1839-42
Flirt, 1840

Florida, 1827
Franklin, 1817-21
General Pike, 1813-15
General Taylor, 1843
Governor Tompkins, 1812
Grampus, 1839-41
Growler, 1812-13
Guerrière, 1815-21
Gunboat No. 5, 1809
Gunboat No. 14, 1806
Gunboat No. 67, 1814
Hamilton, 1813
Hetzel, 1864
Hornet, 1814-19
Hudson, 1828-29
Hunchback, 1865
Independence, 1815-37
Jefferson, 1842
John Adams, 1815-42
Jones, 1814-18
Julia, 1812
Kearsarge, 1876-77
Lady of the Lake, 1813-14
Levant, 1841-42
Lexington, 1830-44
Macedonian, 1820-45
Madison, 1813-14
Marion, 1842
"Miscellaneous" (undated
   rolls and indexes, all
   unidentified, apparently
   before 1825)
Mohawk, 1814-15
Montgomery, 1865
Natchez, 1829-31
Niagara, 1860-61
Nonsuch, 1819-20

North Carolina, 1836-38
Ohio, 1840-45
Oneida, 1810-15
On-ka-hy-e, 1848
Ontario (schooner), 1813
Ontario (ship of war),
   1815-43
Oregon, 1843
Peacock, 1824-37
Pennsylvania, 1842-52
Pequot, 1864
Pert, 1813, with Raven
   and Scourge
Pioneer, 1836-37
Porpoise, 1826-28
Portsmouth, 1859-62
Potomac, 1834-44
Preble, 1841-60
President, 1814
Raven, 1813
Red Rover, 1862
Relief, 1840-42
Revenge, 1821
Richmond, 1869-71
St. Louis, 1839-42
Saranac, 1815-16
Saratoga, 1844-60
Savannah, 1847
Scourge, 1805-47
Shark, 1824-41
Shenandoah, 1885
Spark, 1815-24
Sylph, 1813-15
Torch, 1814-15, with
   Spitfire
Truxtun, 1843
Union, 1844

(3) Loose Records, 1803-85 (continued)

United States, 1810-41
Vandalia, 1829-57
Vincennes, 1840-58

Warren, 1832-41
Washington, 1816-19
Wasp, 1812

Wave, 1840-41
Weasel, 1823
York, 1813
Zouave, 1864

APPENDIX D: LIST OF LOGS AND JOURNALS
OF VESSELS OF THE UNITED STATES NAVY

(The entries in this list, arranged chronologically, refer to subseries of Entry 392. Except as otherwise explicitly indicated, each
entry in this list refers to a single unindexed volume.)

(1) Log of the Continental Schooner Wasp, Commanded by Capt. William
Hallock, on a Voyage from New Providence to Philadelphia (photostat),
Mar. 9 - Apr. 18, 1776. Typed index and introduction. Original in
Public Record Office.

(2) Log of the Continental Ships Ranger, Nov. 26, 1777 - May 14,
1778, and Bonhomme Richard, May 8 - Sept. 24, 1779. 2 vols. (1 a typed
copy, the other a photostat of the typed copy). According to a note
inside the front cover of the log of the Bonhomme Richard, the volume was
purchased in 1824 from a New York baker named Harding by a Captain Boyd
of Greenock. In 1830 both logs came into the possession of Lady Isabella
Helen Douglas, of St. Mary's Isle, Scotland.

(3) Log of the Continental Ship Ranger, Commanded by Capt. Thomas
Simpson (photostat), Aug. 24, 1778 - May 10, 1780. Typed index. Original
in possession of the Rosenbach Co., 15 E. 51st St., New York, in 1933.

(4) Logs of HMS Serapis, Sept. 26 - Nov. 22, 1779, the Continental
Frigate of War Alliance, Nov. 22, 1779 - June 15, 1780, the Continental
Ship of War Ariel, June 16 - Oct. 14, 1780, and the Queen of France, Aug.
20 - Sept. 10, 1782 (typed copies). Prepared from copies in the Naval
Academy. The Serapis was a prize taken Sept. 23, 1779. The Alliance and
the Ariel cruised off the coast of France. The Queen of France sailed
from Delaware Bay for L'Orient. At the end of the volume are lists of
officers and crew of the Bonhomme Richard (June 1779), of deserters from
the same (July 19, 1779), and of officers and crew of the Ariel (undated).

(5) Fragment of a Log Kept by Mdn. John Manley on the General George
Washington, Commanded by Comdr. Joshua Barney, at Havre de Grâce, June 8 -
July 1, 1783. Identified by a deposition of Manley on pages 2-3, dated
Apr. 2, 1845. The log is followed by accounts and computations dated
July 17 and Aug. 7, 1830.

(6) Log of the Constellation, Commanded by Capt. Thomas Truxtun, on
a Cruise to the West Indies and Back to Norfolk (photostat), June 24, 1798 -
Mar. 25, 1800. 1 vol. and loose sheets in 1 package, duplicates. Typed
index. Original in possession of the Historical Society of Pennsylvania.

(7) Journal Kept by James Pity aboard the Constitution, Commanded by M 1030
Capt. Samuel Nicholson, July 23, 1798 - May 11, 1799. In the back of the
volume are accounts, 1800-15.

(8) Logs Kept by Lts. Joseph Strout and William V. Hutchings, Mdn.
John Sale Hickling Cox, Act'g Mdn. Joseph Beale, and Master Abiel R. Story,

during a Cruise of the Herald, Commanded by Capt. James Sever, off the Atlantic Coast, Aug. 22 - Dec. 30, 1798. 5 vols. The cruise began and ended at Boston. The logs of Strout and Hutchings are dated Aug. 22 - Dec. 29; that of Beale is dated Aug. 30 - Sept. 30; that of Story, Sept. 7 - Nov. 25; and that of Cox, Nov. 2 - Dec. 30. All were kept on identical printed forms.

(9) Extracts from the Log of the Constitution, Commanded by Capt. Samuel Nicholson, on a Cruise from Boston to the West Indies (photostat), Dec. 20, 1798 - July 17, 1800. Original in Naval History Society Collection in the Library of the New York Historical Society.

(10) Log Kept by Mdn. Joseph Brown aboard the Merrimack, Commanded by Capt. Joseph Brown, on a Cruise from Boston to the West Indies and Back to Boston (photostat), Jan. 3 - Dec. 8, 1799. Original in possession of the Historical Society of Old Newbury, Mass. The entries are made on a printed form.

(11) Log Kept by Sailing Master Joseph Whitmore aboard the Warren, Commanded by Capt. Timothy Newman and Lt. Joseph Strout, on a Cruise from Boston to the West Indies and Back to Charleston (photostat), Dec. 31, 1799 - Aug. 31, 1800. Original in possession of the Historical Society of Old Newbury, Mass.

(12) Journal Kept by Lt. Isaac Hull aboard the Constitution, Commanded by Capt. Silas Talbot, on a Cruise to the West Indies and Back to Boston (photostat), Feb. 6 - Aug. 25, 1800. The original, in possession of the New York Historical Society, ends with Oct. 20, 1800.

(13) Log Kept by Lt. Thomas Wilkey aboard the Philadelphia, Commanded by Capt. Stephen Decatur, Cruising in the West Indies, May 28, 1800 - Jan. 25, 1801. Several pages at the end of the volume have been torn out. Newspaper clippings were formerly mounted on most of the pages.

(14) Log of the George Washington, Commanded by Lt. Wilson Jacobs, on a Cruise from Philadelphia to the Mediterranean and Back to Philadelphia (photostat), June 14, 1800 - Apr. 19, 1801. Original in the Henry E. Huntington Library and Art Gallery.

(15) Log of the Augusta, Commanded by Lt. Archibald McElroy, Cruising near Cap François, July 6 - Oct. 22, 1800.

(16) Log of the President, Commanded by Capt. Thomas Truxtun, on a Cruise from New York to the West Indies (photostat), Sept. 5, 1800 - Feb. 10, 1801. Original in the collection of Mr. Jonathan Sawyer, 1934.

(17) Extracts from the Log of the Boston, Commanded by Capt. George Little, on a Cruise from Boston to the West Indies and Back to Boston (photostat), Sept. 7, 1800 - July 4, 1801. Sheets stapled in a paper wrapper. Original in the Henry E. Huntington Library and Art Gallery.

(18) Log of the Boston, Commanded by Capt. George Little, Cruising in the West Indies (photostat), Sept. 23, 1800 - May 4, 1801. Original in possession of the Massachusetts Historical Society.

(19) Abstract of Journals Kept by Mdn. Charles Morris, Jr., on a Cruise from New York to the Mediterranean and Back to Cape Henry (photostat), June 20, 1803 - Sept. 25, 1805. Original in possession of Mrs. C. E. Fox, 1926. Midshipman Morris served on the Constitution (June 20, 1830 - Apr. 17, 1804), the Scourge (Apr. 17 - Aug. 8, 1804), the Argus (Aug. 8 - Nov. 1, 1804), and the President (Nov. 1, 1804 - Sept. 25, 1805).

(20) Journal of Mdn. Frederick Cornelius De Krafft Kept on a Cruise from Philadelphia to the Mediterranean and Back to Gosport, aboard the Siren, Commanded by Lt. Charles Stewart, and the Scourge, Aug. 6, 1803 - Feb. 13, 1805. Midshipman De Krafft left the Siren Sept. 27, 1804, and on Sept. 29 took command of the Scourge, a prize, which he brought to the United States.

(21) Log Kept by Comdr. Isaac Hull, Commanding the Argus on a Cruise from Algeciras to the Mediterranean and Alexandria, Va. (photostat), Nov. 9, 1803 - Nov. 29, 1804.

(22) Journal Kept by Mdn. Charles Morris, Jr., Cruising in the Mediterranean on the Constitution, Commanded by Commo. Edward Preble, Mar. 18-21, 1804, and the Argus, Commanded by Comdr. Isaac Hull, Aug. 9-24, 1804 (photostat). Original in possession of Mrs. C. E. Fox, 1926.

(23) Journal Kept by Hezekiah Loomis, Steward, aboard the Vixen, Commanded by Lt. John Smith and Comdr. George Coxe, Cruising in the Mediterranean, and the Congress, Returning to Washington (typed copy), Oct. 28, 1804 - Nov. 29, 1805. Original in possession of Mr. Louis F. Middlebrook, Hartford, Conn., 1925. The writer was transferred to the Congress Aug. 19, 1805. At the back of the volume are lists of officers and crew of the Vixen.

(24) Journal Kept by Mdn. Charles Morris, Jr., aboard the President, Commanded by Capt. James Barron, on a Cruise from Malta to Cape Henry (photostat), Nov. 2, 1804 - Sept. 1, 1805. Original in possession of Mrs. C. E. Fox.

(25) Journal Kept aboard the Argus and the Nautilus, Commanded by Lt. William Crane, Cruising near New York, Oct. 13, 1811 - July 15, 1812. Lieutenant Crane, apparently the writer, was transferred to the Nautilus Jan. 23, 1812.

(26) Log of Gunboat No. 10, Commanded by Master Squire Fisk, at New York, July 14, 1812 - July 6, 1813.

(27) Extract from the Log of the Constitution, Commanded by Capt. Isaac Hull (photostat), Aug. 20-21, 1812. Reproduction of 2 sheets relating to the engagement of the Constitution and HMS Guerrière.

(28) Log of the Cartel Ship <u>Analostan</u>, Commanded by Master William Peters Smith, on Cruises from Washington to the West Indies and Nova Scotia, Apr. 22, 1813 - Sept. 18, 1815. Alexis Luckett, Master, is named on the flyleaf as writer of the log, but entries in it were made by several officers.

(29) Log Kept aboard the <u>Peacock</u>, Commanded by Lt. Lewis Warrington, on a Cruise off the Atlantic Coast of France (photostat), Apr. 15 - Aug. 31, 1814. Original in possession of R. A. James H. Oliver, Shirley, Va., 1927.

(30) Log of the Cartel Ship <u>Perseverance</u>, Commanded by Master Joseph H. Dill, on a Voyage from Providence, R. I., to Halifax, N. S., and Back to Providence, May 20 - July 28, 1814.

(31) Journal of Peter M. Potter, Captain's Clerk aboard the <u>Spitfire</u> on a Voyage from New York to the Mediterranean and Back to New York (photostat), May 20 - Nov. 23, 1815.

(32) Log of the Cartel Ship <u>Perseverance</u>, Commanded by Master Joseph H. Dill, on a Voyage from Providence, R. I., to Plymouth, Eng., and Back to Norfolk, June 8 - Aug. 30, 1815.

(33) Log Kept by Mdn. William Rice aboard the <u>Independence</u> (Flagship of Commo. William Bainbridge), Commanded by Capt. William Crane, on a Voyage to the Mediterranean, July 3 - Oct. 16, 1815.

<u>M902</u> (34) Journal and Correspondence of Capt. James Biddle, Commanding the <u>Ontario</u> on a Cruise from New York to the Columbia River and Back to Norfolk, Oct. 4, 1817 - Apr. 23, 1819. Transmitted to the Secretary of the Navy with a letter dated Apr. 23, 1819.

<u>1875</u> (35) Journal Kept by Lt. Charles Gauntt on the <u>Macedonian</u>, Commanded by Capt. John Downes, on a Cruise from Boston to Guayaquil and Back to Boston, July 29, 1818 - June 18, 1821.

<u>M876</u> (36) Journal Kept by Charles J. Deblois, Captain's Clerk, aboard the <u>Macedonian</u>, Sept. 21, 1818 - July 9, 1819.

(37) Log of the <u>Spark</u>, Commanded by Lt. Raymond H. Perry, Cruising in the Mediterranean (photostat), Nov. 13, 1819 - June 7, 1820. Original in Farragut Collection, National Museum.

(38) Journal Kept by Lt. Charles Gauntt aboard the <u>Macedonian</u>, Commanded by Capt. James Biddle, on a Voyage from Boston to Cape Haitien, Mar. 21 - June 20, 1822, and the <u>Warren</u>, Commanded by Comdr. Lawrence Kearny, on a Cruise from Boston to the Mediterranean and Back to Baltimore, Dec. 13, 1826 - May 5, 1829. At the end of the volume are copies of correspondence of Capt. James Biddle relating to the duties of first lieutenants, May 27, 1819 - Apr. 22, 1822.

(39) Journal Kept by Mdn. Charles Wilkes, Jr., Commanding the Merchant Vessel O'Cain on a Voyage from Valparaiso to Boston, Mar. 26 – Oct. 15, 1823. The title written by Wilkes on the flyleaf appears to be "Journal on Board the Ship O'Cain of Boston, Charles Wilkes, Jr., Captain," though in 1823 Wilkes was a midshipman. In the back of the volume are notes labeled "Pendulum Experiments" (probably prepared by Wilkes while in charge of the Dépôt of Charts and Instruments in the 1830's), penciled notes on the proposed exploring expedition of 1838–42 (which Wilkes commanded), and rough drafts of letters.

(40) Journal of Commo. Daniel T. Patterson, Commanding the North Carolina on a Mediterranean Cruise (typed copy), Mar. 26 – Aug. 13, 1825. Original in possession of Miss Harriett Patterson Winslow, 1943.

(41) Journal Kept by Mdn. William Johnson Slidell aboard the North Carolina, on a Cruise from Hampton Roads to the Mediterranean and Back to Hampton Roads, Mar. 27, 1825 – July 29, 1827.

(42) Journal Kept by Mdn. Stephen C. Rowan aboard the Vincennes, Commanded by Commo. Isaac Chauncey, on a Cruise to Chile, Peru, and Tahiti, May 28, 1825 – Aug. 12, 1827. Deals at length with manners and customs. Many pages are torn out.   M180

(43) Extract from the Journal of Capt. Charles Morris, Commanding the Brandywine Conveying General Lafayette from Washington to France (photostat), Sept. 1 – Oct. 1, 1825. Original in possession of Mrs. C. E. Fox. The rest of vol. 1 and all of vol. 2, relating to an inspection of French and British dockyards, are omitted from the photostat.

(44) Journal of Lt. Thomas A. Dornin on Voyages to the Pacific, June 24, 1826 – Feb. 10, 1830, Apr. 1, 1831 – Jan. 29, 1834. Voyages on the Brandywine (Capt. Jacob Jones, cruising off Chile and Peru, June 24, 1826 – May 9, 1829), the Falmouth (Comdr. William B. Finch, sailing to Tahiti, Hawaii, Canton, and Manila, May 9, 1829 – Feb. 10, 1830), and again the Falmouth (Capt. Francis H. Gregory, cruise from New York to Mazatlán and back to New York, Apr. 1, 1831 – Jan. 29, 1834); and notes, accounts, clippings, and directions for gardening, as late as 1840.   M981

(45) Journal Kept by Act'g Mdn. Peter L. Gansevoort aboard the Sabina on a Voyage from Guayaquil to Canton and Manila, July 28, 1827 – Feb. 25, 1828. Only partly legible.

(46) Journal Kept by Ass't Surgeon John C. Mercer aboard the Constellation, Cruising in the Mediterranean, Apr. 21, 1832 – Nov. 4, 1834. The end of the journal is lost.

(47) Log Kept by Lt. William Mervine, Commanding the Experiment on a Cruise from Washington to Boston, Apr. 22, 1832 – May 21, 1833.

(48) A Midshipman and an Old Lady: Journal of a Cruise Made by P. Stuyvesant Fish, in the Years 1832 and 1833 (privately printed by

Stuyvesant Fish, Jan. 1931). Selections, with interspersed editorial comments, from a log kept by Act'g. Mdn. Peter Stuyvesant Fish on a voyage to the Mediterranean aboard the United States, commanded by Capt. John B. Nicholson, July 3 - Sept. 7, 1833.

(49) Log Kept by Mdn. William P. Gamble aboard the Fairfield, Commanded by Comdr. Elie A. F. La Vallette, on a Cruise along the Pacific Coast of America, Jan. 1, 1834 - Aug. 10, 1835.

(50) Journal Kept aboard the Brandywine, Commanded by Capt. David Deacon, and the Boxer, Commanded by Lt. Hugh N. Page, on a Cruise from New York to the Pacific Coast of America, Apr. 28, 1834 - Feb. 13, 1837. The anonymous writer was transferred to the Boxer at Callao, June 18, 1835.

(51) Journals Kept by Mdn. John Julius Guthrie aboard the John Adams, Commanded by Capt. David Conner and Comdr. Silas H. Stringham, on a Cruise from Norfolk to the Mediterranean and Back to New York, July 18, 1834 - June 19, 1835, Jan. 1, 1836 - May 6, 1837. 2 vols. At the end of the second volume are copies of Guthrie's correspondence, June 14, 1833 - Oct. 1, 1841; a summary statement of his Naval services, June 22, 1834 - July 16, 1853; and watch, quarter, and station bills of the John Adams.

(52) Log Kept by Mdn. William H. Macomb aboard the Potomac, Commanded by Capt. Joseph J. Nicholson, on a Cruise from Boston to the Mediterranean and Back, Sept. 19, 1834 - Mar. 19, 1837. 2 vols.

(53) Journal of the Experiment, Commanded by Lt. George S. Blake, Aug. 4, 1835 - Nov. 11, 1838, and the Nautilus, Commanded by Lieutenant Blake and Lt. Oliver Todd, Apr. 28, 1839 - Nov. 8, 1841, Surveying the Waters off the Atlantic Coast.

(54) Log Kept by Comdr. William Mervine, Commanding the Natchez on a Cruise from New York to Vera Cruz, July 23, 1836 - Nov. 25, 1837.

(55) Log Kept by Mdn. Abram Davis Harrell aboard the North Carolina (Flagship of Commo. Henry E. Ballard), Commanded by Lt. Thomas O. Selfridge, on a Cruise in the Pacific, Jan. 13, 1837 - June 25, 1839.

(56) Log Kept by Mdn. C. R. Perry Rodgers aboard the Fairfield, Commanded by Comdr. Isaac Mayo, on a Voyage from Norfolk to Montevideo, Apr. 5, 1837 - Oct. 31, 1838.

(57) Journals or Notebooks of Lt. Henry A. Wise, July 1837 - Nov. 9, 1860. 14 vols. These volumes were apparently designed as raw materials to be eventually combined and revised as an extensive autobiography. All are unofficial and informal, with scraps of original verse, quotations, witticisms, rough drawings, clippings, maps, and cryptograms on the fly-leaves, inside the covers, and scattered through the text. Some of the volumes are wholly or partly in pencil. They consist of the following: (a) notes on seamanship, accounts, and watch and quarter bills, July 1837 - Jan. 1842; (b) journal on the Cyane, cruising in the Mediterranean,

July 2, 1838 - Dec. 25, 1839 (3 vols.); (c) journal on the Gallatin, from Philadelphia and back, Sept. 13, 1843 - Feb. 16, 1844; (d) journal on the Plymouth and in Europe, Aug. 8, 1844 - Feb. 21, 1845; (e) journal on the Independence, from California to Hawaii and Valparaiso, Sept. 19, 1846 - Mar. 2, 1849 (2 vols., the second beginning with page 9 of chapter 28 of an unidentified treatise); (f) letter book and original poems composed during the writer's service in coast-survey work at Cambridge, Mass., Aug. 11 - Sept. 11, 1851, with poems and prose copied from various sources as late as 1873 (though Wise died in Apr. 1869); (g) journal on the Cumberland, from Boston to the Mediterranean, Apr. 23, 1852 - Dec. 5, 1853 (2 vols.); (h) journal of a vacation voyage from New York to Stockholm and other cities of Europe, May 22, 1858 - July 16, 1859 (2 vols.); and (i) journal on the Niagara, commanded by Capt. William W. McKean, on a voyage from New York to Hongkong to convey members of the staff of the Japanese Embassy to Japan, July 11 - Nov. 9, 1860. Many leaves have been cut out of the earlier volumes. References in several of the volumes suggest that the foregoing list does not contain all the journals and notebooks of the writer.

(58) Journal Kept by Mdn. John Julius Guthrie aboard the Columbia, Commanded by Commo. George C. Read, on a Cruise from Norfolk to Ceylon, China, Hawaii, and Back to Boston, Jan. 13, 1838 - May 14, 1839. At the end is an abstract of the writer's Naval services, May 6, 1838 - Apr. 13, 1858.

(59) Journal Kept by Mdn. John Colt Beaumont on a Cruise to the Gulf of Mexico and the Coast of Africa, June 1, 1838 - May 31, 1842. 2 vols. Service on the Erie (Comdr. Abraham S. Ten Eick, June 1 - July 25, 1838, at Pensacola), the Constellation (Commo. Alexander J. Dallas, Aug. 1-13, 1838, at Pensacola), the Ontario (Lt. Ebenezer Farrand and Comdr. John D. Williamson, Aug. 15, 1838 - Apr. 21, 1840), the Erie (Comdr. William V. Taylor, Apr. 26 - July 22, 1840, Pensacola to Boston), and the Constellation (Commo. Lawrence Kearny, Oct. 27, 1840 - May 31, 1842, Boston to Africa). The second volume begins Apr. 26, 1840.

(60) Journal Kept aboard the Marion, Commanded by Comdrs. William J. Belt and Louis M. Goldsborough, Cruising between Rio de Janeiro and Montevideo, Dec. 20, 1839 - June 20, 1842. The writer was probably Mdn. George W. Harrison, whose name appears on the flyleaf and elsewhere in the volume.

(61) Journal of a Cruise of the Potomac, Commanded by Capt. Lawrence Kearny, from Norfolk to Rio de Janeiro, May 12 - July 3, 1840. The same volume contains directions compiled by Commo. Charles Morris relating to signals and evolutions in general, 1843.

(62) Extract from a Journal Kept by William H. Meyers, Gunner aboard the Cyane, Commanded by Comdr. Cornelius K. Stribling, on a Voyage to and from the Pacific (photostat), July 23, 1841 - June 6, 1844. Original in possession of the Hon. Nelson B. Gaskill. Illustrated with various drawings.

(63) Log Kept by Lt. Stephen C. Rowan aboard the <u>Delaware</u> (Flagship of Commo. Charles Morris), Commanded by Capt. Charles Stewart McCauley, on a Cruise from Norfolk to Montevideo and the Mediterranean, Aug. 28, 1841 - Feb. 6, 1844.

M180

(64) Abstracts of Journals Kept by Lt. John Julius Guthrie aboard Various United States Ships, Jan. 14, 1842 - Apr. 13, 1858. Cruises on an unnamed vessel (cruising in the Gulf of Mexico, Jan. 14 - May 31, 1842), the <u>Union</u> (Lt. Henry H. Bell, Norfolk to Galveston and back to Norfolk, May 12 - Dec. 30, 1844), the <u>On-ka-hy-e</u> (Lt. Arthur Sinclair, Norfolk to Corpus Christi and back to Norfolk, July 31, 1845 - Jan. 7, 1846), the <u>Flirt</u> (Lt. Arthur Sinclair, Norfolk to Tampico and back to Norfolk, Mar. 11 - Nov. 1, 1846), the <u>Brandywine</u> (Commo. George W. Storer, Norfolk to Montevideo and back to New York, July 2, 1847 - Dec. 6, 1850), the <u>Saranac</u> (Capt. John C. Long, Philadelphia to Rio de Janeiro and back to Norfolk, Sept. 15, 1851 - July 8, 1853), and the <u>Levant</u> (Comdr. William Smith, New York to Cape Town, China, Manila, Cape Town, and back to Boston, Oct. 16, 1855 - Apr. 13, 1858).

(65) Journal Kept by Comdr. Thomas A. Dornin, Commanding the <u>Dale</u>, on a Cruise from Callao to California and Philadelphia, Apr. 21, 1842 - Oct. 20, 1843, and the <u>Portsmouth</u>, on a Cruise from Boston to Martinique, Nov. 21, 1851 - Feb. 21, 1852.

M981

(66) Log Kept by Passed Mdn. John Colt Beaumont aboard the <u>Constellation</u> (Flagship of Commo. Lawrence Kearny), on a Cruise from Canton to Manila, Callao, and the United States, June 1, 1842 - Apr. 30, 1844.

(67) Journal of Vice-Admiral Stephen C. Rowan, June 2, 1843 - ca. 1869. Abstracts of logs of the <u>Dale</u> (Mazatlán to Philadelphia, June 2 - Oct. 15, 1843), the <u>Cyane</u> (Norfolk to California and back to Norfolk, June 20, 1845 - Oct. 11, 1848), and the <u>Relief</u> (New York to Rio de Janeiro, Mar. 24, 1854 - Oct. 20, 1855); and a private journal kept by Admiral Rowan during his command of the Asiatic Squadron, Aug. 1, 1867 - ca. 1869, containing comments on the manners and customs of the Japanese.

M180

(68) Journal of Mdn. William Sharp, Nov. 3, 1843 - May 27, 1845. Cruises on the <u>United States</u>, flagship of Commo. Thomas ap Catesby Jones (Capt. James Armstrong, Callao to Mazatlán and Boston, Nov. 3, 1843 - Oct. 15, 1844), the <u>St. Mary's</u> (Comdr. John L. Saunders, Washington to Gosport, Dec. 13, 1844 - Jan. 18, 1845), and the <u>Jamestown</u>, flagship of Commo. Charles W. Skinner (Comdr. Robert B. Cunningham, Norfolk to Porto Praia, Jan. 18 - May 27, 1845).

(69) Log Kept by Mdn. Meriwether Patterson Jones aboard the <u>Constitution</u>, Commanded by Capt. John Percival, on a Cruise from New York to Madagascar, China, Hawaii, Mexico, and Chile, May 20, 1844 - July 5, 1846.

M 1030

(70) Journal of Mdn. James Charles P. De Krafft, Oct. 1, 1844 - Dec. 31, 1846, June 15 - Nov. 23, 1847. Cruises on the <u>Raritan</u>, flagship of Commo. Daniel Turner (Capt. Francis H. Gregory, Rio de Janeiro to Montevideo and

Vera Cruz, Oct. 1, 1844 - Dec. 2, 1846), the Cumberland (Capt. Francis H. Gregory, Vera Cruz to Norfolk, Dec. 2-31, 1846), and the Ohio (Capt. Silas H. Stringham, New York to Rio de Janeiro, June 15 - Nov. 23, 1847).

(71) Log Kept aboard the Portsmouth, Commanded by Comdr. John B. Montgomery, on a Cruise from Callao to San Francisco, May 12, 1845 - Oct. 5, 1846. This volume was received by the Office of Naval Records and Library as part of the Gansevoort Papers. Mdn. Stanwix Gansevoort, an officer on the voyage, was probably the writer of the log.

(72) Journal of Capt. William Mervine, Commanding the Cyane and the Savannah on a Cruise from Norfolk to Monterey, Calif., July 26, 1845 - Nov. 16, 1846. Captain Mervine turned over the command of the Cyane to Lt. Stephen C. Rowan July 7, 1846, and thereafter remained at Monterey in command of the United States Forces on Shore till Sept. 22, 1846, when he took command of the Savannah, which remained in or near Monterey Harbor.

(73) Journal Kept by Lt. George S. Blake, Commanding the Perry, on a Voyage to Vera Cruz and Back to Philadelphia, May 16 - Dec. 8, 1846, and the Germantown, on a Voyage from Philadelphia to Norfolk and Back to Philadelphia, Dec. 9, 1846 - Jan. 19, 1847.

(74) Journal Kept by Lt. Tunis Augustus M. Craven aboard the Dale on a Voyage from Rio de Janeiro to San Francisco and Guaymas, June 14, 1846 - Apr. 9, 1848. A postscript is dated December 24, 1848.

(75) Journal Kept by Mdn. Philip C. Johnson, Jr., aboard the Ohio and the Savannah, on a Voyage from Boston to Monterey, Calif., Dec. 14, 1846 - Nov. 14, 1848. The log of the Ohio closes at sea; that of the Savannah begins Jan. 21, 1848.

(76) Extract from the Journal Kept by Mdn. Philip C. Johnson, Jr., aboard the Ohio, Commanded by Capt. Cornelius K. Stribling (photostat), Mar. 29, 1847 - Sept. 10, 1848.

(77) Log of the Colonel Cross, Commanded by Capt. William C. Rogers, on a Voyage from Philadelphia to Vera Cruz and Back to New Orleans, Sept. 23, 1847 - Apr. 30, 1848.

(78) Journal Kept by Past Mdn. Nicholas H. Van Zandt aboard the Columbus (Flagship of Commo. Thomas Biddle), Commanded by Capt. Thomas W. Wyman, on a Voyage from Valparaiso to Hampton Roads, Oct. 14, 1847 - Mar. 15, 1848, and the Relief, Commanded by Lt. Benjamin J. Totten, on a Voyage from New York to Porto Praia, Oct. 27 - Dec. 12, 1849.

(79) Journal Kept by Lt. Tunis Augustus M. Craven aboard the Dale, Commanded by Comdr. John Rudd, Aug. 3, 1848 - Aug. 19, 1849.

(80) Journal of Lt. William Reynolds, June 12, 1849 - July 28, 1865. Steam log of the Alleghany on a Voyage from Malta to Washington, Pensacola, and back to Washington, Jan. 12 - Oct. 1, 1849; navigation log of the Alleghany, Aug. 20 - Oct. 6, 1849; a long penciled account of the Hawaiian

Islands, where the writer served as naval storekeeper, Feb. 1857 - Nov. 1861; and a paragraph sketching later events. Many pages have been cut out.

(81) Log of the Excellent, Commanded by Lt. Guert Gansevoort, on a Voyage from an Unnamed Port to Norfolk, Apr. 25 - June 20, 1850. According to the title page, the log was kept by Ebenezer Andrews, Jr., but it contains entries by several watch officers.

(82) Journal Kept by Passed Mdn. Robert R. Carter aboard the Rescue, on a Voyage in Search of Sir John Franklin in the Arctic, Beginning and Ending at New York (photostat), May 13, 1850 - Oct. 5, 1851. Original in possession of R. A. James H. Oliver.

M981 (83) Journal of Comdr. Thomas A. Dornin, Commanding the Portsmouth on a Cruise from Rio de Janeiro to San Francisco, Honolulu, and Tahiti and back to Hampton Roads, Feb. 22, 1852 - Apr. 4, 1855.

(84) Journal Kept by Frederic Donald Stuart, Draftsman and Assistant Astronomer on the Vincennes, Flagship of the North Pacific Expedition Commanded by Comdr. Cadwalader Ringgold, May 31, 1853 - Mar. 13, 1854. At the front is an introduction, setting forth the purposes of the expedition, and a list of vessels and officers engaged in it. The writer served as secretary to Commander Ringgold. For other journals of the expedition, see Entry 272.

(85) Journal Kept by Act'g Lt. Jonathan H. Carter aboard the John P. Kennedy in the North Pacific Expedition, Beginning at New York and Ending at Norfolk, June 11, 1853 - Feb. 14, 1856.

(86) The Razee: A Journal Kept by Chaplain Fitch W. Taylor during a Cruise among the Samoan Islands aboard the Independence, ca. 1854. Consists chiefly of comments upon the manners and morals of the Samoans. Many pages are cut out and others are canceled.

(87) Medical Journal Kept by Ass't Surgeon R. P. Daniel aboard the San Jacinto, Commanded by Comdr. Henry H. Bell, on a Cruise from New York to Hongkong and Back to New York (typed copy), Oct. 25, 1855 - Aug. 1858. Copy prepared by the State Office, Jacksonville, Fla., Historical Records Survey, from original owned by Dr. R. P. Daniel, Jacksonville.

(88) Journal Kept by Lt. William H. Macomb aboard the Portsmouth, Commanded by Comdr. Andrew H. Foote, on a Cruise from Hampton Roads to Cape Town, Canton, and Back to Boston, Apr. 5, 1856 - June 23, 1858.

(89) Journal Kept by Mdn. Weld N. Allen aboard the Cyane, Commanded by Comdr. Robert G. Robb, on a Cruise from Boston to Aspinwall, Colombia (now Colón, C. Z.), and Back to Norfolk, Oct. 25, 1856 - Jan. 12, 1858, and the Perry, Commanded by Lt. Richard L. Tilghman, on a Voyage from Norfolk to Montevideo, Jan. 21 - May 4, 1858.

(90) Diary of First Lt. Henry W. Queen, USMC, on a Cruise from the Mediterranean to Bluefields, Nicaragua, Jan. 1 - Dec. 31, 1857

("Agenda"). In pencil and barely legible. The ship to which Lieutenant Queen was attached is not named.

(91) Log of the Wabash, Commanded by Capt. Samuel Barron, on a Voyage from New York to Smyrna, May 25 - Sept. 29, 1858.

(92) Abstract of the Log of the Metacomet, Renamed the Pulaski, Commanded by Lt. William H. Macomb, on a Cruise from Warrington, Fla., to Montevideo, Dec. 8, 1858 - Mar. 7, 1862. Notice was received Dec. 15, 1859, that the name of the Metacomet had been changed to the Pulaski.

(93) Journal Kept by Mdn. Francis B. Blake aboard the Minnesota, Commanded by Capt. Samuel F. Du Pont, on a Voyage from the Mozambique Channel to Boston, Mar. 21 - June 2, 1859.

(94) Log Kept by Mdn. George C. Remey aboard the Hartford (Flagship of the East India Squadron), Commanded by Capt. Charles Lowndes, on a Cruise from Boston to Hongkong and Back to Philadelphia, June 14, 1859 - Dec. 6, 1861.

(95) Journal Kept by First Ass't Engineer Richard C. Potts aboard the Powhatan on a Voyage from China to San Francisco and Philadelphia, June 15, 1859 - Aug. 13, 1860. Indexed.

(96) Journal Kept by Second Ass't Engineer Edward B. Latch aboard the Sumter, Aug. 1859 - Feb. 1860, and the Hartford, Jan. 1862 - May 1863.

(97) Journal Kept by Passed Mdn. Francis B. Blake aboard the Mohican, Jan. 19 - May 30, 1860, and the Marion, Aug. 13 - Oct. 1, 1860, on a Voyage from New York to São Paulo de Loanda and Back to Portsmouth, N. H.

(98) Journal of the Mississippi (Flagship of Commo. William Mervine, Commanding the Gulf Squadron), May 2 - July 12, 1861, and the Colorado, July 15 - Sept. 22, 1861.

(99) Reminiscences of Lt. Comdr. William Barker Cushing, May 1861 - Feb. 1865. 3 vols., consisting of manuscript original, a ribbon copy, and a carbon copy. A connected narrative of the writer's naval services at M1034 sea and on shore.

(100) Log of the Santee, Commanded by Capt. Henry Eagle, on a Cruise from Portsmouth, N. H., to Galveston and Back to Boston, June 7, 1861 - Aug. 26, 1862.

(101) Journal Kept by Comdr. Stephen D. Trenchard, Commanding the Rhode Island, July 31, 1861 - Aug.17, 1865. 3 vols.

(102) Log of the Lexington, Commanded by Comdr. Roger N. Stembel and Lt. James W. Shirk, Mississippi Squadron, Aug. 16, 1861 - June 21, 1862.

(103) Journal of the Augusta, Commanded by Comdr. Enoch G. Parrott, South Atlantic Blockading Squadron, on a Cruise Beginning at New York and Ending at Philadelphia, Oct. 16, 1861 - Sept. 4, 1862.

(104) Journal Kept by Comdr. George F. Emmons, Commanding the Hatteras, West Gulf Blockading Squadron, on a Voyage Beginning at Philadelphia, Nov. 1, 1861 - June 30, 1862.

(105) Journals Kept by Carpenter's Mate William M. C. Philbrick aboard the Portsmouth, West Gulf Blockading Squadron, Nov. 20, 1861 - Apr. 4, 1865. 3 vols. Two of the journals, in pencil, Jan. 12 - Nov. 29, 1862, and June 4, 1863 - Apr. 4, 1865, are probably sources from which the main journal, Nov. 20, 1861 - Aug. 8, 1864, was later compiled. The main journal seems not to have been finished.

(106) Journal of Commo. Henry H. Bell, Commanding the Brooklyn on and near the Lower Mississippi, Jan. 2, 1862 - July 3, 1863. 6 vols. In pencil.

(107) Journal Kept by Second Ass't Engineer Isaac DeGraff aboard the Hartford, West Gulf Blockading Squadron, on a Cruise Beginning and Ending at New York, Jan. 25, 1862 - Dec. 20, 1864, and the Tennessee, on a Voyage from Boston to Cartagena, Colombia, and Back to Philadelphia, Feb. 4 - May 13, 1865. 2 vols.

(108) Log of the Ino, Commanded by Act'g Volunteer Lt. Josiah P. Cressy, on a Voyage (Beginning and Ending at Boston) in Pursuit of the Confederate States Ship Sumter, Feb. 5 - June 3, 1862.

(109) Journal Kept by Lt. John Colt Beaumont, Commanding the Aroostook, Feb. 20 - July 8, 1862, the Dakota, Mar. 15 - Apr. 10, 1863, and the Mackinaw, Apr. 23, 1864 - Mar. 31, 1865, Serving in the North Atlantic Blockading Squadron.

(110) Log of the Monitor, Commanded by Lt. John L. Worden, Cruising off the Atlantic Coast of the United States, Feb. 25 - Sept. 10, 1862.

(111) Correspondence and Journal of Comdr. George M. Ransom, Feb. 1862 - Dec. 2, 1870. 3 vols. Commander Ransom commanded the Kineo (West Gulf Blockading Squadron, 1862-63), the Mercedita (West India Squadron, 1863), the Grand Gulf (North Atlantic Blockading Squadron, 1863-64), the Muscoota (East Gulf Blockading Squadron, later Gulf Squadron, May 18 - Nov. 7, 1865), the Algonquin (New York Navy Yard, 1866), and the Terror (Boston to Key West, Dec. 3, 1869 - Dec. 2, 1870).

(112) Extracts from the Diary of R. A. David G. Farragut (photostat), Apr. 24, 1862, Mar. 14, 1863, and Aug. 5 - Dec. 13, 1864. 2 vols. Original in possession of Mr. George T. Keating, New York, 1939.

(113) Journal of the Ram Lancaster No. 3, Serving in the Vicinity of Memphis and Vicksburg, June 19 - July 16, 1862.

(114) Abstract of the Log of the Tioga, Commanded by Comdr. Albert G. Clary, West India Squadron, on a Cruise from Boston to Bermuda, June 30, 1862 - Mar. 1, 1863. In pencil.

126

(115) Log of the Genesee, Commanded by Comdr. William H. Macomb, on a Cruise from Boston to the Mississippi, July 3, 1862 – Sept. 16, 1863.

(116) Journal Kept by Capt. George F. Emmons, Commanding the R. R. Cuyler from Mobile to Donaldsonville, Nov. 20, 1862 – July 15, 1863, the Monongahela from Donaldsonville to New Orleans, July 17 – Aug. 10, 1863, and the Brooklyn from New Orleans to New York, Aug. 12-26, 1863.

(117) Log of the Rachel Seaman, Commanded by Act'g Master Quincy A. Cooper, on a Cruise from Sabine Pass, Texas, to New York, Dec. 1, 1862 – Aug. 29, 1863. The front of the same volume, labeled on the flyleaf "United States, Book of Record, Public Property, October 1, 1850," with index, contains copies of affidavits made in and near Pensacola relative to naval purchases, Oct. 1, 1850 – Jan. 27, 1859.

(118) Log of the General Headquarters of the East Gulf Blockading Squadron, Key West, July 19, 1863 – July 23, 1864 ("Arrivals, Departures, & General Movements of U. S. Vessels, at Key West, Fla.").

(119) Journal Kept by Charles H. Guider aboard the Commodore Read, on a Cruise from New York to Washington, Aug. 25, 1863 – July 12, 1864, and the Vanderbilt, on a Voyage from New York to San Francisco and Back to New York, Apr. 7, 1865 – Apr. 6, 1868. 2 vols.

(120) Journal and Letter Book of Capt. George F. Emmons, Commanding the Brooklyn on Duty near Charleston and on a Voyage to Baltimore, Sept. 18 – Dec. 13, 1863.

(121) Journal Kept by J. C. Gregg aboard the Brooklyn, on a Cruise from New York to Mobile and Back to New York (typed copy), May 10, 1864 – Jan. 31, 1865. Original in possession of Lt. F. C. Sachse, 1932.

(122) Log of the Cowslip, West Gulf Blockading Squadron, Cruising off Pensacola and Mobile, June 14 – Aug. 30, 1864.

(123) Logs of the Prize Steamer Matagorda, Alias Alice, Commanded by Lt. Simeon P. Gillett, in a Voyage Beginning at Sea and Ending at Boston, Sept. 20-29, 1864. 2 vols. Logs dated Sept. 20-29 and 22-29.

(124) Abstract of Logs Kept by Comdr. Richard Graham Davenport, Sept. 29, 1864 – Dec. 25, 1900. At the end of the volume is a reference to a second volume, which has not been found.

(125) Journal Kept by Capt. George F. Emmons, Commanding the Lackawanna on a Cruise from New York to Galveston and Back to New York, Oct. 12, 1864 – June 30, 1865, and the Pensacola, on a Cruise from Norfolk to New York, Feb. 28 – Mar. 31, 1866. Contains notes on the writer's shore service between the 2 voyages.

(126) Journal and Correspondence of Lt. Comdr. William W. Low, Commanding the Octorara, West Gulf Blockading Squadron, Dec. 5, 1864 – Apr. 23, 1865. The journal begins Mar. 20, 1865.

(127) Steam Log of the James Adger, Commanded by Act'g Volunteer Lt. Comdr. John MacDearmid, Cruising off Aspinwall, Colombia (now Colón, C. Z.), Oct. 1 – Dec. 31, 1865.

(128) Remark Book Kept by Act'g Master Anthony F. Holmes aboard the James Adger, on a Voyage from Aspinwall, Colombia, to New York, Jan. 1 – May 2, 1866. This volume is apparently not by the writer of (127).

(129) Remark Book of the Lackawanna, Commanded by Capt. William Reynolds, on a Cruise from New York to Honolulu and Back to San Francisco, June 11, 1866 – Jan. 9, 1869. Signed by Reynolds but not in his hand.

(130) Journal of the South Atlantic Squadron (Flagship Guerrière), on a Cruise from Boston to Buenos Aires and Rio de Janeiro, June 19, 1867 – June 25, 1869, Submitted by Comdr. Francis M. Ramsay, Chief of Staff, to R. A. Charles H. Davis, Commanding the Squadron. 2 vols.

(131) Log of the Plymouth, Commanded by Capt. William H. Macomb, on a Cruise from New York to Europe and Back to Portland, Me., Jan. 20, 1869 – Jan. 26, 1870.

(132) Log of the Colorado, Commanded by Capt. George H. Cooper, on a Voyage from New York toward China, Feb. 15 – Apr. 16, 1870.

(133) Journals, Accounts, and Correspondence of Lt. Comdr. George C. Remey, Engaged in the Naval Survey of the Isthmus of Tehuantepec under the Command of Capt. Robert W. Shufeldt, Commanding the Mayflower, Nov. 11, 1870 – Apr. 27, 1871. 2 vols. The larger volume begins and ends at Minatitlán. The smaller is a penciled diary of surveys, Feb. 12 – Apr. 4, 1871.

(134) Journal Kept by Mdn. James H. Bull aboard the Guard, Commanded by Comdr. Thomas O. Selfridge, in Charge of the Darien Interoceanic Canal Surveying Expedition, on a Voyage Beginning and Ending at New York, Dec. 3, 1870 – July 22, 1871.

(135) Journal Kept by Lt. Charles H. Rockwell aboard the Palos, Cruising off China and Japan, Jan. 1 – Dec. 31, 1871.

(136) Journal Kept by N. Hayes aboard the Polaris on an Exploring Voyage to Greenland, July 27, 1871 – Aug. 16, 1872. 2 vols. Sheets of a preface to the journal lie loose in the second volume.

(137) Surveying Journals of the United States Naval Nicaragua Surveying Expedition, Commanded by Comdr. Chester Hatfield, Kept by Lts. Jacob E. Noel, Eugene H. C. Leutze, and William W. Rhoades, May 1 – June 12, 1872. 2 vols. Surveys of the Sapoa route by Noel, May 1–24; the Ochomogo route by Leutze, May 27 – June 6; and the Brito route by Rhoades, May 1–12. The journals were submitted as reports to Commander Hatfield.

(138) Log Kept by Cadet Mdn. Nathaniel R. Usher aboard the Constellation, on a Summer Cruise from Annapolis to Newport and Back to Annapolis,

June 9 - Sept. 25, 1872. Apparently a smooth copy of a log that contained entries by all the watch officers.

(139) Log Kept by Charles E. Cany, Captain's Clerk aboard the California (Flagship of the North Pacific Squadron), Commanded by Capt. James Charles P. De Krafft, on a Cruise from San Francisco to Hongkong, Nov. 27, 1872 - Feb. 27, 1875. 2 vols.

(140) Log of the Kearsarge, Commanded by Capt. David B. Harmony, on a Cruise from San Francisco to China and Back to Hampton Roads, Dec. 8, 1873 - Oct. 28, 1875. 3 vols.

(141) Log Kept by Cadet Mdn. Nathaniel R. Usher aboard the Constellation on a Cruise from Annapolis to Newport and Back to Annapolis, June 12 - Sept. 24, 1874.

(142) Log Kept by Ens. Nathaniel R. Usher aboard the Tennessee (Flagship of the Asiatic Squadron), on a Cruise from New York to Japan, China, and Egypt, June 23, 1875 - Nov. 17, 1877. 2 vols.

(143) Journal Kept by Mdn. Alfred L. Hall aboard the Monongahela, Commanded by Capt. William E. Fitzhugh, on a Cruise from New York to Yokohama, Aug. 1, 1877 - May 15, 1879, and the Constellation, Commanded by Comdr. Edward E. Potter, on a Voyage from New York to Dublin and Back to Annapolis, Mar. 18 - June 13, 1880.

(144) Record of Observations to Determine Ship's Position Made by Lt. George W. De Long on a Voyage from Havre de Grâce to San Francisco, July-Dec. 1878. Chiefly in pencil.

(145) Journal Kept by Cadet Mdn. Albert W. Grant aboard the Lackawanna, on a Cruise from San Francisco to Newfoundland and Portsmouth, N. H., Sept. 24, 1878 - Sept. 3, 1880, and the Iroquois, on a Cruise from San Francisco to Paita, Peru, Apr. 12, 1882 - Jan. 27, 1883.

(146) Journal Kept aboard the Jeannette and on the Ice by Lt. Comdr. George W. De Long, Commanding the Arctic Expedition from San Francisco to the Seas North of Siberia, July 8, 1879 - Oct. 30, 1881. 4 vols. The Jeannette was crushed in the ice and sunk June 12, 1881, at 77° 15′ N, 155° 0′ E. The last volume, labeled "DeLong's Ice Diaries," recounts the wanderings of the survivors on foot. The whole journal is a smooth copy, not in Commander De Long's handwriting.

(147) Journal Kept by Ens. Albert Parker Niblack aboard the Lackawanna, on a Cruise from Chinibote to Apia, Honolulu, and Panama, Sept. 17, 1880 - Apr. 3, 1883, and the C. P. Patterson, on a Surveying Cruise from Hampton Roads to Alaska and Back to Port Townsend, Wash., July 30, 1884 - May 5, 1886.

(148) Journal of the Charleston, Commanded by Capt. George C. Remey, on a Cruise from San Francisco to China and Back to San Francisco, Dec. 26, 1889 - Mar. 10, 1892.

(149) Journal Kept by Ens. Edward H. Watson aboard the Maine, on a Cruise from Hampton Roads to New York, July 1, 1895 - Apr. 25, 1896.

(150) Journal Kept by Naval Cadet Arthur St. Clair aboard the Indiana on a Cruise from New York to Santiago de Cuba, June 19, 1897 - July 9, 1898. Contains numerous mounted photographs.

(151) Extracts from the Diary of Adm. George Dewey in the Philippines and the United States (photostat), Jan. 10, 1898 - Oct. 3, 1899. 2 vols. Original in possession of the Chicago Historical Society.

(152) Journal of the Illinois (Red Star Line), Commanded by Lt. Edward V. Roberts, and the Supply, on a Voyage from Philadelphia to Cuba and Back to Philadelphia, Mar. 14 - July 9, 1898. The log of the Illinois ends at Philadelphia May 6; that of the Supply begins the next day. The Illinois did not leave Philadelphia.

(153) Journal of the North Atlantic Squadron, Commanded by R. A. William T. Sampson (carbon copy), Apr. 21 - May 14, 1898. Chiefly copies of correspondence and orders.

(154) Engineering Log Kept by Passed Ass't Engineer William H. Perkins aboard the Frolic, on a Cruise from Portsmouth, N. H., to Norfolk, July 6 - Sept. 27, 1898.

(155) Log of the Supply, Commanded by Lt. Comdrs. Royal R. Ingersoll, Edward V. Roberts, and William W. Kimball, on a Cruise Beginning and Ending at New York, July 9, 1898 - Feb. 2, 1899.

(156) Journal Kept by Naval Cadet Charles E. Courtney aboard the Newark, on a Cruise from New York to Cavite, Feb. 1, 1899 - Mar. 31, 1901, and for Short Periods on the Isla de Cuba, the New York, the Don Juan de Austria, the Buffalo, the Hancock, and the Hartford, 1901-04. The entries on the Newark are detailed; those made later are scattered and brief. The volume is illustrated with numerous mounted photographs.

(157) Journal Kept by Ens. Dudley W. Knox, Commanding the Albany in the Philippines, Jan. 25 - Mar. 23, 1900.

(158) Log of the Hospital Ship Relief, Cruising in the Philippines, Dec. 1, 1900 - June 17, 1901.

(159) Journal Kept by Mdn. Richard Wainwright, Jr., aboard the Massachusetts, on a Cruise Beginning and Ending at New York, May 21 - Sept. 13, 1902, and the Indiana, at New York, Sept. 18, 1902.

(160) Rough Logs of the Mayflower, Cruising between Washington and New York, Feb. 1-28, 1907, and June 1-30, 1908. 2 vols. Form NEq. 21.

APPENDIX E: LIST OF OFFICERS' LETTER BOOKS

(The entries in this list, arranged chronologically, refer to subseries
of Entry 395. Except as otherwise indicated, each entry in this list
refers to a single unindexed volume.)

(1) Letters Sent by Capt. John Paul Jones, Commanding the Ranger and
the Bonhomme Richard, Mar. 1778 - July 1779. 4 vols. Photostat of a
letter book presented to the Naval Academy by James Carson Brevoort, of
Brooklyn, Sept. 20, 1829; and a typed copy (3 vols.) of the same.

(2) Letters Sent by Capt. Thomas Truxtun, Commanding the Constellation on a Cruise to the West Indies (photostat of handwritten copies)
May 1798 - Dec. 1799. Original in the Library of the Historical Society
of Pennsylvania.

(3) Correspondence of Commo. Thomas Tingey, Commanding the Ganges
on a Cruise to the West Indies, and Establishing the Washington Navy Yard
(handwritten copies), Sept. 1798 - Sept. 1799, Feb.-June 1800, July 1801.
Typed index.

(4) Correspondence of Capt. Alexander Murray, Commanding the Constellation, the Insurgente, and the Adams (handwritten copies), June 1799 -
Dec. 1805. Typed index. These vessels cruised in the West Indies and
the Mediterranean.

(5) Letters Sent by Capt. Thomas Truxtun, Commanding the President
on a Cruise to the West Indies (photostat of handwritten copies), June
1800 - June 1801. Original in the Library of the Historical Society of
Pennsylvania.

(6) Letters Sent by Capt. Richard Dale (Flagship President), Commanding the Mediterranean Squadron (photostat), May 1801 - Jan. 1802. Typed
index. Original in possession of Edward C. Dale, Bryn Mawr, Pa.

(7) Correspondence of Commo. Isaac Hull (Flagship Argus), Commanding
the Mediterranean Squadron (handwritten copies), May 1803 - May 1806.
2 vols. Indexed. (a) Letters received, May 1803 - May 1806; and (b)
letters sent, Jan. 1804 - May 1806.

(8) Letters Sent by Lt. Daniel S. Dexter, aboard Gun Vessel 162 and
the Louisiana in the Gulf of Mexico (handwritten copies), Sept. 1811 -
Nov. 1813.

(9) Letters Sent by Commo. Isaac Hull, Commanding the United States
on a Cruise from Hampton Roads to Callao, Nov. 1823 - Mar. 1827.

(10) Correspondence of Commo. John Rodgers, Commanding the North
Carolina on a Cruise from the Mediterranean to Hampton Roads (photostat),
June 1825 - July 1827. Loose sheets tied between boards. Original in
possession of a member of the Rodgers family.

(11) Letters Sent by Capt. George W. Rodgers, Commanding the Warren (handwritten copies), Dec. 1831 - May 1832.

(12) Letters Sent by Lt. William H. Macomb (handwritten copies), Apr. 1834 - Dec. 1855. Begins with the service of the writer as a midshipman, and includes not only letters but various computations and rough notes.

(13) Letters Sent by Commo. Jesse D. Elliott (Flagship Constitution), Commanding the Mediterranean Squadron (handwritten copies), Mar. 1835 - Mar. 1837.

(14) Correspondence of R. A. William Mervine (handwritten copies), July 1836 - Aug. 1868. 8 vols. Indexed. (a) Letters sent and received, 1836-56 (2 vols.); (b) letters received, 1855-57 (2 vols.); (c) letters sent, 1855-60 (3 vols.); and (d) a miscellaneous volume probably copied from the first volume of letters sent and received, with later additions, 1836-47, 1861-68. In the first volume of letters sent and received, pages 1-73 are stapled firmly together in such a way that they cannot be read. Captain Mervine (promoted to Rear Admiral in Aug. 1866) commanded the Constellation (Home Squadron, 1836-37), the Cyane (Pacific Squadron, 1845-46), the Savannah (Pacific Squadron, 1846-47), and the Powhatan (Pacific Squadron, 1852), and served as commanding officer of the Pacific Squadron (Flagship Independence, 1854-57) and the Gulf Blockading Squadron (Flagships Mississippi and Colorado, 1861). His later services were confined to shore duties.

(15) Correspondence of Commo. Daniel Turner (Flagship Constitution), Commanding the Pacific Squadron (handwritten copies), Jan. 1839 - Nov. 1841. Captain Turner assumed command of the Pacific Squadron in Mar. 1841, when the vessel that he had commanded in the Pacific Squadron since 1839 became the flagship.

(16) Correspondence of Lt. Comdr. C. R. Perry Rodgers, Commanding the Phoenix off the Coast of Florida (handwritten copies), July 1839 - Mar. 1842.

(17) Correspondence of Lt. James Charles P. De Krafft (handwritten copies), Oct. 1841 - Jan. 1861. Includes service in the Coast Survey Office, on the John Adams in a voyage from Valparaiso to Panama (1856-57), and on the Michigan at Erie, Pa.

(18) Correspondence of the Commanding Officer of the African Squadron (handwritten copies and some originals), 1842-55. 2 vols. Indexed. The first volume is labeled "Public Documents from Commodores Perry, Read, Skinner, Bolton, Cooper, Gregory, and Lavallette, Transferred to Commodore Mayo, and by Him to His Successor, Commodore Crabbe, and by Him to Flag Officer Thos. A. Conover."

(19) Letters Sent by Commo. Daniel Turner (Flagships Columbia, Columbus, and Raritan), Commanding the Brazil Squadron (handwritten copies), Apr. 1843 - Mar. 1845.

(20) Correspondence of Capt. Joel Abbot, Commanding the Decatur, African Squadron (handwritten copies), June 1843 - Dec. 1844. Indexed.

(21) Letters Sent by Commo. David Conner (Flagships Potomac, Falmouth, Cumberland, and Raritan), Commanding the Home Squadron (hand-written copies), Dec. 1843 - May 1847. 5 vols. Letters to (a) the Navy Department, Dec. 1843 - May 1847 (2 vols.), and (b) the Squadron, Dec. 1843 - Mar. 1847 (3 vols.), including service at Vera Cruz.

(22) Correspondence of Comdr. John B. Montgomery, Commanding the Portsmouth off the Coasts of California and Mexico (handwritten copies). Oct. 1844 - Nov. 1848. 4 vols. (a) Letters sent, Oct. 1844 - Nov. 1848 (3 vols.), and (b) orders received and sent, Feb. 1845 - Oct. 1846, Dec. 1847 - Nov. 1848. Commander Montgomery served as Military Governor of San Diego under Commodore Stockton, Governor of California.

(23) Letters Sent by Commo. William C. Bolton (Flagship Jamestown), Commanding the African Squadron (handwritten copies), Sept. 1847 - Jan. 1849. 2 vols. The first volume is labeled "Miscellaneous Letters, Orders, & Instructions"; the second, "Letter Book." These volumes may serve as a partial substitute for the missing originals of Commodore Bolton's letters to the Secretary of the Navy during this period.

(24) Orders Received by Capt. William Jamesson, Commanding the Cumberland, Home Squadron (typed copies), Dec. 1847 - May 1848.

(25) Correspondence of Capt. George S. Blake, Commanding the Independence, Mediterranean Squadron (handwritten copies), Sept. 1849 - Nov. 1851. 2 vols. Indexed.

(26) Correspondence of Surgeon James C. Palmer, Jan. 1853 - May 1876. 4 vols. and 1 adhesive binder. (a) Original letters received and hand-written copies of letters sent, mounted as a single sequence in 2 blank books, Jan. 1853 - May 1876; (b) register of letters to and from medical officers of the West Gulf Blockading Squadron, Aug. 1863 - Oct. 1865; (c) press copies of letters sent, Dec. 1868 - June 1873; and (d) printed copies of orders received and issued, Mar. 1869 - Apr. 1873 (1 adhesive binder). The writer served on the receiving ship at Baltimore (1854-57), in the Mediterranean Squadron aboard the Niagara and the Macedonian (1857), as Fleet Surgeon of the West Gulf Blockading Squadron during the Civil War, in the Naval Hospital at New York, and (June 1872 - July 1873) as Surgeon General of the Navy. According to a note on the flyleaf of the earliest volume, he assembled these materials for his daughters, and had discarded earlier correspondence that did not seem to warrant preserva-tion. According to a note on the flyleaf of the register, he had destroyed most of the correspondence registered in that volume.

(27) Orders Received by Lt. Henry Rolando, Commanding the Vincennes, from Commo. Cadwalader Ringgold, Commanding the North Pacific Exploring Expedition (handwritten copies), June 1853 - Jan. 1854.

(28) Letters Sent by Vice-Adm. Stephen C. Rowan, with Summaries of His Naval Services (handwritten copies), Feb. 1854 - Mar. 1890. Indexed. Labeled on the flyleaf, "Copies of Letters Written by S. C. Rowan, U. S. Navy, from Feby 22, 1854 to Jan 21, 1880, and Transferred, Jany 1882, from Various Letter Books: Also Notes of His Services and List of Battles & Engagements in Which He Took Part during Mexican War and War of 1861.2.3.4.5." He served on the _Relief_ on a voyage to Rio de Janeiro (1854); on the _Pawnee_, the _Delaware_, and the _Philadelphia_ off North Carolina (1861-62); on the _New Ironsides_ off Charleston (1863-64); as commanding officer of the Asiatic Squadron (1867-70); as Commandant of the New York Navy Yard; and in other capacities.

(29) Orders Received by Lt. Joshua Bishop (originals), Oct. 1854 - June 1864. During the Civil War Lieutenant Bishop commanded the _General Bragg_, Mississippi Squadron.

(30) Correspondence of Comdr. Guert Gansevoort, Commanding the _Decatur_, Pacific Squadron (handwritten copies), Oct. 1855 - Mar. 1856. 2 vols. Indexed.

(31) Letters Sent by Lt. C. R. Perry Rodgers, Assistant to the United States Coast Survey, Commanding the _Gallatin_ and the _Bible_ in Surveys from New England to South Carolina (handwritten copies), Oct. 1855 - Mar. 1858. 2 vols.

(32) Letters Received by Comdr. John Rodgers and Lt. Matthew F. Maury, Office of the North Pacific Exploring Expedition, Washington (handwritten copies), Sept. 1856 - Oct. 1860. The letters (occupying only 10 pages) relate chiefly to proposed publication of results of the exploring expedition.

(33) Letters Sent by John B. Rittenhouse, Purser of the _Susquehanna_, Mediterranean Squadron (press copies), Jan.-Oct. 1857. Barely legible.

(34) Letters Sent by Henry Myers, Paymaster of the _Marion_, African Squadron (handwritten copies), May 1858 - Oct. 1860.

(35) Letters Sent by Lt. William H. Macomb, Commanding the _Metacomet_, Renamed the _Pulaski_, Brazil Squadron (handwritten copies), Nov. 1858 - May 1860.

(36) Correspondence of Comdr. Henry Walke, Commanding the Store Ship _Supply_, Stationed at São Paulo de Loanda, Vera Cruz, and Pensacola (handwritten copies), Aug. 1859 - Feb. 1861.

(37) Letters Sent by Comdrs. Henry J. Hartstene, Stephen C. Rowan, and Percival Drayton and Lt. Comdr. James G. Maxwell, Commanding Officers of the _Pawnee_, Stationed at Vera Cruz, Washington, Hatteras Inlet, and Port Royal (handwritten copies), June 1860 - Feb. 1862.

(38) Letters Sent by Flag Officer Garrett J. Pendergrast (Flagships _Powhatan_, _Cumberland_, and _Roanoke_), Commanding the Home Squadron and

later the West India Squadron (handwritten copies), Oct. 1860 – Sept. 1861. Typed index. On and after May 14, 1861, Flag Officer Pendergrast signed his letters as "Comdg. West India Squadron."

(39) Correspondence of Comdr. Henry Walke, Commanding the Gunboats Taylor and Carondelet and the Ram Lafayette, Mississippi Squadron (handwritten copies), Nov. 1860 – Aug. 1863.

(40) Letters Sent by Lt. Penrod G. Watmough, Commanding the Potomska and the Memphis, South Atlantic Blockading Squadron (handwritten copies), Jan. 1861 – Jan. 1863.

(41) Letters Sent by Capt. Henry Eagle, Commanding the Santee off Galveston Bay (handwritten copies), June 1861 – Feb. 1862. Indexed.

(42) Letters Received by Lt. Joshua Bishop, Commanding the General Bragg, Mississippi Squadron (originals), July 1861 – Feb. 1864.

(43) Letters Sent by Capt. Maxwell Woodhull, Commanding the Supply Ship Connecticut on Service between New York and Key West (handwritten copies), Aug. 1861 – June 1862.

(44) Letters Sent by Capt. Andrew H. Foote, Commanding the United States Naval Forces on Western Waters, Stationed at St. Louis and Cairo (handwritten copies), Sept. 1861 – Feb. 1862.

(45) Letters Sent by R. A. Louis M. Goldsborough (Flagship Minnesota), Commanding the North Atlantic Blockading Squadron (handwritten copies), Sept. 1861 – Sept. 1862. 4 vols.

(46) Correspondence of R. A. David G. Farragut (Flagship Hartford), Commanding the West Gulf Blockading Squadron, Sept. 1861 – Dec. 1864. 15 vols. Some volumes indexed. (a) Letters received and sent, Sept. 1861 – July 1863 (handwritten copies, 2 vols.); (b) letters to the Navy Department, Jan. 1862 – July 1863, Dec. 1863 – Dec. 1864 (press copies, 4 vols.); (c) orders issued, Nov. 1862 – May 1863 (handwritten copies, 1 vol.); (d) letters to the Squadron, Jan. 1862 – July 1863, Jan.–Nov. 1864 (press copies, 7 vols.); and (e) detachments, June–Nov. 1864 (press copies, 1 vol.). Admiral Farragut was detached from the Squadron to other duty in Aug. 1863 and returned in Jan. 1864; during his absence Commo. Henry H. Bell commanded the Squadron.

(47) General Orders Issued by R. A. Samuel F. Du Pont, Commanding the South Atlantic Blockading Squadron (printed and handwritten copies), Oct. 1861 – June 1863. 1 adhesive binder.

(48) Correspondence of Capt. George F. Emmons, Commanding the Hatteras, the R. R. Cuyler, and the Brooklyn, South Atlantic Blockading Squadron, Oct. 1861 – Sept. 1863, and Journal of the Blockading of Berwick Bay, S. C., by the Hatteras, July–Nov. 1862 (handwritten copies).

(49) Correspondence of Comdr. Daniel Ammen, Commanding the Seneca, the Sebago, and the Patapsco, South Atlantic Blockading Squadron (handwritten copies and some originals), Oct. 1861 – June 1864. Indexed.

(50) General Orders Received by the Mohican, Oct. 1861 – Feb. 1863, and General Orders Issued by R. A. David D. Porter, Commanding the North Atlantic Blockading Squadron, Oct. 1864 – Jan. 1865.

(51) Letters Sent by Comdr. Thomas H. Stevens (handwritten copies), Oct. 1861 – July 1865. Commander Stevens commanded the Gunboat Ottawa, cruising along the coast of Florida; the Maratanga, in Chesapeake Bay; the Sonoma, West India Squadron (1862-63); the Patapsco, along the coast of Georgia (1864); and the Oneida, cruising between New Orleans and Galveston (1864-65).

(52) Letters Sent by Flag Officer William W. McKean (Flagship Niagara), Commanding the Gulf Blockading Squadron, Later the East Gulf Blockading Squadron (press copies), Nov. 1861 – June 1862. Indexed.

(53) Letters Sent by Capt. C. R. Perry Rodgers, Commanding the Wabash, South Atlantic Blockading Squadron (handwritten copies), Nov. 1861 – May 1863. Indexed.

(54) Letters Sent by Act'g R. A. Charles H. Davis (Flagships Benton and Eastport), Commanding the Mississippi Squadron (handwritten copies), Dec. 1861 – Sept. 1862. 6 vols. Admiral Davis took command of the Squadron in May 1862.

(55) Letters Sent by Comdr. William E. Le Roy, Commanding the Keystone State, South Atlantic Blockading Squadron, and the Oneida and the Ossipee, West Gulf Blockading Squadron (handwritten copies), Dec. 1861 – Sept. 1865. 2 vols. The writer was in command of the Keystone State till June 1863 and of the Oneida Sept. 1863 – Apr. 1864.

(56) Correspondence of Comdr. Henry K. Davenport, Commanding the Hetzel, in the Sounds of North Carolina, and the Lancaster, Pacific Squadron (handwritten copies), Dec. 1861 – Apr. 1866. 7 vols. Indexed. (a) Letters sent Dec. 1861 – Apr. 1866 (6 vols.); and (b) register of orders received from Act'g R. A. Samuel Phillips Lee, Mar. 1863 – May 1864. Commander Davenport was detached from the Hetzel in June 1864 and assigned to the Lancaster in Sept. 1864.

(57) Orders and Circulars Issued and Received by the South Atlantic Blockading Squadron (chiefly printed and mounted), Jan. 1862 – May 1865. 2 vols.

(58) Letters Sent by Capt. Henry A. Wise, Ass't Inspector of Ordnance, Later Chief of the Bureau of Ordnance, Jan. 1862 – Apr. 1868. 4 vols. Indexed. Handwritten copies, Jan. 1862 – Nov. 1864 (1 vol.), and press copies, Jan. 1862 – Apr. 1868 (3 vols.). Captain Wise served as Chief of the Bureau of Ordnance from June 1863 to June 1868.

(59) Orders Issued by the Commanding Officer of the Potomac Flotilla (handwritten copies), Feb. 1862 - June 1865. Indexed.

(60) Letters Sent by Comdr. Thomas H. Patterson, Commanding the Chocura, North Atlantic Blockading Squadron, and the James Adger, South Atlantic Blockading Squadron (handwritten copies), Mar. 1862 - Oct. 1864, May-June 1865. 2 vols. Commander Patterson was in charge of the James Adger 1862-65.

(61) Correspondence of Comdr. John M. B. Clitz, Commanding the Penobscot, North Atlantic Blockading Squadron, the Juniata, West India Squadron, and the Osceola, North Atlantic Blockading Squadron, May 1862 - Dec. 1866. 6 vols. (a) Handwritten copies of correspondence (5 numbered vols.); and (b) orders and circulars received, Jan. 1863 - Apr. 1865.

(62) Letters Sent by Capt. Guert Gansevoort, Commanding the Adirondack, Wrecked in the Bahama Islands (handwritten copies), July-Sept. 1862.

(63) Letters Sent by Capt. Maxwell Woodhull, Commanding the Cimerone, Serving in the James River Flotilla, Later in the Blockade of the St. Johns River, Fla. (handwritten copies), July 1862 - Jan. 1863.

(64) Correspondence of Comdr. George W. Rodgers, Commanding the Tioga, the Wachuset, and the Catskill (handwritten copies), July 1862 - July 1863. Indexed. The Tioga and the Wachuset were employed under Act'g R. A. Charles Wilkes in the James River Flotilla and the West India Squadron, 1862; the Catskill served in the South Atlantic Blockading Squadron, 1863.

(65) Correspondence of Commo. Andrew A. Harwood, Commanding the Potomac Flotilla, July 1862 - Dec. 1863. 11 vols. (a) Letters sent, July 1862 - Dec. 1863 (handwritten copies, 3 vols.); and (b) letters received, Aug. 1862 - Dec. 1863 (originals, 8 vols. with typed indexes; overlapping chronologically, perhaps because of some method of classification by correspondents that is not obvious).

(66) Correspondence of Commo. Henry H. Bell, Commanding the Brooklyn and the Pensacola, West Gulf Blockading Squadron, July 1862 - July 1864. 5 vols. and 1 adhesive binder. (a) Letters sent, July 1862 - July 1863 (handwritten copies, 2 vols.); (b) letters to the Navy Department, Aug. 1863 - Jan. 1864 (press copies, 1 vol., indexed); (c) letters to the Squadron, Aug. 1863 - Jan. 1864 (press copies, 3 vols., indexed); and (d) letters received, May 1863 - July 1864 (originals, 1 adhesive binder). In the absence of R. A. David G. Farragut, Aug. 1863 - Jan. 1864, Commodore Bell commanded the Squadron.

(67) Correspondence of Comdr. William H. Macomb, Commanding the Genesee, West Gulf Blockading Squadron, the Shamrock, Sounds of North Caronlia, and the Chattanooga, the Kenosha, and the Plymouth, European Squadron, July 1862 - July 1870. 9 vols. (a) Letters sent, July 1862 - Mar. 1870 (handwritten copies, 4 vols., indexed); (b) letters sent,

Nov. 1864 - Mar. 1865, July 1866 - July 1870 (press copies, 2 vols., indexed); (c) letters received, July 1862 - Aug. 1863 (originals, 2 vols.); and (d) abstracts of letters received, Dec. 1863 - Nov. 1864 (1 vol.). Commander Macomb had charge of the Genesee till Sept. 1863, the Shamrock Dec. 1863 - Mar. 1865, and the other vessels July 1866 - July 1870.

(68) Orders and Circulars Received and Issued by the North Atlantic Blockading Squadron (chiefly printed), Aug. 1862 - Apr. 1865. Table of contents.

(69) Correspondence of Capt. Thomas G. Corbin, Commanding the Wabash, South Atlantic Blockading Squadron, and the Augusta, North Atlantic Blockading Squadron (handwritten copies), Aug. 1862 - Apr. 1867. Captain Corbin commanded the Wabash till July 1863 and the Augusta Mar. 1864 - Jan. 1865.

(70) Correspondence of Capt. Cicero Price, Commanding the Jamestown in Chinese and Japanese Waters (handwritten copies), Sept. 1862 - Sept. 1865. 2 vols.

(71) Correspondence of R. A. David D. Porter (Flagship Black Hawk), Commanding the Mississippi Squadron, Oct. 1862 - Oct. 1864. 44 vols. and 2 adhesive binders. Indexed. (a) Letters from the Navy Department, Oct. 1862 - May 1864 (2 vols.); (b) telegrams received, Oct. 1862 - Dec. 1863 (1 binder); (c) letters from the Bureau of Ordnance, Oct. 1862 - Aug. 1864 (1 binder); (d) letters from officers of the Squadron, Mar. 1863 - Sept. 1864 (27 vols., many overlapping chronologically as if they belonged to different sequences, though no basis for classifying them is found); (e) letters to the Secretary of the Navy, Oct. 1862 - Oct. 1864 (press copies, 4 vols.); (f) letters to bureaus, Oct. 1862 - Sept. 1864 (press copies, 1 vol.); and (g) letters to other persons, chiefly officers of the Squadron, Dec. 1862 - Oct. 1864 (press copies, 10 vols., labeled "General Letters").

(72) Letters Sent by Comdr. William Reynolds, Commanding the Vermont, South Atlantic Blockading Squadron (handwritten copies), Nov. 1862 - Nov. 1864. 5 vols. Indexed.

(73) Correspondence of Comdr. John C. Beaumont, Commanding the Sebago and the Nantucket, South Atlantic Blockading Squadron (handwritten copies), Dec. 1862 - Sept. 1863.

(74) Correspondence of Act'g R. A. Theodorus Bailey (Flagships St. Lawrence, Magnolia, San Jacinto, and Dale), Commanding the East Gulf Blockading Squadron, Dec. 1862 - Aug. 1864. 11 vols. and 1 adhesive binder. Indexed. (a) Reports from officers of the Squadron, Dec. 1862 - July 1864 ("Reports of Captures and Expeditions," 4 vols.); (b) letters from the Secretary of the Navy, Feb.-Aug. 1864 (1 binder); (c) letters to the Secretary of the Navy, Dec. 1862 - Aug. 1864 (press copies, 2 vols., "I" and "J"); (d) orders issued, Dec. 1862 - Aug. 1864 (press copies, 3 vols., "K," "M," and "N"); (e) miscellaneous letters sent, Mar. 1863 - Jan. 1864 (press copies, 1 vol., "L"); and (f) letters of requisition issued for ships' fittings at Key West, Mar. 1863 - July 1864 (press copies, 1 vol.).

(75) Orders and Circulars Received and Issued by the East Gulf
Blockading Squadron, Jan. 1863 - June 1865. 2 vols.

(76) Correspondence of Act'g Master William Tell Street, Commanding
the Primrose and the Fuchsia, Potomac Flotilla, Mar. 1863 - Aug. 1865.
2 vols. (a) Letters sent, Mar. 1863 - Aug. 1865 (handwritten copies);
and (b) orders received, Jan. 1864 - June 1865.

(77) Orders Issued by Lt. Comdr. K. Randolph Breese, Commanding the
Black Hawk, Mississippi Squadron (press copies), Apr. 1863 - Sept. 1864.
Indexed.

(78) Correspondence of Capt. Henry Walke, Commanding the Sacramento
on Special Service in European Waters (handwritten copies), Sept. 1863 -
Aug. 1864.

(79) Letters Sent by Comdr. C. R. Perry Rodgers, Commanding the
Iroquois on Special Service in South American and European Waters (handwritten copies), Oct. 1863 - Oct. 1865. Indexed.

(80) Letters Sent by Lt. Comdr. James Charles P. De Krafft, Commanding
the Conemaugh, West Gulf Blockading Squadron and Atlantic Squadron (handwritten copies), Nov. 1863 - Mar. 1866. Arranged by classes of persons
addressed.

(81) Letters Sent by Lt. Comdr. Penrod G. Watmough, Commanding the
Kansas, North Atlantic Blockading Squadron (handwritten copies), Dec. 1863 -
Feb. 1865.

(82) Letters Sent by Act'g Master William R. Browne, Commanding the
Restless, East Gulf Blockading Squadron (handwritten copies), Jan.-July
1864. Indexed.

(83) Letters Sent by Capt. Guert Gansevoort, Commanding the Roanoke,
North Atlantic Blockading Squadron (handwritten copies), Jan.-Sept. 1864.

(84) Letters Sent by Act'g Volunteer Lt. Charles H. Rockwell,
Commanding the Gem of the Sea, East Gulf Blockading Squadron (handwritten
copies), Jan.-Sept. 1864.

(85) Letters Sent by Capt. Melancton Smith, Commanding the Onondaga
on Service in the Sounds of North Carolina and the James River, Mar.-Aug.
1864. 2 vols. (1 of handwritten copies, 1 of press copies). Indexed.

(86).Correspondence of Comdr. John C. Beaumont, Commanding the
Mackinaw, North Atlantic Blockading Squadron (handwritten copies), Apr.-
Nov. 1864.

(87) Correspondence of Commo. William Radford, Commanding the New
Ironsides, South Atlantic Blockading Squadron, and the Dumbarton and the
Phlox, North Atlantic Blockading Squadron (handwritten copies), Aug. 1864 -
Apr. 1865.

(88) Letters Received by Lt. Comdr. Joshua Bishop, Commanding the Wyoming, Asiatic Squadron (originals), Aug. 1864 - Aug. 1866.

(89) Correspondence of Act'g R. A. David D. Porter (Flagship Malvern), Commanding the North Atlantic Blockading Squadron, Sept. 1864 - May 1865. 21 vols. and 1 adhesive binder. Indexed. (a) Letters from officers, Sept. 1864 - Apr. 1865 ("Officers' Letters, North Atlantic Squadron," 12 vols.); (b) telegrams received, Oct. 1864 - Apr. 1865 (1 binder); (c) letters to the Secretary of the Navy, Oct.-Dec. 1864 (press copies, 1 vol.); (d) letters to bureaus, Oct. 1864 - Apr. 1865 (press copies, 2 vols.); (e) letters to officers, Oct. 1864 - Apr. 1865 (press copies, 4 vols.); (f) orders issued, Oct. 1864 - Apr. 1865 (press copies, 1 vol.); and (g) letters sent relating to courts martial, Dec. 1864 - May 1865 (press copies, 1 vol.).

(90) General Orders and Circulars Received by the Juniata, North Atlantic Blockading Squadron, Commanded by Capt. William R. Taylor, Oct. 1864 - Jan. 1865.

(91) Correspondence of Capt. George F. Emmons, Commanding the Lackawanna off Galveston (handwritten copies), Oct. 1864 - Feb. 1865. 2 vols. (a) Letters sent; and (b) correspondence relating to enlisted men, with lists.

(92) Letters Sent by Act'g R. A. Samuel Phillips Lee (Flagships Black Hawk and Tempest), Commanding the Mississippi Squadron (press copies), Oct. 1864 - Aug. 1865. 2 vols. Indexed. Letters to (a) the Secretary of the Navy and (b) bureaus.

(93) Correspondence of Comdr. Daniel Ammen, Commanding the Mohican, South Atlantic Blockading Squadron, and the Miantonomah, Detained in the Washington Navy Yard (handwritten copies), Oct. 1864 - June 1866. Indexed. Commander Ammen took charge of the Miantonomah in Sept. 1865.

(94) Orders Issued by Act'g Volunteer Lt. Charles H. Rockwell, Commanding the Hendrick Hudson, Nov. 1864 - July 1865, and Observations on the Coast and Harbors of China, Mar. 1868 (handwritten copies).

(95) Letters Sent by Comdr. William Reynolds, Commanding the New Hampshire, South Atlantic Blockading Squadron (handwritten copies), Dec. 1864 - July 1865. 3 vols.

(96) Letters Sent by Act'g R. A. William Radford (Flagship Malvern), Commanding the North Atlantic Blockading Squadron (press copies), Apr.-Oct. 1865. 3 vols.

(97) Letters Sent by Comdr. Edward Y. McCauley, Commanding the Benton, Mississippi Squadron (press copies), Apr. 1865 - Mar. 1872. 2 vols. The first volume is labeled "2," but no predecessor is found.

(98) Letters Sent by R. A. Louis M. Goldsborough (Flagship Colorado), Commanding the European Squadron (handwritten copies), June 1865 - Aug. 1867.

3 vols. Letters to (a) the Secretary of the Navy, June 1865 - Aug. 1867;
(b) ministers and consuls, June 1865 - June 1867; and (c) other persons,
June 1865 - July 1867.

(99) Letters Sent by Lt. Comdr. Francis B. Blake, Commanding the
Nipsic, South Atlantic Squadron (handwritten copies), Jan. 1866 - Oct. 1867.

(100) Letters Sent by Act'g R. A. George F. Pearson (Flagships
Lancaster and Powhatan), Commanding the Pacific and South Pacific Squadrons (press copies), Feb.-Dec. 1866. Indexed.

(101) Letters Sent by R. A. Charles H. Davis (Flagship Guerrière),
Commanding the South Atlantic Squadron (handwritten copies), June 1867 -
July 1869. 12 vols. Letters to (a) the Secretary of the Navy, May 1868 -
July 1869 (2 vols.), (b) bureaus, June 1867 - July 1869 (1 vol.), (c) the
Squadron, July 1867 - May 1869 (7 vols.), and (d) other persons, June 1867 -
July 1869 (1 vol.); and general orders and circulars issued, Aug. 1867 -
May 1869 (1 vol.).

(102) Letters Sent by Capt. William Reynolds, Commanding the
Lackawanna, Pacific Squadron (handwritten copies), Oct. 1867 - Jan. 1869.

(103) Letters Sent by Vice-Adm. Stephen C. Rowan (Flagships Piscataqua
and Delaware), Commanding the Asiatic Squadron (handwritten copies),
Oct. 1867 - Nov. 1870. Indexed.

(104) Correspondence of Lt. Comdr. Thomas H. Eastman, Commanding the
Penobscot, North Atlantic Squadron (handwritten copies), Dec. 1867 -
July 1869.

(105) Letters Received from the Secretary of the Navy by R. A. Thomas
Turner, Commanding the South Pacific and Pacific Squadrons (originals),
Mar. 1868 - Aug. 1870. 1 adhesive binder.

(106) Letters Sent by R. A. William Radford (Flagship Franklin),
Commanding the European Squadron (press copies), Jan. 1869 - Aug. 1870.
2 vols. Letters to (a) the Navy Department and (b) other correspondents.

(107) Night Orders Issued by Capt. William H. Macomb, Commanding the
Plymouth (handwritten copies), Feb. 1869 - Jan. 1870.

(108) Correspondence of Lt. Comdr. Thomas H. Eastman, Commanding the
Nyack in an Expedition to Darien (handwritten copies), Sept. 1869 -
Oct. 1870.

(109) Letters Sent by Capt. John C. Beaumont, Commanding the Powhatan,
North Atlantic Squadron (press copies), Aug.-Dec. 1870, Dec. 1873 -
July 1874.

(110) Letters Sent by Lt. George Rockwell, Commanding the Palos,
Asiatic Squadron (handwritten copies), Oct. 1870 - Oct. 1872.

(111) Letters Received by R. A. Charles A. Gove (originals), June 1871 – June 1919. 1 adhesive binder. Orders received, copies of testimonials, calling cards, and other materials, beginning with Admiral Gove's service as a midshipman.

(112) Letters Sent by Capt. David B. Harmony, Commanding the Kearsarge and the Hartford, Asiatic Squadron (handwritten copies), Dec. 1873 – Oct. 1875. Indexed.

(113) Letters Sent by Comdr. Joseph N. Miller, Commanding the Ajax, North Atlantic Squadron (handwritten copies), Dec. 1873 – May 1876. Indexed.

(114) Letters Received by Comdr. Samuel Dana Greene, Commanding the Juniata, European Squadron (originals), Jan. 1875 – May 1876. 1 adhesive binder.

(115) Letters Sent by R. A. William Reynolds (Flagship Tennessee), Commanding the Asiatic Squadron, June 1875 – Oct. 1877. 9 vols. (a) Press copies of miscellaneous letters, June–Nov. 1875 (1 vol.); and handwritten copies of (b) miscellaneous letters, Dec. 1875 – July 1877 (1 vol.), (c) letters to officers, Nov. 1875 – Oct. 1877 (3 vols.), (d) letters to the Secretary of the Navy, Nov. 1875 – Dec. 1876 (1 vol.), (e) letters to bureaus, Nov. 1875 – Apr. 1877 (1 vol.), and (f) orders issued, Dec. 1875 – June 1877 (2 vols.).

(116) Correspondence of Comdr. Thomas H. Eastman, Commanding the Ajax, North Atlantic Squadron (handwritten copies), May 1876 – Nov. 1877. 2 vols.

(117) Letters Sent by R. A. Stephen D. Trenchard (Flagships Hartford and Powhatan), Commanding the North Atlantic Squadron (press copies), Aug. 1876 – Aug. 1878. Indexed.

(118) Letters Sent by Comdr. George C. Remey, Commanding the Enterprise, North Atlantic Squadron (handwritten copies), Mar. 1877 – Apr. 1878.

(119) Correspondence of R. A. C. R. Perry Rodgers, Superintendent of the Naval Academy (handwritten copies), June 1877 – June 1878. During the latter months of this period the writer was preparing for duty as the commanding officer of the Pacific Squadron.

(120) Orders Issued by Rear Admirals John C. Howell and Robert H. Wyman (Flagships Powhatan and Tennessee), Commanding the North Atlantic Squadron (press copies), Sept. 1878 – June 1880. Barely legible.

(121) Correspondence of Lt. Comdr. George W. De Long (Flagship Jeannette), Commanding the Arctic Exploring Expedition, Mar. 1879 – Oct. 1882. 2 vols. (a) Letters sent on a voyage from New York to Unalaska, Mar.–Aug. 1879 (press copies, 1 vol.); and (b) letters received, press copies of letters sent, notes, and copies of various materials, assembled without observable arrangement (1 vol.).

(122) Orders Received by Passed Ass't Engineer Albert B. Willits (handwritten copies), May 1881 - July 1894.

(123) Letters Sent by Comdr. Charles H. Rockwell, Commanding the Yantic, North Atlantic Squadron (press copies), Feb. 1889 - Aug. 1891. 2 vols.

(124) Reports of Absentees, Sick, Coal on Hand, and Noon Positions, with Memoranda, Received by R. A. John G. Walker, Commanding the Squadron of Evolution in European and South Atlantic Waters (originals), Dec. 1889 - May 1892.

(125) Letters Sent by Lt. Thomas S. Phelps, Jr., Commanding the Palos, Stationed at Kobe, Japan (press copies), July 1890 - Sept. 1891. 2 vols.

(126) Letters Sent by Joseph P. Mickley and Walter F. Worthington, Chief Engineers aboard the Terror, North Atlantic Squadron (handwritten copies), Feb. 1897 - Aug. 1898.

(127) Confidential Memoranda Received from the Office of Naval Intelligence by the Commanding Officer of the Eastern Squadron (Flagship Oregon), Feb.-June 1898. 1 adhesive binder.

(128) Letters Sent by Lt. Comdr. Richard Wainwright, Commanding the Gloucester, North Atlantic Squadron (press copies), May-Oct. 1898. Indexed.

(129) Letters Received by R. A. John W. Philip and by His Widow, June 1898 - Sept. 1900 ("Philip Papers"). During the Spanish-American War Admiral Philip commanded the Texas in Cuban waters. Most of the volume consists of letters, telegrams, and cards of condolence received by his survivors on the occasion of his death.

(130) Letters Sent by Lt. Comdrs. William A. Marshall and Nathan Sargent, Commanding the Scorpion, North Atlantic Squadron (press copies), Aug. 1899 - July 1901. 2 vols. Indexed.

(131) Correspondence of R. A. George C. Remey (Flagship Brooklyn), Commanding the Asiatic Squadron, Apr. 1900 - May 1902. 14 vols., 4 adhesive binders, and 1 looseleaf binder. (a) Telegrams sent and received, Apr. 1900 - May 1902 (4 adhesive binders); (b) letters received and carbon copies of letters sent, Dec. 1901 - May 1902 (1 looseleaf binder); indexed press copies, Apr. 1900 - May 1902, of letters to (c) the Squadron (9 vols., labeled "S"), (d) the Navy Department (3 vols., labeled "M"), and (e) other correspondents (1 vol., labeled "M"); and (f) press copies of orders issued, Sept. 1901 (1 vol.).

(132) Confidential Letters Sent by Rear Admirals George W. Sumner, Benjamin P. Lamberton, and Charles D. Sigsbee, Commanding the South Atlantic Squadron, Later the Caribbean Squadron and the Second Squadron (press copies), Oct. 1902 - May 1906. 2 vols. Indexed.

(133) Letters Sent by Rear Admirals Caspar F. Goodrich and William T. Swinburne (Flagship Chicago), Commanding the Pacific Squadron (press copies), Aug. 1905 – July 1908. 13 vols. (a) Volumes beginning with "5" and forming a chronological sequence (12 vols.), and (b) letters sent relating to courts martial, Aug. 1904 – Mar. 1908 (1 vol.).

APPENDIX F: FILE DESIGNATIONS USED IN THE SUBJECT FILE (Entry 464)

(Copied from a Typed Manual of the Office of Naval Records and Library)

A. NAVAL SHIPS: DESIGN, CONSTRUCTION, ETC. [103 boxes]
    AC. Construction
    AD. Design and general characteristics
    AF. Fittings and equipment
    AH. Hulls
    AL. Laid-up ships: condition, repair, inspections, etc.
        (includes "fitting out" status)
    AO. Boats (small)
    AQ. Qualities, sailing, etc. (including trial trips)
    AR. Repair
    AS. Spars and rigging
    AV. Miscellaneous
    AX. Salvage of wrecks, etc.
    AY. Purchases, sales, and final disposition of naval vessels,
        except prizes (see XZ) and merchant ships (see SY)

B. ORDNANCE [23 boxes]
    BA. Ammunition
    BG. Guns and gunnery
    BH. Hand weapons (cutlasses, rifles, revolvers, etc.)
    BM. Mines and torpedoes
    BO. Ordnance equipment
    BR. Armor and armament, general
    BV. Miscellaneous

D. COMMUNICATION [13 boxes]
    DB. Books, signal and tactical
    DC. Codes, cryptography, and censorship
    DE. Emblems and national flags
    DM. Mail
    DP. Private and special signals
    DR. Radio
    DS. Signals, general
    DT. Telegraph and cable
    DV. Miscellaneous
    DX. Courier and secret service

E. ENGINEERING [11 boxes]
    EA. Auxiliary machinery
    EB. Boilers, steam
    EE. Engines (marine)
    EL. Electrical appliances
    EM. Machinery plants in general
    EP. Propellers and paddles
    EV. Miscellaneous

H. BATTLES AND CASUALTIES TO SHIPS [16 boxes]
  HA. Engagement with enemy war vessels
  HB. Battle casualties to material
  HC. Engagement with enemy commerce raiders (one of ships
      involved to be war ship)
  HF. Fires, explosions, etc.
  HG. Groundings, strandings, foundering, etc.
  HJ. Joint military-naval engagements
  HK. Collisions
  HL. Engagements of ships and naval forces with land forces
      (see OH)
  HM. Merchant ship engagements
  HP. Privateer engagements (with or of enemy, no ship-of-war
      involved)
  HV. Miscellaneous
  HW. Wind and weather casualties to material

I. INSTRUCTIONS, ETC. [5 boxes]
  IC. Circulars
  IG. General orders
  IO. General court-martial orders
  IR. Regulations
  IS. Special orders
  IV. Miscellaneous

K. NAUTICAL TECHNOLOGY AND SCIENCE [12 boxes]
  KH. Hydrography and topography, including surveying (maps)
  KL. Lighthouses and other navigational aids
  KM. Meteorology
  KN. Navigation and astronomy
  KS. Seamanship
  KV. Miscellaneous

M. MEDICAL [17 boxes]
  MA. Administration of hospitals and medical departments
  MC. Charitable and pension admissions to Naval Asylum or
      Hospital
  ME. Equipment and supplies (technical)
  MH. Health conditions, general: hygiene and sanitation
  MK. Casualties, battle, accident, etc.
  ML. Personnel, medical—training, etc.
  MM. Admissions—individual cases
  MN. Discharges from medical custody—individual cases and
      deaths
  MR. Routine health reports
  MS. Special reports, epidemics, special incidents, etc.
  MT. Treatments, methods of
  MV. Miscellaneous
  MX. Medical surveys and examinations of individuals

N. PERSONNEL [158 boxes]
- NA. Complements, rolls, lists of persons serving in or with vessels or stations
- NC. Ceremonies, salutes, courtesies, honors, etc.—military
- NE. Drills, training, and education
- NF. Distribution and transfers
- NH. Heroic acts, commendation, honors, memorials, and medals
- NI. Promotion and privileges; rank, retirement, and reinstatement
- NJ. Discipline (minor) and minor delinquencies
- NK. Technical and professional examinations of individuals
- NL. Living conditions, customs, etc.
- NN. Commissions, appointments, applications, acceptances, oaths, resignations, discharges, and similar documents
- NO. Courts martial, etc.
- NP. Pilots
- NR. Recruiting and enlistments, shipping articles, etc.
- NU. Uniforms, characteristics
- NV. Miscellaneous
- NZ. Desertion and straggling

O. OPERATIONS OF NAVAL SHIPS AND FLEET UNITS [139 boxes]
- OA. Administration and organization (internal)
- OC. Cruises and voyages (special)
- OD. Distribution (general)
- OH. Shore operations—marine, naval, etc. (except HL)
- OI. Inspections of military efficiency
- OJ. Joint military naval operations (except HJ)
- OL. Mobilization and demobilization
- OM. Routine operations
- ON. Strategy and tactics
- OO. Operations of large groups of vessels (routine)
- OP. Pilotage, port movements, port changes, etc.
- OR. Chartered vessels operations (except supply ships; see OX)
- OS. Ships' movements (record of arrivals and departures)
- OT. Training and drills (with ships)
- OV. Miscellaneous
- OX. Lines of supply and supply ships (charter parties)

P. BASES, NAVAL (INCLUDING NAVY YARDS AND STATIONS) [81 boxes]
- PA. Rolls (civil)
- PB. Administration of station
- PD. Dry docks (not docking)
- PF. Frauds and irregularities (civilian)
- PI. Industrial activity
- PL. Labor and civil personel
- PM. Military
- PN. Plant
- PS. Sites and boundaries
- PV. Miscellaneous

R. PRISONERS AND PRISONS (INCLUDING PRISON SHIPS) [53 boxes]
    RA. Prisoners of war rolls and lists (U. S. nationalities)
    RB. Prisoners of war rolls and lists (hostile or foreign
        nationalities)
    RE. Release and exchange, including cartel ships (except
        lists)
    RL. Paroles (except lists)
    RN. Aliens, civilian, in U. S.
    RP. Prisons, shore and ship
    RR. Retaliation and reprisal
    RV. Miscellaneous (impressed seamen)
    RX. Subsistence, clothing, and care

S. MERCHANT SHIPS AND COMMERCE [32 boxes]
    SA. Administration (internal)
    SB. Design and construction
    SC. Commerce, maritime (general)
    SD. Distribution
    SG. Illegal service, including blockade-running, slave trade,
        piracy, smuggling, etc. (except H and O papers)
    SM. Mercantile business
    SN. Personnel
    SO. Operations, voyages, etc.
    SP. Privateers and privateering (except HP)
    SR. Registry, clearance papers, port charges, etc.
    SS. Naval assistance to (except political aspects—see VP)
    SV. Miscellaneous
    SY. Purchases and sales (except for naval use—see AY)
    SZ. Prizes (merchant ships and private property captured by
        U. S. Ships, and American captured by enemy), except
        legal and financial aspects—see XZ

V. GOVERNMENTAL RELATIONSHIPS—DOMESTIC AND FOREIGN [46 boxes]
    VA. Administration and organization, Navy Department
        (internal)
    VC. National policy
    VD. Diplomatic negotiations, treaties, etc.
    VI. International relations and politics
    VL. Law, international
    VM. Military policy
    VN. Naval policy
    VP. Protection of individuals and property abroad
    VR. Marine Corps, general policies
    VU. Revenue Cutter, Coast Guard, Lighthouse, Marine Hospital,
        Life Saving, and other maritime governmental services—
        general policies (Texas Navy)
    VV. Miscellaneous

X. SUPPLIES (INCLUDING FINANCE) [105 boxes]
    XA. Accounting and finance (not accounts)
    XD. Claims (except in prize cases)

X. SUPPLIES (continued)
    XF. Fuel and water
    XN. Naval stores afloat
    XO. Clothing and food
    XP. Pay, naval, and allowances
    XS. Naval supplies ashore
    XU. Supplies for Navy Department (internal)
    XV. Miscellaneous
    XY. See AX and AY
    XZ. Prizes, prize money, and prize sales (legal and financial
        aspects)

Y. PENSIONS AND PENSIONERS
    YL. Pension laws, regulations, etc.

Z. HISTORY[1]
    ZB. Biography [alphabetical by person]
    ZC. Ships [alphabetical by ship]
    ZE. Places [including continents, islands, nations, States of
        the Union, cities, shore establishments, etc., in a
        single alphabet]
    ZO. Operations, military or naval [various subjects, such as
        visits of American vessels to Central America, the mari-
        time wars of the early eighteenth century, privateers
        and privateering, naval operations at New Orleans, naval
        militia, etc.; chiefly wars, arranged alphabetically by
        names of wars]
    ZR. Sources of historical material
    ZV. Miscellaneous [alphabetical; such subjects as aviation,
        burial of the dead, celebrations, chronology, duels,
        legal holidays, Marine Corps, "misc. papers falling
        under no special head, and of minor importance," monu-
        ments and other memorials erected to officers of the
        Navy, officers of the Navy, priests in the Philippines,
        salutes, signals, songs, State navies, torpedoes, and
        other subjects]

---

[1]Custody of materials in the Z classification has been retained by
the Office of Naval Records and Library. They consist largely of reference
correspondence and notes of that Office, relating to the Navy both before
and after 1910. They also include, however, original papers previous to
1910 attached to the correspondence for purposes of reference and not
filed under earlier letters of the alphabet.